Crowdfunding in the United States and European Union: Markets, Platforms, Critics, and Future Prospects

Irini Liakopoulou

Crowdfunding in the United States and European Union: Markets, Platforms, Critics, and Future Prospects

Irini Liakopoulou

Academica Press
Washington~London

Library of Congress Cataloging-in-Publication Data

Names: Liakopoulou, Irini author. |
Title: Crowdfunding in the united states and european union : markets, platforms, critics, and future prospects / Irini Liakopoulou
Description: Washington : Academica Press, 2020. | Includes references.
Identifiers: LCCN 2020938771 | ISBN 9781680530957 (hardcover)

CONTENTS

Dedicated to Sofia and Dimitris

INTRODUCTION

This book investigates the crowdfunding phenomenon, deepening the implications for the various stakeholders deriving from this funding collection mechanism and the role it has assumed in recent years, especially in the processes of business creation and spread of entrepreneurship.

The actors involved, i.e. the promoters of the initiatives, the supporters and the platforms through which the campaigns are launched, constitute an ecosystem in continuous evolution, which is increasingly growing over the years and is allowing the spread of this form of financing from the bass.

In this work, conducted with the "multiple paper thesis" method, original and innovative contributions are presented, in some cases applying techniques and methodologies so far not used for this topic, which can lead to new reflections on this financing instrument. The aim is to participate in the current debate on crowdfunding and to extend a literature that is still at an early stage, as well as to broaden the knowledge of areas that are under-research and on which clarity has not been made completely. The present work begins with a first chapter, in which crowdfunding is briefly discussed, describing: Origins, functioning, ecosystem, market, models, regulations, numbers and literature.

These brief notes are useful to provide a first overview of this alternative form of financing which is supportive of understanding its evolution and how it has currently become significant in the world economy. In the following three chapters, the focus is placed on the companies successfully financed, analyzing the factors that influence the amount of funding received and the investors involved.

The second chapter analyzes the signals used by entrepreneurs, which influence the success of the initiative through crowdfunding, measured both in terms of the amount of funding raised and in terms of the number of investors who have financed the initiative. The analysis was conducted with reference both to initiatives that made use of the equity-based crowdfunding model, considering a sample of 235 campaigns, and to the reward-based model, considering a sample of 108 campaigns, in both cases they were analyzed projects that have achieved (or exceeded) the target in terms of funding. The focus is on three types of signals, namely the qualities of the company (consisting of human capital, information on the establishment of the company and information on the status of the company), the level of information that the company provides to reduce the degree of uncertainty (the presence of a business plan and the company share hold) and the qualities of the crowdfunding campaign (updates, comments, average contribution and supporters). The main objective of this chapter is to analyze what information influences financing and to what extent it acts towards investors.

The third chapter analyzes, through a dataset of 103 projects, the qualities of the founders (project proponents) and funders, which determine the amount obtained in successful, or funded, initiatives. The objective of this chapter is to analyze the internal social capital created in the platforms, represented by the bonds established by the founders and funders, measured in terms of supported projects, followed and created previously by both actors (all with reference to a date prior to the launch of the initiative analyzed), and how it affects the result of the initiative, or on the capital raised.

The fourth chapter analyzes the networks underlying crowdfunding, considering the projects launched as ego-centered networks (formed by a founder "ego" and financiers "alters"). This chapter aims to investigate the characteristics of the networks and the impact they have on the success of the initiative, analyzing a dataset of 103 projects. The goal is to analyze in particular the role that the connections between the funders have (not considering in this case those with the founder) and the number of bonds of the founder at the time of the launch of the crowdfunding campaign. The contribution aims to analyze how these two elements, measured respectively with redundancy - effective size, and the number of bonds (tie) of the founder, positively influence the volume of funding collected by the successful initiative.

In the fifth chapter, a sample of 30 companies financed through equity crowdfunding were analyzed, which repeated the call on the same platform. The purpose of the investigation is to highlight the effects and implications for companies that have resorted to raising funds through equity crowdfunding portals. In particular, the focus is placed on the evolution of the companies over the years following the use of this mechanism, primarily as regards their value, especially in the event that they have launched more than one fundraising campaign.

The sixth chapter represents a study of post-crowdfunding, or what happens after completing a crowdfunding campaign, both in case of success or failure of the initiative. The focus is on the different possible scenarios for both the founders and the funders, analyzed through the logic of real options.

Finally, the book closes with the conclusions and future research hypotheses that may derive from this work, also extending its study to other contexts.

CHAPTER 1

Crowdfunding definition, models and economic analysis

1. Definition and origins of the crowdfunding concept

The crowdfunding, literally funded by the crowd, is an alternative funding source to traditional methods, which has undergone a strong evolution in the last decade.

A definition of what crowdfunding is has been provided by the Framework for European Crowdfunding: "Crowdfunding can be defined as a collective effort of many individuals who network and pool their resources to support efforts initiated by other people or organizations. This is usually done via or with the help of the Internet. Individual projects and businesses are financed with small contributions from a large number of individuals, allowing innovators, entrepreneurs and business owners to utilise their social networks to raise capital."[1]

The definition shows in particular the role of the supporters who make the network, creating communities, and the importance, now fundamental, of the web for the global diffusion of campaigns through platforms, accessible to anyone and everywhere.

Further definitions have been provided in the literature by several authors, among the best known is the description of Kleemann,[2] which was revised by Belleflamme et al., who offered this redefined version: "Crowdfunding involves an open call, mostly through the Internet, for the provision of financial resources either in the form of donation or in

---

1DE BUYSERE K, GAJDA O, KLEVERLAAN R. and MAROM, D., *A Framework for European Crowdfunding.* Resource Document, European Crowdfunding Network, 2012, p.9.

2KLEEMANN F., VOSS G.G. and RIEDER K., *Un(der)paid innovators: The commercial utilization of consumer work through crowdsourcing,* in *Science, Technology and Innovation Studies,* vol. 4, n.1, 2008, pp. 5-26.

exchange for the future product or some form of reward to support initiatives for specific purposes."[3]

Several other descriptions referred to specific types of crowdfunding, such as the equity-based[4] or the reward-based[5] model.

Crowdfunding represents a new concept of financing and support used both to launch new ideas and initiatives, and from start-ups already established or in the expansion phase. The concept of crowdfunding is rooted in the broader concept of crowdsourcing,[6] where the role of the

---

3BELLEFLAMME P., LAMBERT T., SCHWIENBACHER A., *Crowdfunding: Tapping the right crowd*, in *Journal of Business Venturing*, vol. 29, n.5, 2014, p. 585ss.

4AHLERS G.K.C., CUMMING D., GÜNTHER C., SCHWEIZER D., *Signaling in Equity Crowdfunding*, in *Entrepreneurship Theory and Practice*, vol. 39, n.4, 2015, pp. 955-980.

5KRAUS S., RICHTER C., BREM A., CHENG C.F., CHANG M.L., *Strategies for reward-based crowdfunding campaigns*, in *Journal of Innovation & Knowledge*, vol.1, n.1, 2016, pp. 13-23.

6The term crowdsourcing was coined in 2005 by two publishers of the Wired Magazine, Jeff Howe and Mark Robinson, from the analysis of the phenomenon of incremental use by companies of the internet platform as a means of outsourcing activities to individuals outside the business. The official definition of the term is published for the first time by Jeff Howe, where the following description is made public: Crowdsourcing is the act of a company or institution to take a function traditionally performed by employees and outsource it to an indefinite (generally large) network of people in the form of an open call. This in turn can take on the structure of peer-production or social production (with the work done collaboratively), but often it is also undertaken by a single individual. Crowdsourcing therefore allows the power of the crowd to conclude tasks that were once the field of competence of a few specialists. Using other words, it consists of taking the principles used in open source software projects and applying them to the whole spectrum of the business world. The fundamental prerequisite is the use of the open call format and the vast network of potential workers. Four fundamental developments have created the environment where crowdsourcing has become practicable inevitable: The revival of amateurism, the emergence of the open source software movement, the growing availability of production tools, the rise of active self-organized focused communities around the interests shared by people. When combined together, these four developments provide fuel for the crowdsourcing engine and create a true mechanism of meritocracy. Moreover, crowdsourcing to date is manifesting itself in at least four very different business scenarios: The use and application of collective intelligence, the production of mass creative works, the filtering and organization of vast information storage and, the use of the collective financial resources of the crowd. When viewed from these different points of view, it becomes clear that the term crowdsourcing is only a heading for what is actually a wide range of activities. The phenomenon is highly adaptive and flexible and therefore capable of emerging in many applications. SAFIRE W., *On Language*, in *New York Times Magazine*, 2009. HOWE J., *Crowdsourcing: Why the Power of the Crowd Is Driving the Future of*

crowd is to make contributions in terms of ideas, feedback and solutions, in the specific case of crowdfunding of economic resources.[7]

The importance of the crowd can be seen from crowdsourcing, which as we said is the basis of crowdfunding, underlining the fundamental support that this brings in various terms (ideas or funding). The focus on the crowd had already been placed years earlier with the concept of "crowd intelligence."[8]

Funding through crowds is a relatively recent phenomenon, and its advent has not been a disruptive one, in fact it has only recently had an important following and development in the global economy. Crowdfunding has risen to the headlines thanks to the establishment of some of the most well-known portals, such as Kickstarter (USA). However, by the late 1990s and early new millennium, this concept had emerged on the occasion of fundraisers made by artists and developers.[9]

The first appearance of the term, however, is traced back to 2006, when it was introduced on the occasion of an incubation system for projects related to the videoblog in which an online collection system of donations was set up.[10]

But the origins of this form of funding are much older. One case considered a "pioneer" of crowdfunding is represented by the fundraising of 1885 to finance the installation of the Statue of Liberty in New York.

Business, Crown Publishing Group New York, NY, USA, 2008. KUPPUSWAMY V., BAYUS B.L., *Crowdfunding creative ideas: The dynamics of project backers in Kickstarter*, UNC Kenan Flager Research Paper, n. 2013-15, SSRN Electronic Journal, 2013, pp. 1-37.

7HOWE J., *Crowdsourcing: Why the Power of the Crowd Is Driving the Future of Business,* Three Rivers Press, New York, USA, 2008. ORDANINI A., MICELI L., PIZZETTI M. and PARASURAMAN A., *Crowd-Funding: Transforming Customers into Investors through Innovative Service Platforms*, in *Journal of Service Management*, vol.22 , n.4, 2011, pp. 443 – 470.

8SUROWIECKI J., *The Wisdom of Crowds: Why the Many are Smarter than the Few and How Collective*, Wisdom Shapes Business, Economies, Societies, and Nations, Doubleday, Anchor, 2005.

9Mark Tapio Kines was the first director in 1997 to use crowdfunding to partially finance a film released in 1999. A few years later, in 2001 "ArtistShare" was born, one of the first internet crowdfunding platforms that represented a completely new business model for creative artists, by putting the latter in contact directly with the fans, with whom they shared emotions, works and materials, and making sure that their works were directly financed by the public through funds. The following year, in 2002, the Blender Foundation launched a campaign aimed at obtaining the necessary funds for an open-source 3D graphics software.

10Fundavlog launched in 2006 by Michael Sullivan.

In this circumstance J. Pulitzer started the financing campaign on World (the well-known New York newspaper), to obtain the necessary funds, setting a goal of 100,000 dollars. The "rewards" consisted of the publication of donor names in the journal. The campaign was successful and showed a strong sense of belonging to the community.

However, the first forms of crowdfunding did not foresee economic returns from financing and crowdfunders recognized the value of the project exclusively in social and emotional factors, in the possibility of realizing something useful or, in some cases, in the non-monetary reward paid. For these reasons, the development of crowdfunding is closely connected to the social web, and it is thanks to the latter that funders have had the opportunity to create peer-investor social networks with common interests.

For a crowdfunding project to be born, the collaboration of the following actors is needed: a) The creator or proposer. It is the subject, the company or the association that proposes the project on a crowdfunding portal. Depending on the different types of projects, the creator can be a subject that raises capital for personal purposes, a company that seeks funding to carry out its business, or an association that raises funds for social, scientific or humanitarian purposes. b) The crowdfunding platform. It is the virtual place where the transfer of capital takes place. The platforms can be divided according to the type of projects that allow financing, on the basis of the proposers and/or investors to whom they turn or on the basis of the geographical area in which they operate. Most of the platforms are connected to the social web and allow you to share projects on the most important social networks. This confirms and underlines the importance of the social component that underlies the crowdfunding phenomenon. c) The crowdfunder. It is the representative of the crowd who makes resources available for the project. It based on the characteristics of the collection and can obtain returns of a completely different nature. These can refer to the social and emotional sphere, or as we will see below, they can be rewards proposed by the creator or contain financial returns.

1.2 Classification and models

Crowdfunding, as mentioned, is a financing mechanism through a crowd of supporters, according to the purposes and the ways in which this instrument is implemented, there are different classifications. The common denominator of the various typologies is that supporters receive monetary and non-monetary benefits in exchange for their financial support. Here, we will present the most used and internationally proposed classification in the literature, which divides the projects according to the nature of the exchange between the proposer and crowdfunders.

The main types of crowdfunding are therefore the following:

1. The reward model is the most popular and used by the main crowdfunding platforms (for example the Kickstarter). This method provides for the definition of different types of rewards, offered by the project promoters to the supporters, based on various levels of amount that the lenders are willing to allocate. Rewards often take the form of tokens of appreciation (for example artist's autograph, T-shirt, etc.) or the prepurchasing of a product or service. There are two subcategories of this type of crowdfunding: The all-or-nothing and the keep-what-you-raise. Moreover, this type of crowdfunding is used to fund movies, music, etc. as well as for the development of new products and innovations. In fact, this category includes projects related to the creative world: Artists who seek funding to produce a book, a record, a film, to organize a tour or an exhibition, and who reward the financier with a reward such as thanks in the titles end of the film and delivery of the disc or book once completed. The economic value of the reward is obviously lower than the funded portion, but this mechanism allows to incentivize the donation by the investor who in many cases recognizes in the reward a greater value than its economic value. A very widespread practice is to offer different reward classes based on the number of units financed in order to encourage crowdfunders to invest greater amounts of money.

2. The donation typology provides that supporters sustain the campaigns without necessarily having to receive something in return. These are mainly social campaigns, charitable causes and non-profit activities. In addition, private projects that seek funds for personal purposes and those proposed by associations or institutions with the aim of financing socially useful activities (cultural events, creation of structures for communities, initiatives related to the world of education, etc.) also belong to the category. The purposes with which they are carried out are precisely mostly philanthropic or linked to solidarity.[11] This mechanism presents benefits but also risks. The points in favor of this type

11We give an example of where the money goes from donations. Particularly, according to the GlobalGiving Foundation: "There are no costs for nonprofits to join GlobalGiving, but GlobalGiving retains a 15% fee on donations. When a donor makes a 100 dollars donation, 85 dollars goes to the project(s) of his/her choosing, and 10 dollars goes to fund the many programs and services we offer nonprofits. Then 3 dollars goes to cover standard credit card on transaction fees, and the remaining 2 dollars goes to administrative costs of running Global Giving."

of crowdfunding summarized in the following arguments: The key benefit is access to cheaper funds regardless of geographical barriers. Using social networks to raise funds helps to give visibility to the campaign and reach individuals outside the beneficiary's immediate social circle. Other benefits include the formalization of donations, advice, basic accounting, marketing, education and training. As for the risks this type of raise funds meets, the most obvious is fraud,[12] either in form of fake campaigns or cyber-attack. Other risks have to do with the cost of the campaign. For example, platforms charge fees and the beneficiaries need to spend extra money to design and run the campaign, manage relationships with donors, administer donations, etc. Another type of risk may be the raise of funds for money laundering or for terrorist financing purposes, particularly where platforms escape the regulatory framework for anti-money laundering and counter terrorist financing due to a gap in their regulation and oversight.[13]

3. Equity based crowdfunding projects consist of risk capital offers from start-ups or companies in general and crowdfunders become owners of the same. This form of crowdfunding is the latest and still evolving. In addition, equity crowdfunding is certainly the most complex type of the four since it involves the acquisition of company shares. We speak of equity-based crowdfunding when through the online investment you buy a real equity investment in a company: In this case, the reward for the financing is represented by the complex of property and administrative rights that derive from the participation in the enterprise.

This model provides a more conventional capital-raising method by offering financial securities to investors. Moreover, its process is carried out on specialized online platforms such as StartEngine and Wefunder.

In general, crowdfunding is a particularly suitable mechanism in the start-up phase, since the newly incorporated companies are entering the market and need initial resources, to fill the existing funding gap.[14]

12GRELLA S., *Fraudulent Crowdfunding Campaing Sets Precedent,* in *Observer,* September 2015, available at: http://observer.com/2015/09/kickstarter/

13For further details on benefits and risks on donation crowdfunding see: JENIK I., LYMAN T., NAVA A., *Crowdfunding and Financial Inclusion, Working Paper-CGAP*, 2017, p.55ss.

14LEY A., WEAVEN S., *Exploring agency dynamics of crowdfunding in start-up capital financing,* in *Academy of Entrepreneurship Journal*, vol. 17, n. 1, 2011, pp. 85-110. MACHT S.A., WEATHERSTON J., *The Benefits of Online Crowdfunding for Fund-Seeking Business Ventures,* in *Strategic Change*, vol. 23, n.1/2, 2014, pp. 1-14.

Equity crowdfunding, in particular, would be a particularly suitable tool if used in the launch phase of the initiative, or in the immediately following period, where the first turnover is achieved. However, the founders of the companies, in some cases, show a tendency to postpone the entry of new members by aiming to recognize a higher value of the project and the possibility of selling, with the same financial resources being equal, a lower share of the company.

Equity crowdfunding, actually, would be a particularly suitable tool if used in the launch phase of the initiative, or in the immediately following period, where the first turnover is achieved. However, the founders of the companies, in some cases, show a tendency to postpone the entry of new members by aiming to recognize a higher value of the project and the possibility of selling, with the same financial resources being equal, a lower share of the company.

GrowVC and Crowdcube are the first two equity crowdfunding platforms that saw the light respectively in 2010 and 2011. GrowVC defines itself as "a new model of community financing" and aims to develop a market to support the technological start-ups with financing of up to one million dollars. The commitment of the subjects involved in the development of this model testifies to the importance that is attached to the tool for supporting start-ups and in general for small and medium-sized enterprises which, in the economic context of the last decade, have struggled to receive capital from traditional financing channels. In fact, the great success of this crowdfunding model can be read in the light of the economic situation of recent years: The credit crunch caused by the crisis that has hit the global economy has impacted start-ups in particular. Being risky companies by definition, they encountered increasing difficulties in obtaining financing from the banking sector, which at the same time had to limit risky investments in response to the new scenario of economic crisis. The development of equity-based platforms, however, was slowed down by the need for new regulations, as the shares purchased by investors were financial securities in all respects. Lawmakers are working to define the rules within which this financing model can develop, which is why today equity crowdfunding is a model that is still evolving and must continuously deal with the introduction of regulations by the authorities.

4. Finally, the lending model, which represents the most relevant in terms of turnover, basically consists of a "loan between private individuals" bypassing traditional intermediaries. In fact, the projects of this class are forms of collective loan and require crowdfunders to lend money to the proposer (company or private individual) who on a pre-established date undertakes to return the principal and interest due. In turn,

these projects are divided into two sub-classes: a) The micro-loan which consists in the provision of financial services to people with low incomes or who have difficulty obtaining money from traditional financing channels. In this case the loan is collected by a group of crowdfunders and is managed by an intermediary who is usually appointed by the platform; b) peer-to-peer loans that take place directly between individuals without the intermediation of financial institutions. In these forms of loan, the relationship between the proposer and the investors is one to many. The promoter requests funding and this is spread across different crowdfunders in order to limit the impact of insolvency risks on the individual person.

The match between the two types of subjects, i.e. those who need money and those who are willing to lend it, therefore takes place through lending crowdfunding platforms, where they can sometimes (as in the case of peer-to-peer) directly contact and establish loan amounts and rates (fixed or variable) that satisfy both parties. Based on the key objective promoted by the platform, we can distinguish commercial, nonprofit and socially oriented lending. Platforms for commercial lending usually do not target specific groups of fundraisers. Examples of these include LendingClub in the United States and Zopa in the United Kingdom. The nonprofit platforms, on the other hand, seek to reach communities with limited access to formal lenders without expectations of a financial return. Examples of these are Zidisha e Kiva, which lend money collected from lenders leveraging local microfinance infrastructures in the hardest to reach places. Finally, socially oriented lending support specific communities or geographic regions. For example, MYC4 enables funders to lend money to SMEs in developing countries in Africa for a small yield.

A further classification that can be found within the different types of crowdfunding is that relating to the model applied by the platforms for financing the campaigns.

The business models are substantially concretized in "all or nothing" (AON) and "keep it all" (KIA), or hybrid forms that derive from the combination of the two.

The first model provides for a goal in terms of funding to be collected, and the funds raised will be given to the proposer only and exclusively in the event that the objective is achieved (or exceeded). This model is particularly risky for entrepreneurs who set ambitious goals.

The second model, unlike the first, allows the founders to obtain the amount collected during the campaign (sometimes with higher fees) regardless of the achievement of the goal.

A classification of the four types mentioned above is proposed below, creating a special matrix. It relates the growth rate on the market of the different types of crowdfunding and the ability of the same four forms to support innovation.

Table 1. Matrix of the 4 types of crowdfunding

		Degree of support for innovation	
Growth rate on the market		High	Low
	Low	Equity	Donation
	High	Reward	Lending

Source: Processing by the author

The equity and reward-based forms have a high degree of sustainability towards innovation, understood as the ability to support and encourage the diffusion of innovations. The two models, in fact, represent considerable support for startuppers both in the launch phase of their business or test of the idea, and in subsequent developments of the entrepreneurial initiative. The two types indicated lend themselves well to supporting the innovative process by the founders, who can for example make prototypes or offer innovative outputs/products in pre-sale (reward) or develop further new technologies and expand the company (equity). Moreover, the equity based model, depending on the country of reference, can pursue precisely the aim of supporting targeted start-ups of an innovative nature.

Instead the donation and lending models have a low ability to support innovation because they pursue other purposes (respectively donations for solidarity and interest loans). As for the market growth rate, as reported by the main world statistics and reports (e.g. the Massolution annual reports or the Cambridge Center for Alternative Finance-CCAF), the lending and the reward model have experienced significant growth in recent years, in particular the former has also become the most representative in terms of market volume of the four types (with over 25 billion dollars in 2015).[15] The growth of the other two types is still slow, in particular equity crowdfunding, which more and more states are considering introducing with specific regulations.

15MASSOLUTION, *2015CF The Crowdfunding Industry Report.* Massolution.com, 2015, available at: http://www.smv.gob.pe/Biblioteca/temp/ catalogacion/C8789.pdf

Finally, in addition to the hybrid forms all or nothing "(AON) and" keep it all (KIA) we can refer to social lending and revenue sharing or royalty based project.

Social lending is a model very similar to lending-based, but with an imposing difference: The proposer undertakes to return the capital to the lenders, but does not pay any interest on the loan. This class combines lending projects with donation-based ones.

Revenue sharing or royalty based projects are similar to equity-based, but the investor does not become a shareholder of the company and the return does not necessarily depend on the profits generated but can be equal to a percentage of the turnover or calculated on the basis of other results of the funded project.

1.3. Classification based on the collection objective

In this paragraph we will propose the subdivision of the projects into four mutually exclusive classes, defined according to the combination of two dimensions: The first variable refers to the objective of the proposer who can be personal or social, the second is linked to the reward of the investment which can be monetary or otherwise. By combining these two dimensions, the four classes are obtained: Business, Patronage, Donation/Charity and Cooperation.

The projects of the "business" class are oriented towards the profile and the creation of economic value from which both the proposer and the investor benefit, to whom a monetary return is recognized. This class includes, with the exception of some exceptions, revenue-sharing projects, equity-based projects and lending-based projects in which the proposer requests the loan with the aim of creating economic value.

The patronage class includes profit-oriented projects, but which do not provide for monetary return for the crowdfunder. This class therefore includes most of the reward-based projects (projects that are not for profit, such as cultural initiatives, are excluded).

In the case of donation/charity, the projects do not foresee monetary rewards. This class includes all those projects for social purposes that are part of the donation-based class.

Finally, projects for social or philanthropic purposes, but which encourage investments by proposing an economic return, are included in the class of cooperation. This class includes a number of projects significantly lower than those of donation/charity.

Table 2. Matrix of the 4 types of crowdfunding based on the collection objective

		Primary objective of the promoter Personal	Social
Reward offered to lender	Monetary	BUSINESS	COOPERATION
	Non monetary	PATRONAGE	DONATION/ CHARITY

Source: Processing by the author

1.4. Ecosystem of crowdfunding

The crowdfunding ecosystem has developed very rapidly in recent years and is characterized by the presence of a multitude of stakeholders. The latter have to do with information problems and risks associated with online campaigns.[16] The main stakeholders can be summarized as follows:

1. The founders (promoters of the initiatives and projects proposed on the online portals);
2. The funders (financiers, those who support projects through funding/donations);
3. The crowdfunding platforms (such as Kickstarter and IndieGoGo, which facilitate the meeting between founder and funder);
4. Policy (institutions, international bodies, regulators and guarantors such as authorities);
5. Associations and NGOs (various non-governmental organizations, non-profit organizations, non-profit organizations);
6. Financial community (banks, venture capital, business angels, professional investors, intermediaries, etc.);
7. Shareholders;
8. Community of users;
9. Workers/employees (various categories are included, including analysts, managers, technicians and employees of portals or internet companies, or start-ups financed with crowdfunding, etc.);
10. Competitors (both in terms of platforms and therefore of the related services, and in terms of projects developed and launched);
11. Developers (who create portals and applications);
12. Producers of web technologies, ICT and mobile devices (devices such as smartphones and tablets);

16VOORBRAAK K.J.M., *Crowdfunding for Financing New Ventures: Consequences of the Financial Model on Operational Decisions.* Eindhoven University of Technology, Eindhoven, 2011.

13. Network operators (such as telecommunications that provide networks and connectivity).

The main roles necessary to realize and implement the funding mechanism through the crowd can be traced back to three, namely the platforms, promoters and financiers.[17] First of all, there is the relevant function of the intermediary that allows the meeting between founders and funders to be considered.[18] With reference to the founders, there are both entrepreneurs and proponents of projects or initiatives of different kinds, who through the platform obtain direct access to the market and implement the collection of funds by supporters who are really interested in financially supporting the campaigns.[19] The latter, or the funders, decide to financially support the campaigns, pending a return and taking on the risks.[20]

A framework of the crowdfunding ecosystem can be provided based on the main activities that stand out in the crowdfunding economy: The development of projects (specially created by the founders), distribution (through crowdfunding portals, on which they are launched and advertised, as in the pitch case to describe the idea or project, and disseminated on the web and social networks), the funding offer (through funders, users and investors).

The activities indicated above, whose actors constitute the core around which the crowdfunding economy runs, depend on a complex support ecosystem consisting of: Policy (such as regulation on the subject, for example the regulation for equity crowdfunding and taxation), the prevailing socio-economic conditions (such as income, demography, education), the system of development and management of the platforms (which can belong to an open ecosystem, or open source), devices (such as smartphones and tablets), infrastructure network etc.

17TOMCZAK A., BREM A., *A conceptualized investment model of crowdfunding*, in *Venture Capital-An International Journal of Entrepreneurial Finance*, vol. 15, n. 4, 2013, pp. 335-359.

18BURKETT E., *A Crowdfunding Exemption? Online Investment Crowdfunding and U.S. Securities Regulation*, in *Transactions: The Tennessee Journal of Business* Law, vol. 13, 2011, pp. 63 – 106.

19ORDANINI A., MICELI L., PIZZETTI M. and PARASURAMAN A., *Crowd-Funding: Transforming Customers into Investors through Innovative Service Platforms*, op. cit.

20MOLLICK E., *The dynamics of crowdfunding: An exploratory study*, in *Journal of Business Venturing*, vol. 29, n.1, 2014, pp. 1-16. ORDANINI A., MICELI L., PIZZETTI M. and PARASURAMAN A., *Crowd-Funding: Transforming Customers into Investors through Innovative Service Platforms*, op. cit.

Platforms play a fundamental role, ensuring access to a multitude of users, both on the demand and supply sides. In fact, they allow the meeting between entrepreneurs/project proponents and investors, and in addition to being considered as intermediaries that facilitate and regulate transactions and payments,[21] they are also considered as a place for social connections.[22]

The platform creates value by facilitating the interactions between the different groups[23] which take the form of network effects. The value of the service offered to the user derives from the number of people using it.[24] The more users are present within the platform, the more successful it will be. In fact, if there are many supporters registered as members of the community, this will lead potential promoters of initiatives (both internal and external to the community) to launch campaigns on the platform, vice versa if there are numerous projects to be financed on the platform, this will attract funders who they will be able to choose from numerous alternative initiatives to support.

Based on the above considerations, we can divide the platforms according to the crowdfunding model used. We will therefore have donation, reward, lending and equity-based platforms; and of course some platforms that are not specialized on a single model, but that allow you to present projects that fall into different classes.

Another way to classify the platforms is based on how the funds raised are treated. We are talking about platforms that apply the all-or-nothing rule and take it all. In the first case, the proposer receives funding only if the fundraiser reaches the minimum funding target. If the funding does not reach the minimum threshold on the due date of the collection, the platform will not proceed with the transfer of the loans to the promoters, but will take care of returning the capital to the crowdfunders. In the second case, the all-or-nothing rule is not applied and at maturity

---

21AHLERS G.K.C., CUMMING D., GÜNTHER C., SCHWEIZER D., *Signaling in Equity Crowdfunding,* in *Entrepreneurship Theory and Practice*, op. cit.

22In fact, the platforms immediately exploited the social web using social networks such as Facebok, Youtube and Twitter and quickly became the symbol of bottom-up financing. COLOMBO M.G., FRANZONI C., LAMASTRA C.R., *Internal Social Capital and the Attraction of Early Contributions in Crowdfunding,* in *Entrepreneurship Theory and Practice*, vol. 39, n. 1, 2015, pp. 75-100.

23OSTERWALDER A., PIGNEUR Y., *Business Model Generation: A Handbook for Visionaries, Game Changers, and Challengers*, Hoboken, Wiley, New Jersey, 2010, pp. 1-288.

24HENDLER J., GOLBECK J., *Metcalfe's Law, Web 2.0, and the Semantic Web*, in *Journal of Web* Semantics, vol. 6, n. 1, 2008, pp. 14 – 20.

they transfer the loans received to the proposer even if the project has not reached the pre-established funding threshold. Finally, some crowdfunding platforms focus only on projects that concern particular issues or objectives. For example, there are platforms that collect projects that concern only the world of music or journalism, equity-based platforms that focus only on start-ups of a particular industrial sector and so on.

In addition, both founders and funders are attracted and driven to use the platforms and require increasingly smart services that are suitable for satisfying and increasing the quality of the user experience. Platform users also seek simple and focused access to security protection by operators, as well as regulated communities.

This representation can provide interesting considerations regarding: Competitiveness areas, key transactions, mechanisms and economic drivers. A description of the crowdfunding phenomenon can be of support to the various stakeholders in understanding the ecosystem, primarily policy makers. In fact, the various governments must try to create the best conditions for promoting the local development of this financing instrument and maximizing its innovative potential, since it can benefit society and the various sectors of the economy. The funded projects, in fact, create new jobs and supporters benefit from various types of rewards, such as pre-orders or company shares.[25]

The importance of the role of the various actors within the network changes according to the geographical distribution and market conditions. The peculiarities and availability of crowdfunding platforms, both on the demand and on the supply side, have now become one of the main new sources of value creation.

With digital disruption,[26] there is a change that occurs when new digital technologies and business models developed with them influence the added value, the value proposition of existing products or services. Thanks to the spread of online portals, as well as devices, platform managers have been able to significantly improve their positioning in the value chain of the crowdfunding industry. On the founders' side, the choice of platform is decisive, to attract investors. Platform managers, in fact, try to attract users, project proponents and supporters to increase the value of the platform itself. This value depends on the number of available projects, users and variety of options available.

25BELLEFLAMME P., LAMBERT T., SCHWIENBACHER A., *Crowdfunding: Tapping the right crowd*, in *Journal of Business Venturing,* op. cit.
26SCHMID E., COHEN J., *The Digital Disruption. Connectivity and the Diffusion of Power*, in *Foreign Affairs*, HeinOnline, 2010.

The new platforms have thus created great possibilities for users to generate value, stimulating continuous innovation and increasing the potential to bring both proposers and supporters closer together.

1.5 Market and innovation

Crowdfunding is a typical example of a two-sided market, where two distinct groups of users are connected in a network.[27]

The spread of the internet and the latest web technologies has reduced the role of physical barriers to digital innovation and the rise of electronic platforms and markets has generated enormous opportunities for entrepreneurs with the reduction of development and distribution costs for outputs and applications furnishings.

Crowdfunding has had enormous success in recent years thanks to some key factors, such as the spread of the "mobile" habit thanks to the constant online connection with devices such as notebooks, smartphones and tablets, the greater availability of ultra-wide bandwidth, the reduced costs for the realization and diffusion of projects and initiatives, and above all a change in the needs of the world population. In fact, more and more people, in particular the so-called "millennials," feel the need for connectivity, that is to be always connected with the rest of the world, exchange information, share experiences, communicate in real time, the desire for perfect information, all this is driving the change in consumer behavior and the increasing adoption of financial services from marketplaces (online).

Crowdfunding represents a fundamental lever for the economic development of countries, especially in times of crisis. Since the first appearances, in fact, this new source of innovation in the modern economy has given a strong boost to the economic recovery, showing significant effects in terms of employment, development of sectors partially affected by the crisis and bringing significant innovations for users.

The incentive to innovate is one of the main tasks of regulators, and this leads to significant positive aspects in terms of efficiency, as well as an optimization of services and the circulation of information.

The advent of crowdfunding platforms certainly represents an event that has had a disruptive impact on the world market, effectively changing its balance and moving established competitors. This innovation,

---

27EISENMANN T., PARKER G., VAN ALSTYNE M.W., *Strategies for Two-Sided Markets*, in *Harvard Business Review*, vol. 84, n. 10, 2006, pp.1-11.

which can be labeled as a "disruptive innovation,"[28] has created new markets and a new population of users/consumers, allowing access to services and products through the portals.

Platform developers, in recent years, have brought significant innovations for users, coming to offer increasingly efficient services that support both the founder and the funder in the various steps, as can be seen from the main world portals through which the project proponents are guided in the launch phases of the initiative, and the same is true for funders in the funding phase.

Particularly, in recent years this form of financing has been ousting the main types of financing (banks, venture capital, business angels), becoming a valid alternative and sometimes a competitor of the latter or even a source capable of integration with the previous ones.[29] In recent years we have witnessed rapid changes in strategies in the financial markets and this has led to actions primarily in pricing policies and strategic partnerships. For example, several portals have strongly encouraged the use of academies or targeted tutorships for users. In response to this, traditional financial systems have recently been improving by increasing the offer of services and technologies available to users.

The focus of crowd funding is increasingly focused on finding solutions for users, aimed at exploiting the enormous potential of the network and portals, strongly oriented towards innovation. In this field, some collaborations and alliances between some of the most important players on the market are strategic, in a logic that we could define as "cooperation in innovation," demonstrating how innovations are a fundamental competitive lever. This logic includes the case of some important companies at a global level, such as for example TIM that has promoted open innovation programs and supports new start-ups and new ideas, both with Tim Ventures, and a Corporate Accelerator called TIM Wcap (working capital), and also with a "TIM WithYouWeDo" crowdfunding platform that promotes and finances various types of initiatives to generate economic value by creating social value through digital technology. Many others are companies at international level that through crowdfunding directly support or finance projects such as Coca Cola, Samsung and Wind. Furthermore, a phenomenon that could be

---

28BOWER J.L., CHRISTENSEN C. M., *Disruptive Technologies: Catching the Wave,* in Harvard Business Review, vol. 73, n. 1, 1995, pp. 43–53.
29TOMCZAK A., BREM A., *A conceptualized investment model of crowdfunding,* in *Venture Capital-An International Journal of Entrepreneurial Finance,* op. cit.

defined as "corporate crowdfunding" is also taking hold, in which some companies, such as IBM and Sony, use crowdfunding platforms to finance the ideas of their employees and encourage their work by continuing with the innovative process. In the case of IBM, this innovative method, which represents one of the first cases of internal crowdfunding, which rewards employee innovations and also constitutes a rewards system, was implemented through the creation of an enterprise crowdfunding program in 2012, sponsored and financed by the same company. The project showed a high rate of employee participation (almost 50%), who were left with the decision on how and where to allocate the funds.[30] The excellent outcome of the initiative has led the company to propose it also in other locations[31] and the success of the experiments has prompted the managers of IBM's IT department to also carry out internal crowdsourcing initiatives,[32] and the CIO division to move the crowdfunding platform in the 2013 creating a CIO Lab that annually offers crowdfunding campaigns and leads to technological innovation in various sectors such as mobile telephony and the cloud.

More and more often companies create specific areas (sometimes real Labs) specifically dedicated to the development of innovations, in which start-ups from outside are incubated or their employees are given the opportunity to develop projects, or an internal venturing process.[33] These initiatives created from within are in fact guided and managed by the internal entrepreneurs themselves (or intrapreneurs). The logic of internal venturing requires reallocations of resources and a level of commitment from top management and/or ownership, for the latter, implementing a corporate crowdfunding policy would allow employees to receive the funding necessary to develop the most interesting projects and with greater prospects of realization. The advantage of this method, which guarantees a certain freedom with respect to the company, is given by the commitment of the employees pushed to finance, voluntarily and

---

30Employees each donated $ 100 and had the opportunity to propose a project, but they could only use the funds to support their colleagues' projects, not theirs. The participation was around 500 employees and 45 projects were proposed.

31At IBM's Almaden Research Center, San Jose, with the initiative most focused on technology projects. Subsequently, the crowdfunding experiment also captured the interest of an IBM IT department, whose executives also decided to experiment with the crowd powered ideation process.

32Also referred to as "the crowd-powered ideation process."

33SORRENTINO M., *L'imprenditorialità interna per lo sviluppo*, in LIPPARINI A. and LORENZONI G., (ed. by), *Imprenditori e imprese*, Il Mulino, Bologna, Italy, 2000.

discretionarily (not on a public portal, but in a private space for the employees themselves) internal initiatives of other employees, highlighting a sense of belonging and promoting innovation. On the other hand, the direction and management provide the necessary spaces and are involved as regards, for example, the pre-selection phase of the projects to be financed, sometimes actively participating with financial support, preferring short/medium-term investments. This process certainly stimulates entrepreneurship, bringing out innovative projects and creative initiatives and sometimes generates fruitful interdepartmental collaborations or a sort of healthy "internal competition," with advantages from the point of view of the quality level of innovations.

There have been numerous start-ups born in recent years that have used crowdfunding, with excellent success rates,[34] as a source for obtaining the first feedback and above all the financial resources necessary for the start-up phase and the launch of production/prototyping, such as Pebble smartwatch that has been successful in getting over $ 10 million on Kickstarter, and the same goes for a huge number of business ideas successfully funded on the portals.

The crowdfunding and the portals with which the interaction between founder and funder takes place, represent an important driver of innovation, and the role of the crowd is increasingly important for the development and support of initiatives and the revitalization of local economies (the campaigns crowdfunding can be both a tool to launch new businesses, but also social initiatives). In fact, in recent years we find the crowd as the main element of the most recent models and paradigms developed, such as crowdsourcing, a type of participatory online activity where the crowd freely and voluntarily carries out a task and brings ideas,[35] and the open innovation[36] model, of open innovation drawing on ideas from the outside, which has recently had a great diffusion, undermining the previous innovation models (such as the demand pull and technology push model), and is used more and more frequently in particular by large companies.

34Kickstarter reported that out of 50 aspiring companies that used crowdfunding to raise seed capital, 45 turned into entrepreneurial initiatives, in 2012.

35HOWE J., *Crowdsourcing. Why the power of the crowd is driving future of business,* op. cit. ESTELLÉS AROLAS E., GONZÁLEZ-LADRÓN-DE-GUEVARA F., *Towards an integrated crowdsourcing definition,* in *Journal of Information Science*, vol. 38, n. 2, 2012, pp. 1-14.

36CHESBROUG H.W., *Open Innovation: The New Imperative for Creating and Profiting from Technology*. Harvard Business School Press, 2003.

For proponents of particularly innovative and successful projects, there is often the trade-off between making a strategic choice oriented to the transfer/sale of the business to a large company or to set up a company in its own right (start-up), it cites the case of Oculus as an emblematic example, financed through Kickstarter (with almost 2 and a half million dollars and over 9,500 supporters) and subsequently sold to Facebook. The development of the crowdfunding sector has accompanied changes in the innovation environment and the growth and spread of entrepreneurship has created an explosion of competition and a proliferation of initiatives.

1.6. The regulatory frameworks for crowdfunding in the US and EU

The crowdfunding is a phenomenon that is becoming increasingly popular in all states and in recent years has attracted the attention of world governments.

This type of financing represents an opportunity for economic recovery for the various countries, especially considering the recent crises, and above all a tool that can be of support for the launch and development of new business initiatives and start-ups.

The crowdfunding regulation refers to the equity-based model, which represents a particularly "delicate" type given its economic-financial implications for investors, who acquire equity investments in companies and implies an offer to the public.

This funding model is not yet legal in most states,[37] where it is not yet regulated, and has only recently been legalized in the United States (Jobs Act-2012) and the European Union (Regulation of the European Parliament and of the Council on European Crowdfunding Service Providers for Business- ECSP 2018).

The JOBS Act (short for The Jumpstart Our Business Startups Act) is a law passed by President Obama in 2012 with the aim of reviving the U.S. economy and encouraging start-ups, which represent an important part of the GDP produced.

In particular, this method is dealt with in Title III of the Jobs Act which describes the methods of raising risk capital through portals, requirements, obligations and exemptions.

In the European Union, the scope of application of the ECSP Regulation concerns only two financial models of crowdfunding: Equity

---

37Among the states where it is not prohibited, they are mentioned as an example: Australia, New Zealand, United Kingdom.

crowdfunding and social lending. In the last decade, crowdfunding has reached technological maturity and, in many states, has proven to be a valid tool for raising funds. However, its development has taken place unevenly among the EU members, leading to the creation of multiple regimes that often diverge from each other. The ECSP should therefore allow to overcome this obstacle by reinforcing the protection of investors and savers through the implementation of transparency to encourage the growth in size and the development of platforms within the EU single market. The aim is to give more and better investment opportunities and encourage the spread of transnational crowdfunding, thus increasing access to finance for entrepreneurs, start-ups, expanding companies and SMEs in general. It is for this reason that crowdfunding forms based on donation and reward are excluded from the scope of the initiative.[38]

1.7. The numbers of crowdfunding

Crowdfunding has slowly established itself on the world scene, reaching impressive numbers in a few years, which are summarized below to better understand the impact and the dimensions assumed by the phenomenon.

The crowdfunding market is expanding in terms of total volume transactions, although the growth rate is decreasing (Figures 1 and 2):

The transaction value is expected to show an annual rate of 12.0% resulting in the total amount of US $ 11,958.6 m by 2023.

8.5 millions in dollars in 2020 with an increase of 23.2% compared to 2019;

6.9 millions in dollars in 2019 with an increase of 30.2% compared to 2018;

5.3 millions in dollars in 2018 with an increase of 35.9% compared to 2017.

38The reason for this exclusion is due to the lack of a financial transaction, or a monetary outlay against a promise of repayment based on an expectation of future cash flows. In this case, there is no specific service or product and the investor assumes a much higher level of risk. CROWDFUNDING CLOUD, *Nuovo regolamento UE sul crowdfunding.* Interview ad D. Valliante. Available at: www.crowdfunding.cloud , 23/04/2018.

Figure 1. Growth in the volume of funding through crowdfunding

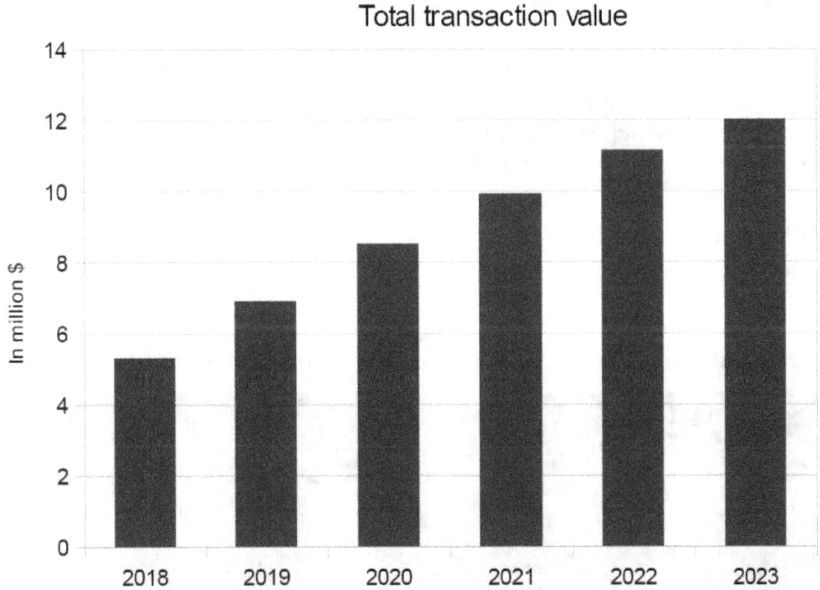

Source: Processing by the author on Crowdfunding data worldwide-Statista 2020

Figure 2. Transaction growth rate in% (2018-2023)

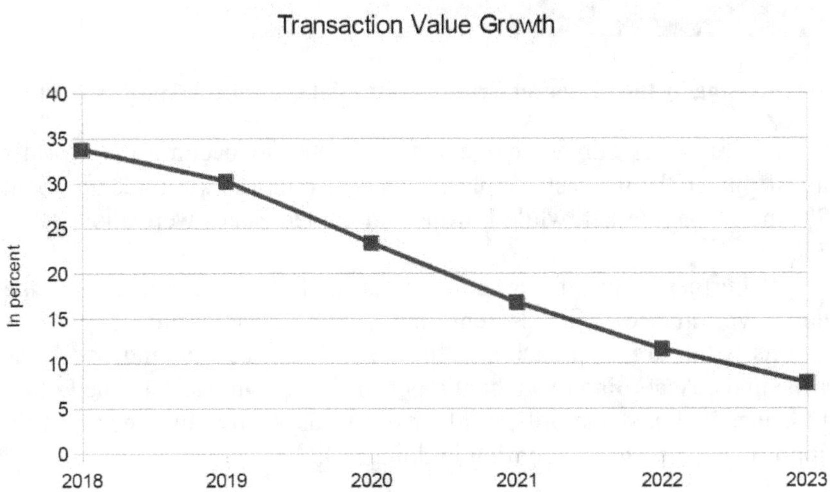

Source: Processing by the author on Crowdfunding data worldwide-Statista 2020

These numbers as evidenced by the "Crowdfunding worldwide-Statista 2020" are expected to further increase reaching US $ 11,985.6m in 2023.

The growth of the phenomenon has occurred in all countries, as can be seen from the data of "Crowdfunding worldwide-Statista 2020" (see Table 3), which records the following data regarding the diffusion for countries with the highest value worldwide: 7,049m of US dollars in China, 782m of US dollars in United States, 100m of US dollars in the United Kingdom, 86m of US dollars in France and 47m of US dollars in Canada.

Table 3:
Diffusion of countries with the highest transaction worldwide

Countries	Total transaction value in m US$ in 2020
China	US $7,049m
United States	US $ 782m
United Kingdom	US $ 100m
France	US $ 86m
Canada	US $ 47m

Source:
Processing by the author on Crowdfunding data worldwide-Statista 2020

China has surpassed the United States to become the world's largest player. In the last couple of years, China market took up about 37% the global market, while Europe and United States were about 18%, 33%.

Further data of particular interest for the evolution of the alternative finance sector is represented by the increasing number of subjects who are approaching this new form of funding, such as Millennials. According to a recent report by Goldman Sachs ("The Future of Finance") almost one Millennial out of two uses crowdfunding (actively supporting campaigns or coming in doing so).

Finally, this alternative form of financing has led to numerous spillover effects, such as the creation of jobs,[39] the advent of numerous crowdfunding platforms[40] and the increase in the proposed projects[41] on them.

39According to a Crowdfund Capital Advisors report, crowdfunding has generated new jobs, in fact 39% of companies hired an average of 2.2 new employees after the crowdfunding campaign, and about half (48%) of companies plan to use the proceeds from crowdfunding to hire new staff.

40The number of crowdfunding platforms present globally in the various countries has been estimated at around 2 thousand (Global Crowdfunding Sites to Choose from by 2016: Top 5 Growth Indicators).

41For example, Kickstarter counts (updates until January 2017) 329,539 projects presented on the platform (of which 117,938 projects successfully funded and 211,601 without success) and a number of supporters of 12,237,155 from almost all countries in the world, and the GoFundMe platform in 2016 reported over 25 million lenders.

CHAPTER 2

Empirical analysis of reward and equity based crowdfunding models

1. Introduction

The "crowdfunding phenomenon" has had a considerable impact on the world economy and significant implications for traditional financing systems and for a multitude of stakeholders.

After the crash of the banking system in 2008,[42] general economic health had an impact on the finance of small businesses.[43] Crowdfunding has begun to receive the attention of world institutions in the post-crisis period and the consequent contraction in the supply of credit, from the so-called credit crunch.[44] This mechanism has started to be considered a concrete source of financing in response to the shortage of funds by small and medium-sized enterprises, and above all to the growing difficulty, particularly for young start-ups, in obtaining financial resources from banks, venture capitalists and business angel.

In recent years, in fact, alternative finance is taking on a significant role, as an opportunity to boost the economic recovery, which is showing particularly significant numbers, as can be seen from the main world benchmarks and reports: In America there was in 2015 a growth in the volume of transactions through online alternative finance platforms of

---

42YAMEN S., GOLDFEDER Y., *Equity Crowdfunding. A Wolf in Sheep's Clothing: The implications of crowdfunding legislation under the JOBS Act,* in *Brigham Young University International Law & Management Review*, vol. 11,n. 1, 2015, p. 40ss, available at: https://digitalcommons.law.byu.edu/ilmr/vol11/iss1/4

43CUMMING D. (ed. by), *The Oxford Handbook of Entrepreneurial Finance,* Oxford, UK, Oxford University Press, 2012.

44 The credit crunch is generally defined as a contraction of the credit supply induced by a fall in the capitalization of banks ("capital crunch"), by reductions in the liquidity of the banking system, or sometimes by a more marked aversion to the risk of banks in granting loans. DE BUYSERE K., GAJDA O., KLEVERLAAN R., MAROM D., *A Framework for European Crowdfunding.* op.cit.

36.49 billion dollars with an increase of 212% compared to 2014 (11.68 billion dollars), while in Europe there were 3 billion euros (to be precise 2,957) in 2014 (+ 144% compared to 2013),[45] and in particular it should be noted that alternative finance in the United Kingdom, which includes crowdfunding, is estimated to have provided working capital in 2014 for 7,189 small and medium-sized enterprises, equal to 2.4% of bank loans to businesses.[46]

The crowdfunding, sometimes also identified as a new form of micro financing,[47] is pushing the traditional banking system and represents a new trend in alternative finance. The financial innovation represented by this form of funding through the crowd has favored the birth and development of various start-ups that have found a favorable ground.[48]

This new typology, through an open call on online platforms,[49] appears to have a key role in startup financing, being a particularly relevant tool in the pre and seed stage.[50]

Through crowdfunding portals, in fact, entrepreneurs can propose projects and request the necessary funds without having to seek risk capital or other traditional sources of investment and without the need for traditional financial intermediaries, being able to receive support directly from the crowd of financiers (crowdfunders).[51]

Technological progress is undermining the traditional European banking model, and in this context, this "new" mechanism, potentially

---

45WARDROP R., ZHANG B., RAGHAVENDRA RAU R., GRAY M., *Moving Mainstream. The European Alternative Finance Benchmarking Report*, University of Cambridge, 2015, available at: https://www.jbs.cam.ac.uk/.../2015-uk-alternative-finance-benc.
46NESTA, *The UK Alternative Finance Industry Report*, 2014.
47BRADLEY D.B., LUONG C., *Crowdfunding: A new opportunity for small business and entrepreneurship,* in *Entreprenurial Executive*, vol. 19, 2014, pp. 95-104. TRAUTMAN L., AHO W., *Crowdfunding, Entrepreneurship, and Start-Up Finance,* in *Entrepreneur & Innovation Exchange,* published online on 8 August 2019, doi: 10.32617/403-5d4c0e0041267
48MEDZIAUSYTE J., NEUGEBAUER P., *Financing success through equity crowdfunding: the case of start-ups and SMEs funded on European crowdfunding platform,* in *International Business School.* Jönköping University, 2017. METELKA A., *Crowdfunding-Startups' alternative funding source beyond banks, business angels and venture capitalists,* in *School of Management.* Blekinge Institute of Technology, 2014.
49MOLLICK E., *The dynamics of crowdfunding: An exploratory study,* op. cit.
50LEY A., WEAVEN S., *Exploring agency dynamics of crowdfunding in start-up capital financing,* op. cit. MANCHANDA K., MURALIDHARAN P., *Crowdfunding: a new paradigm in start-up financing,* Global Conference on Business and Finance Proceedings, vol. 9, n.1, 2014, p. 369.
51MOLLICK E., *The dynamics of crowdfunding: An exploratory study,* op. cit.

disruptive compared to traditional financing systems, is establishing itself as an increasingly widespread model and used by entrepreneurs or aspiring entrepreneurs.

This work examines the initiatives financed successfully through the types of equity and reward-based crowdfunding, launched by already established companies and potential start-ups destined to become companies in the short term. Two separate datasets were used, one for projects financed through an equity model consisting of 235 initiatives proposed on two platforms, and one for projects financed through a reward model consisting of 108 initiatives proposed on a platform. The focus is on the factors that influenced both the total amount of funding obtained and the number of final lenders. In particular, three sets of information and signals were analyzed by the initiative, namely the qualities of the company, the level of information (to reduce the degree of uncertainty) and the qualities of the crowdfunding campaign, to assess its impact on funding final and on investors. Hypotheses have been developed and tested in relation to each type of information, as will be explained below in the next paragraphs, and finally a comparison was made between the initiatives financed through the two types of crowdfunding in question. The purpose of this work, in fact, is to present an empirical examination of both equity and reward crowdfunding, contributing to the current debate on the signals and attributes of the initiatives, so far focused on the only type of equity crowdfunding.

2. Literature review

An increasing number of academics have recently started to become interested in alternative sources of funding, including crowdfunding. This funding collection mechanism, although not yet very simple in its use and with serious problems, has become a tool highly regarded by entrepreneurs and companies, who increasingly use it. This attracted the attention in particular of economics and entrepreneurship scholars, given the implications regarding the birth and growth of businesses.

In fact, several authors have highlighted the importance assumed by crowdfunding for start-ups in the start-up phase, representing a new paradigm in start-up financing[52] capable of bridging the funding gap for

52Cfr.MANCHANDA K., MURALIDHARAN P., *Crowdfunding: a new paradigm in start-up financing,* op. cit. LEY A., WEAVEN S., *Exploring agency dynamics of crowdfunding in start-up capital financing,* op. cit.

the initial phases.[53] Crowdfunding is relatively recent and the main contributions in the literature on this issue are still small and exploratory in nature. In particular, equity crowdfunding, introduced and regulated only a few years ago and limited to a few states, represents a field that is still little investigated and in constant evolution due to the numerous regulatory changes and the implementation of directives by various countries.

Most of the studies are first empirical attempts and have analyzed the determinants of the success or failure of crowdfunding campaigns such as with the works of Mollick,[54] Ahlers et al.,[55] and Cordova et al.[56] Other scholars have focused on the geographical location of the projects such as Agrawal et al.[57] as well as on the different types of crowdfunding for example Belleflamme et al.,[58] Cholakova and Clarysse,[59] Pierrakis and Collins[60] and as regards the business models of the platforms the work of Cumming et al.[61]

As regards the equity model, the most recent contributions have emphasized the options preferred by entrepreneurs in terms of rules on equity crowdfunding, analyzing the trade off regulation - deregulation as

---

53LEY A., WEAVEN S., *Exploring agency dynamics of crowdfunding in start-up capital financing,* op. cit. MACHT S.A., WEATHERSTON J., *The Benefits of Online Crowdfunding for Fund-Seeking Business Ventures,* op. cit.

54MOLLICK E., *The dynamics of crowdfunding: An exploratory study,* op. cit.

55AHLERS G.K.C., CUMMING D., GÜNTHER C., SCHWEIZER D., *Signaling in Equity Crowdfunding,* op. cit.

56CORDOVA A., DOLCI J., GIANFRATE, G., *The determinants of crowdfunding success: evidence from technology projects,* in Procedia-Social and Behavioral Sciences, vol. 181, 2015, pp. 115-124.

57AGRAWAL A., CATALINI C., GOLDFARB A., *Some Simple Economics of Crowdfunding,* in *Innovation Policy and the Economy,* NBER Books, National Bureau of Economic Research, vol. 14, 2013, pp. 63-97.

58BELLEFLAMME P., LAMBERT T., SCHWIENBACHER A., *Crowdfunding: Tapping the right crowd,* op.cit.

59CHOLAKOVA M., CLARYSSE B., *Does the Possibility to Make Equity Investments in Crowdfunding Projects Crowd Out Reward-Based Investments?,* in *Entrepreneurship Theory and Practice,* vol. 39, n.1, pp. 145-172.

60PIERRAKIS Y., COLLINS L., *Crowdfunding: A New Innovative Model of Providing Funding to Projects and Business,* SSRN Electronic Journal, 2013, doi:10.2139/ssrn.2395226.

61CUMMING D.J., LEBOEUF G., SCHWIENBACHER A., *Crowdfunding models: Keep-it-All vs. All-Or-Nothing,* in *Financial Management,* 2019, https://doi.org/10.1111/fima.12262

evidenced by the work of Cumming and Johan[62] and the scenarios from legislative point of view in the works of: Hopkins and Hopkins[63] Dorff,[64] Figliomeni,[65] Hogan,[66] Olson,[67] Houlihan and Curneen.[68]

Belleflamme et al.[69] analyzed the reward (pre-ordering) and equity (profit-sharing) models, comparing utilities and benefits for users, while the work of Cordova et al.[70] highlighted the determinants of success (or failure) reward crowdfunding campaigns focusing exclusively on technological projects.

In literature there are several contributions that, through signaling theory,[71] have analyzed the signals that push investors to finance certain business initiatives. The types of information that guide lenders in their choices vary both on the basis of the nature of the company and on the type of investor. The main references in the literature have placed attention on the signals of start-ups, characterized by a young age and a high infant mortality rate, which induce business angels and venture capitalists to finance them.[72] On the other hand, there is little knowledge of the signals

---

62CUMMING D., JOHAN S., *Demand-driven securities regulation: evidence from crowdfunding,* in *Venture Capital. An International Journal of Entrepreneurial Finance,* vol. 15, n. 4, 2013, pp. 361-379.

63HOPKINS J., HOPKINS K., *Not all that glitters is gold-Limitations of equity crowdfunding regulations,* in *Business Law Journal*, vol. 16, n. 2, 2014, p. 13ss.

64DORFF M.B., *The Siren Call of Equity Crowdfunding,* in *The Journal of Corporation Law,* vol. 39, p. 493.

65FIGLIOMENI M., *Grassroots capitalism or: how I learned to stop worrying about financial risk in the exempt market and love equity crowdfunding,* in *Dalhousie Journal of Legal Studies,* vol. 23, 2014, pp. 105-129.

66HOGAN J., *Like oil and water: equity crowdfunding and securities regulation,* in *Lewis & Clark Law Review,* vol. 18, 2014, pp. 1091-1116.

67OLSON E., *Squalls in the safe harbor: investment advice & regulatory gaps in regulation crowdfunding,* in *Journal of Corporation Law,* vol. 40, 2015, pp. 539-564.

68HOULIHAN C., CURNEEN D., *The regulation of crowdfunding in Ireland,* Dillon Eustace, 2017.

69BELLEFLAMME P., LAMBERT T., SCHWIENBACHER A., *Crowdfunding: Tapping the right crowd,* op. cit.

70CORDOVA A., DOLCI J., GIANFRATE, G., *The determinants of crowdfunding success: evidence from technology projects,* op. cit.

71SPENCE M., *Job Market Signaling,* in *The Quarterly Journal of Economics,* vol. 87, n. 3, 1973, pp. 355-374.

72BOUNCKEN R.B., KOMOREK M., KRAUS S., *Crowdfunding: The Current State of Research,* in *International Business & Economics Research Journal,* vol. 14, n. 3, 2015, pp. 407 ss. COSH A., CUMMING D., HUGHES A., *Outside Enterpreneurial Capital,* in *The Economic Journal,* vol. 119, n. 540, 2009, pp. 1494-1533. ROBB A.M., ROBINSON D.T., *The Capital Structure Decisions of New Firms,* in *The*

that guide small investors, who unlike the two categories just mentioned, do not have experience or even the tools necessary to adequately evaluate projects, or this would require high costs,[73] and therefore there is a high risk of financing initiatives in a less rational way, sometimes not considering economic and financial parameters.

The contributions regarding the signals in the context of crowdfunding are limited to the equity based type, for which there is only a paper produced by Ahlers et al. in 2015,[74] while there are no previous works that have examined the signals also with reference to the start-ups financed through the reward based model.

On equity crowdfunding, in particular a further aspect that has been investigated concerns the motivations and incentives (financial and non-financial) underlying the decisions to invest in an equity crowdfunding context, of which financial returns play a primary role.[75]

Ahlers et al.[76] also analyzed the effectiveness of the signals used by entrepreneurs, which influence the chances of success of fundraising. The authors placed the focus on venture qualities, such as human, social and intellectual capital, and on the level of uncertainty, which induce investors to commit financial resources in a system such as equity crowdfunding. This recent contribution highlights the importance of the level of uncertainty for potential investors and the importance of human qualities, while the remaining two categories of signals (intellectual and social capital) have shown a minimal or insignificant impact.

Starting from the existing literature, this work is aimed at identifying the signals that influence the funding obtained and the investors involved and is the first to also refer to start-ups financed through reward based crowdfunding.

Review of Financial Studies, vol. 27, n. 1, 2014, pp. 153-179. SAUREMANN H., FRANZONI C., SHAFI K., *Crowdfunding scientific research: Descriptive insights and correlates of funding success,* in *PLOS/ONE,* vol. 14, n. 1., 2019, available at: https://doi.org/10.1371/journal.pone.0208384. BESSIERE V., STEPHANY E., WIRTZ P, *Crowdfunding, business angels, and venture capital: an exploratory study of the concept of the funding trajectory,* in *Venture Capital. An International Journal of Entrepreneurial Finance,* 2019, pp. 1-26.

73AGRAWAL A., CATALINI C., GOLDFARB A., *Some Simple Economics of Crowdfunding,* op. cit.

74AHLERS G.K.C., CUMMING D., GÜNTHER C., SCHWEIZER D., *Signaling in Equity Crowdfunding,* op. cit.

75CHOLAKOVA M., CLARYSSE B., *Does the Possibility to Make Equity Investments in Crowdfunding Projects Crowd Out Reward-Based Investments?,* op. cit.

76AHLERS G.K.C., CUMMING D., GÜNTHER C., SCHWEIZER D., *Signaling in Equity Crowdfunding,* op. cit.

The analysis proceeds with the identification of the information channels and the study of the signals both in the reward and equity based context, and by making a comparison between the two types.

3. The success of the initiatives and the influential signals in the contexts of equity and reward crowdfunding

The financing of the projects is characterized by high information asymmetries and by possible problems of adverse selection and moral hazard.[77] In fact, entrepreneurs have information about the initiative that they may not disclose to lenders. Small investors are the most affected, as in the case of crowdfunders, as the collection of information on the initiatives and the status of the initiatives are particularly difficult to find and above all to evaluate. A further problem that emerges in funding contexts through crowdfunding is the lack of clarity on the progress and subsequent steps of the initiatives after being funded. To try to limit some issues related to transparency and clarity, various crowdfunding platforms, both equity and reward based, are requesting more information from the project proposers, such as the description of how the funds will be used, the timing of rewards (in the case of reward) and the status of the company (in the case of equity). However, this issue has not yet been sufficiently addressed by most platform operators, and only recently some regulators, in a still extremely limited number of states, have imposed some information obligations.[78]

In the case of equity crowdfunding, entrepreneurs have often been able to collect substantial amounts of financing through different portals (such as ASSOB), as analyzed by Ahlers et al.[79] highlighting how

---

77BELLEFLAMME P., LAMBERT T., SCHWIENBACHER A., *Crowdfunding: Tapping the right crowd*, op. cit. BELLEFLAMME P., OMRANI N., PEITZ M., *The economics of crowdfunding platforms,* in *Information Economics and Policy,* vol. 33, 2015, pp. 11-28. BEBCZUK N.R., *Asymmetric Information in Financial Markets. Introduction and Applications,* Cambridge, Cambridge University Press, 2013. FIROOZI F., JALILVAND A., LIEN D., *Information Asymmetry and Adverse Wealth Effects of Crowdfunding,* in *The Journal of Entrepreneurial Finance,* vol. 18, n. 1, 2016, pp. 1-8.

78Such as Consob in Italy which has provided for the obligation of a business plan for companies wishing to propose a public offer through an online portal, thus providing a useful information medium for external investors. Position papers - Equity-crowdfunding. Synthetic analysis of the legislation and operational aspects, August 2016.

79AHLERS G.K.C., CUMMING D., GÜNTHER C., SCHWEIZER D., *Signaling in Equity Crowdfunding,* op. cit.

investors have somehow managed to interpret the information and quality signals from businesses. As for reward crowdfunding, it is often noted that companies do not have an adequate level of information and this often turns into a limited number of successfully funded projects, as can be seen, for example, by analyzing the "technology" category, used in this type of study since projects of this type are identified as initiatives destined (potentially) to become businesses over time.[80] In fact, considering the data of the main international reward-based platforms such as Kickstarter (one of the first in the United States)[81] and Ulule (one of the first in Europe),[82] there is a success rate in the Technology,[83] category, respectively less than 20 % (to be precise 19.70%[84])) and 43%.[85]

In this situation of uncertainty, the signals deriving from the observable characteristics of the companies play an important role for the financiers, although not all the information of the companies represents a means to reduce the information asymmetries, since often the qualities and potential of the companies, in different cases young start-ups are not directly observable and easy to grasp.[86]

This work analyzes the signals that guide investment decisions by lenders who approach both an equity and reward-based context. Starting from the first contributions in the literature, some sets of information are analyzed that allow companies to have a positive response from the crowdfunding campaign, both in terms of funding obtained and in the number of investors involved. These two elements, which are associated

---

80CORDOVA A., DOLCI J., GIANFRATE, G., *The determinants of crowdfunding success: evidence from technology projects,* op. cit.

81It is perhaps the most popular of all the crowdfunding sites. It launched some popular products such as Pebble Watch, the Ouya game console and the Reading Rainbow reboot. It follows the all-or-nothing system so the funder's credit card isn't charged until the project meets its goal.

82Ulule is a reward-based platform. It allows you to participate in projects that are successfully funded only if they meet or exceed their fundraising goal. Since its launch in 2010, 16,589 innovative, creative and collective-purpose projects have been funded by users around the world.

83The statistics refer to the projects presented since the birth of the platforms.

84On 27,000 projects launched just over 5,300 were successfully funded. Source: Kickstarter website.

85On 541 projects submitted, 232 were successfully funded. Source: Ulule website.

86BUSENITZ L.W., FIET J.O., MOESEL D.D., *Signaling in Venture Capitalist-New Venture Team Funding Decisions: Does it Indicate Long-Term Venture Outcomes?,* in *Entrepreneurship Theory and Practice,* vol. 29, n. 1, 2005, pp. 1-12. BELLEFLAMME P., OMRANI N., PEITZ M., *The economics of crowdfunding platforms,* op. cit.

with the success of the projects through the use of this funding mechanism, constitute the dependent variables with which the independent variables are connected (see Figure 3).

The success of the initiatives, according to the pre-existing literature, is determined by a series of indications that guide the lenders in the investment, with reference to the characteristics of the entrepreneurial initiative and economic-financial information.

Starting from the work of Ahlers et al. in 2015, with reference to equity-based crowdfunding, in which the determinants of success were analyzed, taking into account the level of uncertainty (equity share and financial projections) and venture qualities (intellectual capital, human and social capital), both in funded projects (fully funded) and in projects not funded (not fully funded), in this paper it is argued that three sets of signals affect the level of funding obtained and the number of investors involved, analyzing both companies financed through reward and equity crowdfunding.

Figure 3. The success factors that determine the amount of funding and the number of investors

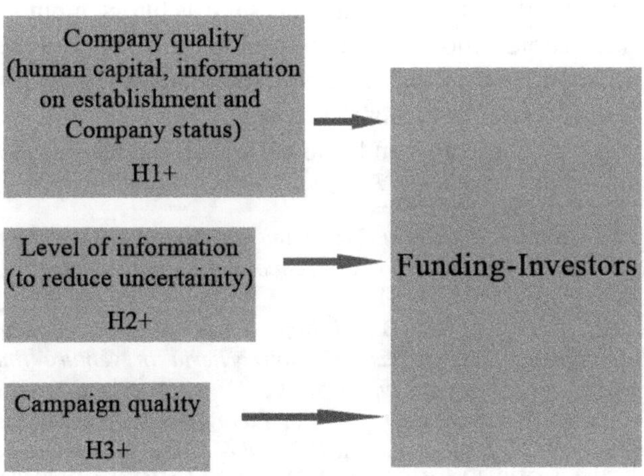

Source: Processing by the author

The first set is represented by the qualities of the company, consisting of information and documents offered by entrepreneurs, which provide indications on the characteristics of the companies.[87]

87AHLERS G.K.C., CUMMING D., GÜNTHER C., SCHWEIZER D., *Signaling in Equity Crowdfunding,* op. cit. BAUM J.A.C., SILVERMAN B., *Picking winners or*

1. Human capital, represented by the team (members of the company or initiative being set up) and the staff (subjects who work for the company, but are not part of the team). Human capital represents an important element for corporate strategies,[88]and is associated with their success;[89]

2. The information on the establishment of the enterprise, represented by the years (since the establishment of the company) and the innovation of the activity carried out (intended as an innovative enterprise or not, or if the main object is a traditional or high activity innovative content).[90] The nature of the company plays a considerable role in the financing choices made by investors, as well as the years in which the company operates in a business. In the reward-based context there is also an indication on the establishment of the company or not, as these are not companies that are already certainly founded as in the case of equity crowdfunding;

3. Information on the state of the firm, represented by previous rounds of financing (whether the firm has previously concluded rounds or not), the number of rounds of funding, awards (i.e. if the firm has received prizes , participated and/or won business plan competition, and other types of awards), tutors (the number of subjects such as tutors, mentors, business angels or incubators who have supported or still support the initiative and/or even recommended the same, until the launch of the crowdfunding campaign). This type of information represents an element that highlights the quality of the company, and allows lenders to receive news on the

---

building them? Alliance, intellectual, and human capital as selection criteria in venture financing and performance of biotechnology startups, in *Journal of Business Venturing,* vol. 19, n. 3, 2004, pp. 411-436.

88BAUM J.A.C., SILVERMAN B., *Picking winners or building them? Alliance, intellectual, and human capital as selection criteria in venture financing and performance of biotechnology startups,* op. cit.

89DOMS M., LEWIS E., ROBB A., *Local labor force education, new business characteristics, and firm performance,* in *Journal of Urban Economics,* vol. 67, n. 1, 2010, pp. 61-77. UNGER J.M., RAUCH A., FRESE M., ROSENBUSCH N., *Human capital and entrepreneurial success: A meta-analytical review,* in *Journal of Business Venturing,* vol. 26, n. 3, 2011, pp. 341-358. AHLERS G.K.C., CUMMING D., GÜNTHER C., SCHWEIZER D., *Signaling in Equity Crowdfunding,* op. cit.

90The term “innovative” does not refer to innovative start-ups, but refers to the nature of the company, or whether it has an innovative activity or project as its object. For example, consider a company that has created a robot or has patented a new type of fuel, which fall into the “innovation” category, unlike, for example, a traditional restaurant (example of a category present in the equity model, in particular in several campaigns on Crowdcube in the UK) which sells an equity stake to find new liquidity.

company's progress and developments. In particular, the awards are a signal of the company's activity.

With reference to this first category, the following two hypotheses have been formulated:

(1) The qualities of the company, represented by human capital (a), information on the establishment of the company (b) and information on the status of the company (c), positively influence the total amount of funding raised.

(2) The qualities of the company, represented by human capital (a), information on the establishment of the company (b) and information on the status of the company (c), positively influence the number of investors involved.

The second category of signals is represented by the level of information that the company provides to reduce the degree of uncertainty that characterizes the initiative, allowing investors registered in the crowdfunding platform to better evaluate the initiative launched. This category includes:

1.The equity offered, represented by the share of equity that the company sells to new investors (and therefore future shareholders) through equity crowdfunding platforms. A quality signal is represented by the share of the company held by entrepreneurs, correlated with the value of the company. The amount of equity sold is a signal that allows investors to know the level of shares that shareholders hold and the power held.

2. The business plan: The presence of a business plan by the company, which indicates economic and financial strategies and elements, is a tool capable of supporting investors to analyze risks and opportunities.

With reference to this second category, the following two hypotheses have been formulated:

(3) the level of information (to reduce the degree of uncertainty) positively influences the total funding raised.

(4) the level of information (to reduce the degree of uncertainty) positively influences the number of investors involved.

The last category is represented by the qualities of the crowdfunding campaign, considered in literature to be elements positively related to the success of the initiatives. They fall into this category:

1. Updates and comments, both the number of updates made by the proponents of the initiative, and the comments written by investors, are quality signals associated with a positive outcome of the crowdfunding campaigns.

2. The average contribution and the number of supporters, both the average amount of the contribution of each lender and the number of

the same, are identifying the higher or lower level of participation and relevance in helping a project to be successful.[91]

With reference to this third category, the following two hypotheses have been formulated:

(5) The qualities of the campaign positively influence the total funding raised.

(6) the qualities of the campaign positively influence the number of investors involved.

4. Methodology and data used

4.1. Data set and data collection

For this type of work, two separate datasets have been created, one with reference to companies financed through equity crowdfunding and the other with reference to reward crowdfunding.

As for the first, the data of the companies that were successfully financed through two of the most well-known equity crowdfunding portals, Crowdcube (UK) and Companisto (Germany), were collected, referring to all the projects financed since the origin of the platforms (therefore respectively from 2011 for the first and from 2012 for the second) until the beginning of 2019 for both. The sample thus obtained is made up of 235 companies (respectively 173 from the first platform and 62 from the second). The currency used was the euro, therefore the amounts of the projects financed through the Crowdcube platform (UK) were transformed from pounds into euros according to the exchange rate at the time of the end of the campaign, while as regards the amounts of the projects on Companisto they are already present in euro.

Instead, with reference to the reward-based model, the data of the projects successfully financed on the Kickstarter portal (USA), one of the main reward crowdfunding portals worldwide, was collected, considering only the Technology category and referring to 2018. The choice to limit the sample to this category only is due to the fact that it concerns both already established companies and potential start-ups which, given the nature of the proposed initiative, are destined to be set up in a short time (unlike equity crowdfunding where the companies must already be set up and sell an equity stake); while the choice to refer to only one year is due to the need to create a complete sample, given the breadth of the number

---

91CORDOVA A., DOLCI J., GIANFRATE, G., *The determinants of crowdfunding success: evidence from technology projects,* op. cit.

of projects presented over the years and the difficulty in finding the data completely.[92] The sample thus obtained is 108 projects successfully financed through a reward model (the currency expressed in dollars for this type has been maintained, since the comparison between systems is on volumes).

Description of the variables

The variables used are listed and described below.

Dependent variables

Two variables were used to measure success: 1) Ln Funding: the logarithmic transformation (natural logarithm) of the total funding raised by the initiatives; 2) The Investors LN: The logarithmic transformation (natural logarithm) of the number of financiers who contributed to the success of the initiative.

Independent variables

These are:

1) The Team. The number of the team that proposes the initiative;

2) The staff. The number of staff who work for or collaborate with the company;

3) Years of activity. The number of years in which the company carries out its activity, since its foundation;

4) Innovation. Dichotomous variable (0.1) that indicates whether the nature of an initiative is innovative or not;

5) The financing round. Dichotomous variable (0.1) that indicates the presence or absence of previous financing rounds obtained from the initiative until the launch of the crowdfunding campaign;

6) The number of financing round. The number of financing rounds that have been obtained from the initiative until the launch of the crowdfunding campaign;

7) Acknowledgments. The number of prizes or various acknowledgments received by the initiative so far;

8) The tutor. The number of subjects such as tutors, mentors, business angels or incubators who supported the initiative or even recommended it, until the launch of the crowdfunding campaign;

92Projects presented on crowdfunding platforms can sometimes, at the request of the proposer, be canceled, no longer making the information available.

9) The equity offered:[93] The share of equity, expressed in percentage terms, that the company sells;

10) The business plan. The dichotomous variable (0.1) indicates the presence or absence of a business plan that indicates the future prospects of the initiative and the way in which the funds will be used;

11) Updates. The number of updates made by the company during the crowdfunding campaign;

12) Comments. The number of comments present during the crowdfunding campaign, written by the lenders and to which the proposer may or may not have replied;

13) The state of initiative.[94] The dichotomous variable (0.1) indicates whether a company is incorporated (1) or not yet established (0);

14) Ln average amount. The logarithm of the amount of the average contribution of each lender;

15) Supporters: The number of financiers who financed the initiative;

Table 4. Descriptive statistics - Equity crowdfunding (Funding)

Variables	Obs	Mean	Std. Dev.	Min	Max
Ln Funding	235	12.08744	1.115421	9.181941	15.83041
Team	235	3.434043	1.960865	1	13
Staff	235	3.32766	8.605745	0	110
Years of activity	235	2.617021	2.412159	1	15
Innovation	235	.6765957	.468774	0	1
Financing round	235	.8680851	.3391205	0	1
n. financing round	235	1.544681	1.216484	0	7
Acknowledgments	235	2.140426	1.821484	0	10
Tutor	235	1.92766	1.571338	0	9
Equity offered	235	17.83718	13.4056	1.07	100
Business Plan	235	.7361702	.4416488	0	1
Updates	235	13.37872	11.37874	1	97
Comments/Notes	235	35.69362	37.57829	0	271

93Variable presented only in equity-based crowdfunding, as the sale of equity shares is presented only in this model.

94Variable presented only in reward-based crowdfunding, as the use of this financing mechanism is not limited to companies already established, unlike the equity model, as it can be used both by companies and by entrepreneurs or aspirants.

Ln average amount	235	6.979246	.9558221	4.869136	11.3022
Supporters	235	317.3872	414.9798	1	3503

Note: This table shows the descriptive statistics on successfully funded equity crowdfunding projects (dependent variable: Funding). It shows the mean (mean), the standard deviation (Std. Dev.) and the minimum (min) and maximum (max) values for each variable used.

Table 5. Descriptive statistics - Reward crowdfunding (Funding)

Variables	Obs	Mean	Std. Dev.	Min	Max
Ln Funding	108	10.12042	1.862524	4.990433	14.89592
Team	108	2.435185	2.296984	1	20
Staff	108	2.166667	3.030993	0	22
Years of activity	108	1.657407	3.144977	0	20
Innovation	108	.75	.4350314	0	1
Initiative status	108	.6111111	.4897708	0	1
Financing round	108	.5648148	.4980926	0	1
n. financing round	108	.7592593	.8523784	0	4
Acknowledgments	108	1.361111	1.423818	0	12
Tutor	108	1.055556	1.303004	0	11
Business Plan	108	.4722222	.5015552	0	1
Updates	108	21.87037	19.13654	0	141
Comments/Notes	108	256.3704	539.291	0	3116
Ln average amount	108	4.415041	1.013291	2.235222	7.647356
Supporters	108	852.6852	1512.001	4	9236

Note: This table shows the descriptive statistics on successfully funded reward crowdfunding projects (dependent variable: Funding). It shows the mean (mean), the standard deviation (Std. Dev.) and the minimum (min) and maximum (max) values for each variable used.

Table 6. Descriptive statistics - Equity crowdfunding (Investors)

Variables	Obs	Mean	Std. Dev.	Min	Max
Ln Investors	235	5.108193	1.185419	0	8.161375
Team	235	3.434043	1.960865	1	13
Staff	235	3.32766	8.605745	0	110
Years of activity	235	2.617021	2.412159	1	15

Innovation	235	.6765957	.468774	0	1
Financing round	235	.8680851	.3391205	0	1
n. financing round	235	1.544681	1.216484	0	7
Acknowledgments	235	2.140426	1.821484	0	10
Tutor	235	1.92766	1.571338	0	9
Equity offered	235	17.83718	13.4056	1.07	100
Business Plan	235	.7361702	.4416488	0	1
Updates	235	13.37872	11.37874	1	97
Comments/Notes	235	35.69362	37.57829	0	271
Ln average amount	235	6.979246	.9558221	4.869136	11.3022

Note: This table shows the descriptive statistics on successfully funded equity crowdfunding projects (dependent variable: Investors). It shows the mean (mean), the standard deviation (Std. Dev.) and the minimum (min) and maximum (max) values for each variable used.

Table 7. Descriptive statistics - Reward crowdfunding (Investors)

Variables	Obs	Mean	Std. Dev.	Min	Max
Ln Investors	108	5.705381	1.51228	1.386294	9.130864
Team	108	2.435185	2.296984	1	20
Staff	108	2.166667	3.030993	0	22
Years of activity	108	1.657407	3.144977	0	20
Innovation	108	.75	.4350314	0	1
Initiative status	108	.6111111	.4897708	0	1
Financing round	108	.5648148	.4980926	0	1
n. financing round	108	.7592593	.8523784	0	4
Acknowledgments	108	1.361111	1.423818	0	12
Tutor	108	1.055556	1.303004	0	11
Business Plan	108	.4722222	.5015552	0	1
Updates	108	21.87037	19.13654	0	141
Comments/Notes	108	256.3704	539.291	0	3116
Ln average amount	108	4.415041	1.013.291	2.235222	7.647356

Note: This table shows the descriptive statistics on successfully funded reward crowdfunding projects (dependent variable: Investors). It shows the mean (mean), the standard deviation (Std. Dev.) and the minimum (min) and maximum (max) values for each variable used.

Table 8. Correlation matrix and VIF - Equity crowdfunding (Funding)

(1-15)																VIF
1.Ln funding	1.0000															
2.Team	0.3269	1.0000														1.20
3.Staff	0.3336	0.1017	1.0000													1.31
4.Years of act.	0.0367	0.0353	0.1971	1.0000												1.22
5.Innovation	0.3995	0.1580	0.0899	-0.0306	1.0000											1.27
6.Financing r.	0.3149	0.1764	0.1042	0.0529	0.1875	1.0000										1.50
7.n. Fin. Round	0.5862	0.2749	0.2956	0.2636	0.3102	0.4753	1.0000									2.74
8.Acknowl.	0.5975	0.2258	0.3534	0.2788	0.2086	0.3414	0.6596	1.0000								2.36
9.Tutor	0.6623	0.3209	0.3007	0.1347	0.2988	0.3670	0.7071	0.6605	1.0000							2.75
10.Equity of.	0.0488	-0.0328	-0.1038	-0.0815	-0.0947	0.0585	0.0034	0.0192	0.0129	1.0000						1.08
11.B. Plan	0.4872	0.1772	0.1128	0.0371	0.3705	0.4514	0.4038	0.3491	0.3788	0.0512	1.0000					1.61
12.Updates	0.1354	0.1311	0.0542	0.1395	0.0183	0.1514	0.1731	0.2912	0.1605	0.0859	0.0200	1.0000				1.21
13.Com./Notes	0.2964	0.2166	0.2011	-0.0697	0.0096	0.0870	0.1946	0.2713	0.3154	-0.0067	0.0142	0.2235	1.0000			1.60
14. LN AVAm.	0.3529	-0.0923	0.0775	0.1295	0.1136	0.1800	0.2060	0.1525	0.1314	0.1285	0.3089	-0.0053	-0.3420	1.0000		1.57
15.Supporters	0.6208	0.3384	0.3658	0.0047	0.2227	0.1259	0.4213	0.4251	0.5446	-0.0208	0.2031	0.0336	0.5024	-0.2697	1.0000	2.27
$p \leq .05$																Mean VIF 1.69
VIF: Variance Inflation Factor																

Note: The sample has no heteroskedasticity (Breusch Pagan test) and there is no autocorrelation (Durbin Watson test).

The average VIF is 1.69 and the individual values are lower than the critical thresholds (5-6), therefore there are no problems related to multicollinearity.

Table 9. Correlation matrix and VIF -Reward crowdfunding (Funding)

(1-15)																VIF
1.Ln funding	1.0000															
2.Team	0.2379	1.0000														1.97
3.Staff	0.3109	0.1694	1.0000													1.37
4.Years of act.	0.1822	0.4607	0.2276	1.0000												2.50
5.Innovation	0.3068	0.0631	0.1453	0.0188	1.0000											1.33
6.In. Status	0.3725	0.1352	0.2581	0.4224	0.1097	1.0000										2.13
7.Fin. Round	0.4843	0.1344	0.3023	0.3991	0.2696	0.6789	1.0000									4.00
8.n. Fin. Round	0.3573	0.2306	0.3195	0.5651	0.1386	0.5572	0.7855	1.0000								4.05
9.Acknowl.	0.3925	0.5945	0.3844	0.6665	0.2226	0.3775	0.5136	0.6653	1.0000							3.68
10.Tutor	0.5046	0.3478	0.3763	0.3012	0.1896	0.3710	0.4552	0.4245	0.4022	1.0000						2.24
11.B. Plan	0.2706	0.2175	0.3412	0.1331	0.3320	0.3741	0.4188	0.2903	0.2955	0.3742	1.0000					1.65
12.Updates	0.5455	0.1444	0.1075	0.0044	0.3239	0.2429	0.2892	0.1482	0.2044	0.2926	0.2284	1.0000				1.66
13.Com./Notes	0.6134	0.2422	0.2196	0.0393	0.2400	0.2002	0.2847	0.2724	0.2761	0.5578	0.1187	0.4149	1.0000			2.91
14. LN AVAm.	0.5852	0.1275	0.1588	0.1951	0.2227	0.3542	0.3489	0.2409	0.1828	0.2769	0.2603	0.4874	0.2411	1.0000		1.67
15.Supporters	0.5799	0.1856	0.2486	0.0056	0.1484	0.1393	0.2572	0.2745	0.2142	0.5510	0.0385	0.2075	0.7361	-0.0273	1.0000	2.94
$p \leq .05$																Mean VIF 2.44
VIF: Variance Inflation Factor																
Note: The sample has no heteroskedasticity (Breusch Pagan test) and there is no autocorrelation (Durbin Watson test).																

The average VIF is 2.44 and the individual values are lower than the critical thresholds (5-6), therefore there are no problems related to multicollinearity.

Table 10. Correlation matrix and VIF -Equity crowdfunding (Investors)

(1-14)	1	2	3	4	5	6	7	8	9	10	11	12	13	14	VIF
1.Ln Investors	1.0000														
2.Team	0.3828	1.0000													1.18
3.Staff	0.2514	0.1017	1.0000												1.22
4.Years of act.	-0.0699	0.0353	0.1971	1.0000											1.21
5.Innovation	0.2843	0.1580	0.0899	-0.0306	1.0000										1.26
6.Fin. Round	0.1512	0.1764	0.1042	0.0529	0.1875	1.0000									1.47
7.n. fin. Round	0.3855	0.2749	0.2956	0.2636	0.3102	0.4753	1.0000								2.71
8.Acknowl.	0.4393	0.2258	0.3534	0.2788	0.2086	0.3414	0.6596	1.0000							2.35
9.Tutor	0.5173	0.3209	0.3007	0.1347	0.2988	0.3670	0.7071	0.6605	1.0000						2.56
10.Equity of.	-0.0577	-0.0328	-0.1038	-0.0815	-0.0947	0.0585	0.0034	0.0192	0.0129	1.0000					1.07
11.B. Plan	0.2094	0.1772	0.1128	0.0371	0.3705	0.4514	0.4038	0.3491	0.3788	0.0512	1.0000				1.59
12.Updates	0.1317	0.1311	0.0542	0.1395	0.0183	0.1514	0.1731	0.2912	0.1605	0.0859	0.0200	1.0000			1.18
13.Com./Notes	0.5546	0.2166	0.2011	-0.0697	0.0096	0.0870	0.1946	0.2713	0.3154	-0.0067	0.0142	0.2235	1.0000		1.47
14. LN AVAm.	-0.4742	-0.0923	0.0755	0.1295	0.1136	0.1800	0.2060	0.1525	0.1314	0.1285	0.3089	-0.0053	-0.3420	1.0000	1.39
$p \leq .05$															Mean VIF 1.59

VIF: Variance Inflation Factor

Note: The sample has no heteroskedasticity (Breusch Pagan test) and there is no autocorrelation (Durbin Watson test).

The average VIF is 1.59 and the individual values are lower than the critical thresholds (5-6), therefore there are no problems related to multicollinearity.

Table 11. Correlation matrix and VIF -Reward crowdfunding (Investors)

(1-14)															VIF
1.Ln Investors	1.0000														
2.Team	0.2076	1.0000													1.96
3.Staff	0.2765	0.1694	1.0000												1.35
4.Years of act.	0.0937	0.4607	0.2276	1.0000											2.46
5.Innovation	0.2287	0.0631	0.1453	0.0188	1.0000										1.33
6.In. Status	0.2214	0.1352	0.2581	0.4224	0.1097	1.0000									2.13
7.Fin. Round	0.3627	0.1344	0.3023	0.3991	0.2696	0.6789	1.0000								3.99
8.n. Fin. Round	0.2786	0.2306	0.3195	0.5651	0.1386	0.5572	0.7855	1.0000							4.00
9. Acknowl.	0.3610	0.5945	0.3844	0.6665	0.2226	0.3775	0.5136	0.6653	1.0000						3.66
10.Tutor	0.4359	0.3478	0.3763	0.3012	0.1896	0.3710	0.4552	0.2245	0.4022	1.0000					2.03
11.B. Plan	0.1588	0.2175	0.3412	0.1331	0.3320	0.3741	0.4188	0.2903	0.2955	0.3742	1.0000				1.59
12.Updates	0.3452	0.1444	0.1075	0.0044	0.3239	0.2429	0.2892	0.1482	0.2044	0.2926	0.2284	1.0000			1.66
13.Com./Notes	0.5939	0.2422	0.2196	0.0393	0.2400	0.2002	0.2847	0.2724	0.2761	0.5578	0.1187	0.4149	1.0000		1.84
14. LN AVAm.	0.0507	0.1275	0.1588	0.1951	0.2227	0.3542	0.3489	0.2409	0.1828	0. 2769	0.2603	0.4874	0.2411	1.0000	1.50
$p \leq .05$															Mean VIF 2.27
VIF: Variance Inflation Factor															

Note: The sample has no heteroskedasticity (Breusch Pagan test) and there is no autocorrelation (Durbin Watson test).

The average VIF is 2.27 and the individual values are lower than the critical thresholds (5-6), therefore there are no problems related to multicollinearity.

5. Results and method

Both with reference to the reward and the equity-based context, two separate analyzes were carried out to test the proposed hypotheses. For both types, the OLS Regression method was used, since the dependent variables follow a normal distribution and there are no problems related to multicollinearity (verified through the VIF), autocorrelation or the presence of heteroskedasticity, as described in the previous tables (Tables 8 -11). In total, four models were performed, statistically significant[95] and for which the respective R^2 indices are indicated, two regarding the funding obtained in the two types of crowdfunding and two regarding the number of investors, always in relation to the two indicated types. In this way it is possible, using common variables, to identify the relevant signals for companies both with reference to the funding received and the number of investors (using the same regressors), and to make a comparison between the two financing systems.

As regards the amount of funding raised, the two models are proposed and discussed below, Model 1 (Table 12) with reference to Equity crowdfunding (with R^2 equal to 78%) and Model 2 (Table 13) with reference to the Reward crowdfunding (with R^2 equal to 76%).

Table 12. Model 1: Equity Crowdfunding – Funding

Source	SS	Df	MS		
				Number of obs	= 235
				F (14,93)	= 57.08
Model	228.289843	14	16.3064173	Prob > F	= 0.0000
Residual	62.8443309	220	.285656049	R-squared	= 0.7841
				Adj R-squared	= 0.7704
Total	291.134173	234	1.24416313	Root MSE	= .53447

	Coef.	Std. Err.	t	P>t	[95% Conf.	Interval]
Team	.0410732	.0195592	2.10	0.037	.0025259	.0796206
Staff	-.0010648	.0046387	-0.23	0.819	-.0102068	.0080773
Years of activity	-.0398536	.0159873	-2.49	0.013	-.0713615	-.0083458
Innovation	.283731	.0840342	3.38	0.001	.118116	.449346

95(Prob F > 0.0000).

Financing round	-.0548557	.1261653	-0.43	0.664	-.3035031	.1937917
n. financing round	.0156981	.0475646	0.33	0.742	-.0780425	.1094388
Acknowledgments	.0963844	.0294853	3.27	0.001	.0382746	.1544942
Tutor	.0732482	.0368755	1.99	0.048	.0005736	.1459227
Equity offered	-.0003899	.0027035	-0.14	0.885	-.0057181	.0049383
Business Plan	.2423531	.1002948	2.42	0.016	.0446916	.4400147
Updates	.0035842	.003377	1.06	0.290	-.0030713	.0102396
Comments/ Notes	.0027801	.0011746	2.37	0.019	.0004653	.005095
Ln Average Amount	.534456	.0458468	11.66	0.000	.4441009	.624811
Supporters	.0013456	.0001269	10.61	0.000	.0010956	.0015956
_cons	7.062307	.3301592	21.39	0.000	6.411628	7.712987

p<0.05

Table 13. Model 2: Reward Crowdfunding - Funding

Source	SS	Df	MS			
				Number of obs	=	108
				F (14,93)	=	22.20
Model	285.310817	14	20.3793441	Prob > F	=	0.0000
Residual	85.8716062	93	.923350605	R-squared	=	0.7688
				Adj R-squared	=	0.7334
Total	371.182424	107	3.46899461	Root MSE	=	.96092

	Coef.	Std. Err.	t	P>t	[95% Conf.	Interval]
Team	-.0484209	.0567867	-0.85	0.396	-.161188	.0643462
Staff	.0132946	.0358888	0.37	0.712	-.0579735	.0845627
Years of activity	.0100987	.0467108	0.22	0.829	-.0826597	.102857
Innovation	-.0290977	.2467114	-0.12	0.906	-.5190176	.4608221
Initiative status	-.0046179	.2768973	-0.02	0.987	-.5544811	.5452453
Financing round	.7998784	.3730047	2.14	0.035	.0591649	1.540592
n. financing round	-.5403144	.2194016	-2.46	0.016	-.9760025	-.1046262
Acknowledgments	.3225678	.1251095	2.58	0.011	.0741251	.5710105
Tutor	-.1255981	.1066944	-1.18	0.242	-.3374722	.0862759

Business Plan	.1386494	.2380163	0.58	0.562	-.3340039	.6113027
Updates	.0129064	.0062521	2.06	0.042	.000491	.0253218
Comments/Notes	.0000582	.0002936	0.20	0.843	-.0005249	.0006413
Ln Average Amount	.8991892	.1184685	7.59	0.000	.6639343	1.134444
Supporters	.0006985	.0001053	6.63	0.000	.0004894	.0009076
_cons	4.94117	.4890769	10.10	0.000	3.969961	5.91238

$p<0.05$

In the equity-based model (Table 12), with reference to the first hypothesis, or the correlation of the qualities of the company with the amount of funding, the following significant variables are noted (while the variables not mentioned are not significant):

The team (with a coeff. of 0.0410 which corresponds to an increase of approximately 4.2% of the funding for an increase of one team unit) which, although not to a particularly high extent, is positively correlated with the funding obtained (considering that this amount can also be quite large), confirming hypothesis 1 a, and therefore the role played by human capital. In this case the team is associated as a quality element of the companies (for example considering the composition of the team, it may be that it is more or less numerous, and probably with different and complementary characteristics among the members).

The innovation, or the nature of the initiative, (with a coefficient of 0.2837 corresponding to an increase of approximately 33% of the funding for a unitary increase in innovation), represents significant evidence of the positive correlation with the amount funding, confirming hypothesis 1 b. However, with reference to the other variable of the information on the establishment of the company, or the years of activity, it is, albeit to a modest extent, negatively associated with the funding received (with a coefficient of -0.0398 corresponding to a decrease in the approximately 4% of funding), a symptom that companies that have been in the business for several years and decide to sell equity shares can be viewed with distrust by investors. In fact, the lenders can interpret the number of years of activity as synonymous with a phase of the company that is no longer of growth but of maturity and probably of decline (some companies have in fact gone bankrupt in a short time post-crowdfunding), highlighting a preference for start-ups, in particular innovative and capable of expanding (scalability), which can guarantee future economic returns. Therefore, hypothesis 1 b is confirmed only with reference to the first variable in question and not also to the second.

The number of awards (coeff. 0.0963 or a 10% increase in funding for a unit increase in awards) and tutors (coeff. 0.0732 or a 7.6% increase in funding for a unit increase in tutors), which fall into the category of information on the state of the company, are positively correlated with the funding obtained, confirming hypothesis 1 c. Both the awards received and the number of subjects who support the initiative are two significant signals that the lenders consider as quality elements and that somehow express the reputation of the company perceived from the outside.

With reference instead to the third hypothesis, that is the level of information to reduce the degree of uncertainty, there is a statistically significant empirical evidence, namely that the presence of business plan is positively correlated with the amount of funding received from the investors (coeff 0.2423 corresponding to a 27.4% increase in funding). This confirms hypothesis 3.

The third set of information, i.e. the qualities of the campaign, are positively correlated, albeit in a modest way, to the funding collected, confirming hypothesis 5. In particular, the number of supporters is a sign of quality, with a small impact (coeff. 0,0013 or an increase of 0.13% of funding for a unit increase of supporters), the average contribution (ln) (coeff. 0.5344 or for each increase of 10% of the average contribution corresponds to an increase of 5.2% of funding) and the number of comments (coeff. 0.0027 or a 0.3% increase in funding for a unitary increase in comments), also with a modest impact on the funding received.

In the reward-based model (Table 13), with reference to the first hypothesis, that is the qualities of the company, significant variables are found only in the information on the status of the company, while the signals regarding human capital and the establishment of the company are not significant. The number of awards, like companies funded through equity crowdfunding, are positively correlated with funding (coeff. 0.3225 corresponding to a 38% increase in funding for a unit increase in awards), a symptom that also in the reward context-based on the various prizes and awards received constitute a quality signal that pushes investors to finance the initiative more. Surprisingly, the rounds of financing have a very positive effect on funding received (coeff. 0.7998), highlighting how having received previous rounds of financing helps lenders to have a better perception of the initiative, since it has already been supported in previously and therefore has already received a first feedback, unlike companies that for the first time are testing their business and the comparison with the market; while the increase in the number of rounds of financing that have been received (coeff. -0.5403), corresponds to a negative effect on the amount of funding, this is presumably due to the fact that companies that have already received several rounds of financing they are probably not the best target for a mechanism such as crowdfunding, especially reward based, since the lenders prefer to support initiatives in the initial stages of their life and support them in the launch and diffusion, thus highlighting the strong effect of the "community." Hypothesis 1 c is therefore partially confirmed, considering the first two variables indicated (acknowledgments and financing rounds), while funding does not find a positive correlation in the number of rounds.

As for hypothesis 3, with reference to the level of information, the presence of a business plan in the choices of the lenders to support a project through reward-based crowdfunding is not significant. This is explained by the nature of this type which, unlike the equity based model, does not require specific supporting documentation, although they could be an aid in the choices, and which seems more suitable for companies that test their business ideas and prototypes on the market.

Finally, hypothesis 5, in relation to the quality of the crowdfunding campaign, is confirmed, highlighting a positive correlation with the funding obtained, both in the number of updates (coeff. 0.0129 or an increase of 1.3% in funding for unit increase of updates), which has an impact, albeit small, unlike the equity model (where there was a slight impact of the comments), and the average contribution (ln) (coeff. 0.8991 or for each increase 10% of the average contribution corresponds to an increase of approximately 9% of funding), while the number of supporters (coeff. 0.0007 or an increase of 0.07% of funding) has an almost negligible impact.

As regards the number of investors involved, the two models are proposed and discussed below, Model 3 (Table 14) with reference to Equity crowdfunding (with R^2 equal to 71%) and Model 4 (Table 15) with reference to the Reward crowdfunding (with R^2 equal to 48%).

Table 14. Model 3: Equity Crowdfunding – Investors

Source	SS	Df	MS			
				Number of obs	=	235
				F (14,93)	=	41.85
Model	233.840848	13	17.9877575	Prob > F	=	0.0000
Residual	94.980414	221	.429775629	R-squared	=	0.7111
				Adj R-squared	=	0.6942
Total	328.821262	234	1.40521907	Root MSE	=	.65557

	Coef	Std. Err.	t	P>t	[95% Conf.	Interval]
Team	.072328	.0237173	3.05	0.003	.025587	.119069

Staff	.0116206	.0054975	2.11	0.036	.0007865	.0224548
Years of Activity	-.0517594	.0195614	-2.65	0.009	-.0903103	-.0132086
Innovation	.3706645	.102584	3.61	0.000	.1684965	.5728325
Financing round	-.2288393	.1534395	-1.49	0.137	-.5312312	.0735527
n. financing round	.0685346	.0580214	1.18	0.239	-.0458115	.1828807
Acknowledgments	.1225324	.0360397	3.40	0.001	.0515069	.1935579
Tutor	.1748987	.0436769	4.00	0.000	.0888222	.2609752
Equity offered	.0017078	.0033073	0.52	0.606	-.00481	.0082256
Business Plan	.3479588	.1224128	2.84	0.005	.1067129	.5892046
Updates	-.0023442	.0040851	-0.57	0.567	-.0103949	.0057065
Comments/Notes	.006313	.0013816	4.57	0.000	.0035903	.0090357
Ln Average Amounts	-.6310214	.052879	-11.93	0.000	-.735233	-.5268099
_cons	8.122646	.3859589	21.05	0.000	7.362015	8.883277

$p<0.05$

Table 15. Model 4: Reward Crowdfunding – Investors

Source	SS	Df	MS		
				Number of obs	= 108
				F (14,93)	= 6.76
Model	118.209961	13	9.09307389	Prob > F	= 0.0000
Residual	126.497902	94	1.34572236	R-squared	= 0.4831
				Adj R-squared	= 0.4116
Total	244.707863	107	2.28698937	Root MSE	= 1.1601

	Coef.	Std. Err.	t	P>t	[95% Conf.	Interval]
Team	-.0201258	.0683616	-0.29	0.769	-.1558594	.1156077
Staff	.0446752	.0429484	.1.04	0.301	-.0405999	.1299503
Years of Activity	-.0314382	.0558822	-0.56	0.575	-.1423936	.0795172
Innovation	.0412395	.2975652	0.14	0.890	-.5495831	.6320621
Initiative status	-.0108858	.3342802	-0.03	0.974	-.674607	.6528353
Financing round	.9271197	.4497112	.2.06	0.042	.0342076	1.820032
n.financing round	-.3782893	.2632243	-1.44	0.154	-.9009272	.1443487
Acknowledgments	.2615552	.1506287	1.74	0.086	-.0375217	.560632
Tutor	.091058	.1226219	0.74	0.460	-.1524107	.3345268
Business Plan	-.1583059	.2822149	-0.56	0.576	-.7186501	.4020383

Updates	.0119582	.0075458	.1.58	0.116	-.0030242	.0269406
Comments/Notes	.0012395	.0002819	.4.40	0.000	.0006799	.0017992
Ln Average Amounts	-.3535485	.1354212	-2.61	0.011	-.6224304	-.0846667
_cons	6.053249	.5546595	.10.91	0.000	4.951959	7.154538

$p<0.05$

In the equity-based model (Table 14), as regards hypothesis 2, or the correlation of the qualities of the company on the number of investors, the following significant variables are noted (while the variables not mentioned are not significant):

The team (coeff. 0.0723 which corresponds to an increase of about 7.5% of the investors per unit increase of the team) and the staff (coeff. 0.0116 or an increase of about 1.2% of the investors per increase unitary staff), are positively correlated with the number of investors involved (even if the staff has little impact), thus confirming hypothesis 2a on the positive influence of human capital on the lenders involved.

The years of activity (coeff. -0.0517 or a 5.3% decrease in the number of investors) are negatively correlated with the number of investors, as happened for the funding received always with reference to the equity model, while the variable innovation (coeff. 0.3706 or an increase of about 45% of investors), positively affects the number of investors. Hypothesis 2 b is therefore only partially confirmed, finding confirmation only in the second variable mentioned.

The number of awards (coeff. 0.1225 which corresponds to a 13% increase in the number of investors per unit increase in awards) and the number of tutors (coeff. 0.1748 which corresponds to a 19% increase in investors for a single increase in the tutors), positively influence the number of investors involved. Hypothesis 2 on the positive correlation between information on the state of the company and the number of investors is confirmed.

With reference instead to the fourth hypothesis, or the level of information to reduce the degree of uncertainty, there is a positive correlation between the presence of the business plan and the number of investors involved (coeff. 0.3479 corresponding to an increase of 41.6 % of investors). This confirms hypothesis 4.

Finally, in the equity model, hypothesis 6 is not confirmed, since the impact of the comments is rather small (coeff. 0.0063 or an increase of 0.6% of the investors per unit increase of comments) and the average contribution (ln) has an impact, albeit limited, negative (coeff. -0.6310 or a decrease of about 6% of investors).

In the reward-based model (Table 15), the only significant variables are: The financing rounds (coeff. 0.9271), which positively affect the number of investors, thus confirming hypothesis 2 c (positive correlation between the information on the status of the company and the lenders involved), the comments (coeff. 0.0012) and the average contribution (coeff. -0.3535). The latter two variables do not have a significant impact on the number of investors (respectively an increase of 0.12% and a decrease of approximately 3%), thus not confirming hypothesis 6, like the equity model.

6. Conclusions and implications

This work constitutes a first examination of the effectiveness of the signals that determine the success of the initiatives through crowdfunding, referring to both the amount of funding received and the number of investors involved. The contribution is the first that analyzes the information with reference both to companies that have resorted to equity crowdfunding, and to companies that have resorted to reward crowdfunding.

The analyzed data highlight the importance of the qualities of the company, in particular information on the status of the company, such as the number of awards received (common in both types of crowdfunding), tutors (in the equity model) and round of financing (in the reward-model). In particular, these signals are elements that take on particular importance in the success of the initiative, since they are identified by investors as information capable of influencing their decision-making process, and consequently they are elements to be kept in strong consideration also by those who promote initiatives, as they are able to influence the success of the campaigns. The awards received from the initiatives are a quality factor, capable of representing a "photograph" of what the company has been able to do so far. The achievement of various awards (including prizes, certificates in various capacities, participation in competitions, etc.), both as regards the equity and reward based context, highlights the successes achieved so far by the company, and in a certain sense "certifies" the goodness of the initiative which has already had a positive "external" validation so far. Therefore, lenders are more predisposed to investing to support a company that is having positive results.

The presence of tutors is a very important factor for companies, which can be supported during their development. This element only affects the crowdfunding equity model, in which the presence of tutors is perceived as an "added value," capable of guiding and supporting companies during their growth path; while in the reward model this presence is not considered by the funders to be a relevant element, probably given the nature of this type of crowdfunding, which is characterized by business still in a test and validation phase.

Unlike equity crowdfunding, reward based crowdfunding highlights the role of previous financing rounds in the investment process.

Human capital and information on the constitution seem to influence only for companies financed through equity-based crowdfunding (in particular they positively influence team and innovation, while the years are negatively correlated). In fact, unlike the reward model, more weight is given to the nature of the initiative and to the team, which are considered significant information for investors who must decide to invest in companies through online portals.

As for the level of information that the company provides to reduce the degree of uncertainty that characterizes the initiative, the presence of a business plan is a quality signal positively associated with both the funding obtained and the number of investors, only in the case of equity crowdfunding. In particular, this document has a "communication" function and its presence represents an element on which investors can base their investment decisions, being able to better evaluate the company and analyze its prospects. This distinction between equity and reward model, in terms of the relevance of the business plan, is evident from the most recent regulations introduced in the last few years, regarding the collection of online loans through portals by companies; in fact, in several countries, this document is mandatory with reference to equity crowdfunding portals (and not in reward based).

Finally, the campaign signals are, both for the equity and the reward model, having an impact only on the amount of funding and not on investors.

The contribution from Ahlers et al. on equity crowdfunding highlighted the importance for potential investors of financial projections and the level of equity offered, while in this work the equity offered, unlike the presence of a business plan, is not correlated with the two variables that measure the success of the initiative. The importance of the qualities of the company is common in both contributions, in particular as regards human capital, although in the previous work the level of education of the members of the board was also considered as a quality element (expressed by the possession of MBA).

The success of crowdfunding initiatives, however, is determined by a series of elements, sometimes not measurable and difficult to identify, which push lenders to support one initiative rather than another and to a different extent (for example in the case of motivations and rewards of non-monetary nature).

This contribution highlights the information perceived as quality signals by lenders, providing valid indications for companies and entrepreneurs in launching financing campaigns. This work can also provide support in particular to policy makers, who promote types of financing to support start-ups and entrepreneurs, and must make decisions regarding capital raising tools.

The information and signals, in fact, constitute elements for reflection by the regulators, who draw useful indications from them to better direct their measures with the aim of improving the conditions of the users and promoting the development of the initiatives as well as the use of the financing mechanism through the crowd.

Further research developments with reference to the proposed topic may concern the replication of the model in other contexts, as well as the expansion of the sample in question (in particular for the reward model) and the implementation of models with additional variables.

CHAPTER 3

Comparison between the main crowdfunding platforms in the US and the EU: Empirical analysis of social capital

1. Introduction

Crowdfunding is a funding mechanism through the crowd, which originates from crowdsourcing.[96]

Fundraising takes place on special online platforms, promoting interaction between the various actors involved in the mechanism.[97] This form of bottom-up financing allows anyone to be able to perform a first test on the validity of their business idea or to test products and obtain the necessary financial resources without financial intermediaries.[98]

Thanks to crowdfunding, in fact, people with ideas can have an initial push to start (a start-up push), giving importance also to those who have not been taken into consideration by traditional credit access channels, the so-called "long tail."[99]

The main crowdfunding platforms, including Ulule and Kickstarter, two of the best known reward-based models in the world (respectively they have been considered one of the first in Europe and one of the first in the United States), show a trend of projects presented in constant growth, as the number of supporters has risen

96HOWE J., *Crowdsourcing. Why the power of the crowd is driving future of business,* op.cit. KLEEMANN F., VOSS G.G. and RIEDER K., *Un(der)paid innovators: The commercial utilization of consumer work through crowdsourcing,* op. cit.
97AGRAWAL A., CATALINI C., GOLDFARB A., *Some Simple Economics of Crowdfunding,* op. cit. MOLLICK E., *The dynamics of crowdfunding: An exploratory study,* op. cit.
98LAMBERT T., SCHWIENBACHER A., *Crowdfunding: Tapping the right crowd,* op. cit. MOLLICK E., *The dynamics of crowdfunding: An exploratory study,* op. cit.
99VASSALLO W., *Crowdfunding nell'era della conoscenza. Chiunque può realizzare un progetto. Il futuro è oggi,* Franco Angeli, Milan, 2016, pp.112.

significantly, highlighting above all a "globalization" effect which has now led to the participation of people from all parts of the world in the initiatives.

Currently the members of the community on Ulule are over 2,852,709 from 195 countries, and the total funds raised, since the creation of the platform, are over 159 million euros, highlighting a constantly increasing trend over the years (see Figure 4). In fact, the increase in funds raised in 2017 was 11.57% compared to 2016 (going from 25.09 to 27.99 million euros), in 2018 10.54% compared to 2017 (going from 27.99 to 30.94 million euros), and finally in 2019 it shows for the first time a slight decrease of -6.07% compared to 2018 (going from 30.94 to 29.07 million euros).

Figure 4. The funds raised on the Ulule platform

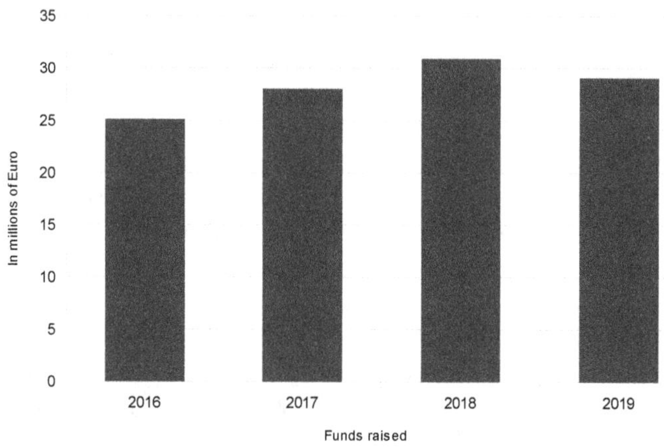

Source: Processing by the author on Ulule data

In the Kickstarter platform (USA), there are currently 17,457,963 members of the community, and the total funds raised since the platform's creation are 4,798,290,228 dollars, highlighting a mixed trend over the years (Figure 5). We start with a small decrease of -5.61% from 2015 to 2016 (going from 686.17 to 649.69 million dollars), next year the increase in funds raised in 2017 is 1.43% compared to 2016 (going from 649.69 to 659.15 million dollars) and in 2018 there is again a small decrease of -8.59% compared to 2017 (going from 659.15 to 606.99 million dollars).

Figure 5. Funds collected on the Kickstarter platform

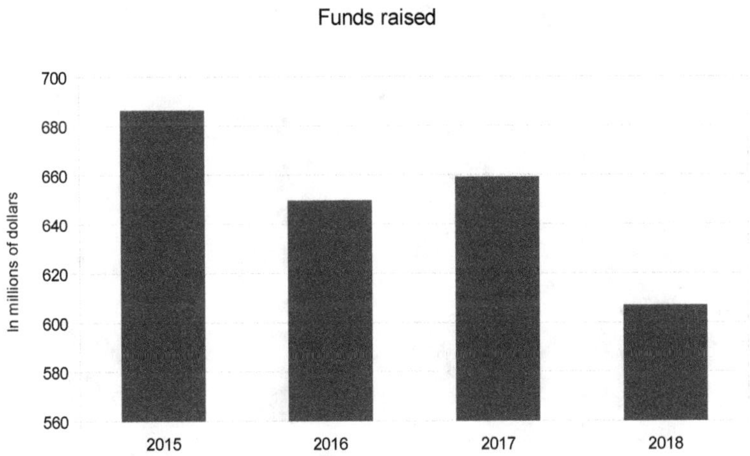

Source: Processing by the author on Kickstarter data (ICO Partners)

As for the number of projects presented on the Ulule platform, since its entry into the market, the overall average success rate is 66%, and in the last year it has been 71%. Also in this case there is a growing trend regarding the number of projects presented (Figure 6). In fact, there is an increase in projects in 2017 of 5.43% compared to 2016 (going from 7.056 to 7.461), in 2018 of 7.58% compared to 2017 (going from 7.461 to 8.073), in 2019 it is highlighted however a drastic drop of 33.02% compared to 2018 (going from 8,073 to 6,069). Finally, at February 2020 the number of projects published on Ulule are 584.

Figure 6. Projects published on the Ulule platform

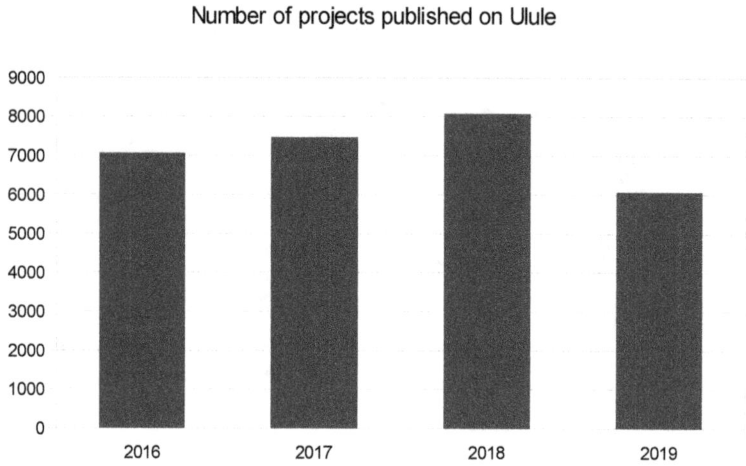

Source: Elaboration by the author on Ulule

With reference to the Kickstarter portal (see Figure 7), after a considerable increase from 2009 to 2015 the number of projects has decreased from 2015 onwards even if the numbers of projects presented remain at high levels. Specifically, in absolute numbers, there is a decrease of -33.0% in 2016 compared to 2015 (going from 77.327 to 58.139), -9.45% in 2017 compared to 2016 (going from 58.139 to 53.116), and finally - 19.35% in 2018 compared to 2017 (going from 53.116 to 44.503).

Figure 7. Projects published on the Kickstarter platform

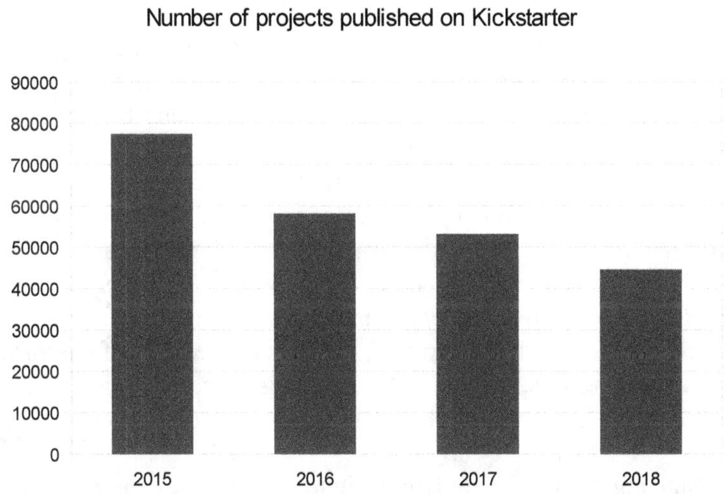

Source: Processing by the author on Kickstarter data (ICO Partners)

A further particularly significant element, which highlights the dimensions of the crowdfunding phenomenon, is represented by the number of supporters who have financed online projects, in fact, referring for example to one of the first and most important portals on the world scene such as Kickstarter, it is noted that the total number of supporters is 17,457,963 from almost all countries of the world.[100] This spread is favored by the expansion of social networks.[101]

2. Literature review

Being a new phenomenon, the contributions in literature are at an early stage. Scholars have investigated the reasons that lead both financiers and entrepreneurs to use a crowdfunding "context."[102]

100Statistiche Kickstarter updated al 01/02/2020.

101MOLLICK E., *The dynamics of crowdfunding: An exploratiry study,*op.cit. COLOMBO M.G., FRANZONI C., LAMASTRA C.R., *Internal Social Capital and the Attraction of Early Contributions in Crowdfunding,* op. cit.

102BELLEFLAMME P., LAMBERT T., SCHWIENBACHER A., *Crowdfunding: Tapping the right crowd,* op. cit. CHOLAKOVA M., CLARYSSE B., *Does the Possibility to Make Equity Investments in Crowdfunding Projects Crowd Out Reward-Based Investments?,* op. cit.

In this mechanism, the interaction that is created between project proponents, crowdfunding platform and supporters is crucial.[103]

The majority of contributions in the literature analyzed the factors that led to successful cases, i.e. achievement (or exceeding) of the objective, and failure (goal not achieved) of the initiatives.[104]

Colombo et al. in the "internal social capital and the attraction of early contributions in crowdfunding," highlighted the role of social capital that is created within the crowdfunding platform. According to the authors, in fact, they "are not only intermediaries of economic transactions, but also places of social connections."[105] In their contribution, it was highlighted how "internal social capital," represented by the number of projects supported by the proposer before launching its crowdfunding campaign, as opposed to external social capital,[106] affects the success of the initiative by attracting supporters, and therefore favoring the contribution of the first contributions, in the initial phase of the launch of the crowdfunding campaign.

Starting from the existing literature, this chapter presents a contribution that focuses on both founder and funder quality, analyzing how these positively affect the success of the initiative, in terms of funding obtained. These qualities are represented by the share capital both referring to the founders, as partially already analyzed in the literature, albeit with different objectives, and to the funders.[107]

No work previously had also analyzed the qualities of the funders, and in fact there are limited contributions to the analysis of the motivations of the subjects.[108] The intuition of this contribution is that funders' share capital also plays an important role in the success of crowdfunding initiatives, or in the amount of funding obtained. The purpose of this

---

103VALANCIENE L., JEGELEVICIUTE S., *Valuation of crowdfunding: Benefits and drawbacks,* in *Economics and Management*, vol. 18, n. 1, 2013, pp. 39-48.

104MOLLICK E., *The dynamics of crowdfunding: An exploratory study,* op. cit. AHLERS G.K.C., CUMMING D., GÜNTHER C., SCHWEIZER D., *Signaling in Equity Crowdfunding,* op. cit. CORDOVA A., DOLCI J., GIANFRATE, G., *The determinants of crowdfunding success: evidence from technology projects,* op. cit.

105COLOMBO M.G., FRANZONI C., LAMASTRA C.R., *Internal Social Capital and the Attraction of Early Contributions in Crowdfunding,* op. cit.

106AGRAWAL A., CATALINI C., GOLDFARB A., *Some Simple Economics of Crowdfunding,* op. cit.

107COLOMBO M.G., FRANZONI C., LAMASTRA C.R., *Internal Social Capital and the Attraction of Early Contributions in Crowdfunding,* op. cit.

108CHOLAKOVA M., CLARYSSE B., *Does the Possibility to Make Equity Investments in Crowdfunding Projects Crowd Out Reward-Based Investments?,* op. cit.

chapter is to contribute to the current debate on crowdfunding and social capital, a topic addressed by different scholars[109] in different areas, but still not very detailed with reference to the new forms of financing that have emerged in recent years, in particular to crowdfunding. The work aims to shed light on the role of the two interpreters of this mechanism and the correlation with the funding received from the lenders.

3. Evolution of lenders

In the literature there are several contributions that have placed the focus on the founders, analyzing the reasons for the decisions to use the crowdfunding platforms to obtain funding,[110] while there are few contributions in reference to the "crowd," in particular by analyzing their motivations, financial and otherwise, which push them to invest,[111] and highlighting the "transformation" of the crowd into "investors"[112] and "small business angels."[113] There are no considerations on a possible transformation of the lenders into "project proponents" and/or "entrepreneurs." Thanks to funding from the crowd, both projects and the number of promoters have increased, a mechanism that over the years has led to a constant increase in the size of the phenomenon, as previously mentioned in numerical terms.

The growing number of founders, who previously supported (see Colombo et al.) or followed initiatives, highlights a sort of "contamination" effect, which leads more and more subjects to launch their business idea or create their own business after the experience carried

109LIN N., *Social capital. A theory of social structure and action,* Cambridge, Cambridge University Press, 2001.

110BELLEFLAMME P., LAMBERT T., SCHWIENBACHER A., *Crowdfunding: Tapping the right crowd,* op. cit. GERBER E.M., HUI J.S., HUO P.Y., *Crowdfunding: Why People Are Motivated to Post and Fund Projects on Crowdfunding Platforms,* in *Proceedings of the International Workshop on Design, Influence, and Social Technologies: Techniques, Impacts and Ethics,* Academic Press, 2012.

111CHOLAKOVA M., CLARYSSE B., *Does the Possibility to Make Equity Investments in Crowdfunding Projects Crowd Out Reward-Based Investments?,* op. cit.

112ORDANINI A., MICELI L., PIZZETTI M. and PARASURAMAN A., *Crowd-Funding: Transforming Customers into Investors through Innovative Service Platforms*, op. cit.

113HORNUF L., SCHWIENBACHER A., *Crowdinvesting-Angel Investing for the Masses?,* in *Handbook of Research on Venture Capital: vol. 3. Business Angels,* 2014, available at SSRN: https://ssrn.com/abstract=2401515.

out as financiers, and driven by a spirit of emulation and by the possibility of carrying out a test on the market at zero cost.[114]

Crowdfunding seems to represent a tool that therefore stimulates funders to promote projects themselves, for example by trying to implement their ideas (business, social, etc.), thus becoming themselves founders. A possible interpretation of the phenomenon is therefore linked to the possibility that crowdfunding is a tool that stimulates "entrepreneurship," since sometimes in funders "shaken" by the example of others, ideas arise, both entrepreneurial ones and in response to certain needs that have emerged and for which a solution has been found.

In this regard, in fact, analyzing the projects presented on the Ulule platform in the four categories used for the dataset (i.e. technology, games, fashion & design and crafts & foods), it emerges that over a quarter of the supporters subsequently in turn become proposer of a project or more projects. A further significant fact is that the same new "promoters" launch campaigns in different categories, therefore not focusing on a specific type of activity.

4. Methodology

4.1. Hypotheses and research objectives

The objective, at this point of the work, is to analyze the qualities of the founders and funders, or the social capital of the same, represented by the bonds established previously in the crowdfunding campaign. These qualities measured in terms of supported projects, followed and created previously by both authors (all with reference to the date prior to the launch of the analyzed initiative), can influence the result of the initiative, or have an impact on the capital raised (dependent variable). Compared to the existing literature, this work aims to verify, in successfully funded projects, the correlation of internal social capital (created in the platform) by both the founders and the funders, with the final amount of funding raised (Figure 8) on the next page.

114COLOMBO M.G., FRANZONI C., LAMASTRA C.R., *Internal Social Capital and the Attraction of Early Contributions in Crowdfunding,* op. cit.

Figure 8. The factors that determine the amount of funding obtained

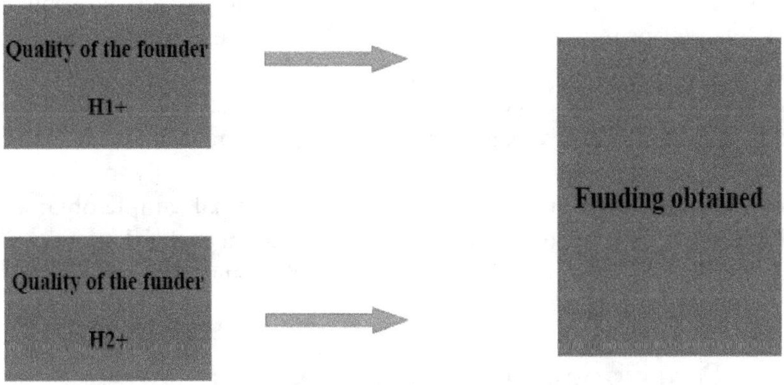

Source: Processing by the author

In this work, it is argued that the funding received is positively correlated with the quality of both the founder and the funder, and we proceed with the formulation of the following two hypotheses.

Hypothesis 1: The qualities of the founders positively influence the total funding raised.

Hypothesis 2: The qualities of the funders positively influence the total funding raised.

The founders' quality category includes the projects created, supported and followed by the founders prior to the launch of the campaign.

The funder quality category includes the projects created and followed by the funders before supporting the campaign, and in addition to representing the previously supported projects, two important variables were identified, namely the number of expert funders (who supported at least one project in previously), the number of projects financed by expert funders and also the number of new supporters is indicated, that is, those who for the first time signed up to the platform and supported an initiative.

Further variables related to control concern updates, comments, the funding objective (the minimum target expected to be reached in order to consider a funded campaign) and the average contribution, already used in literature.[115]

115MOLLICK E., *The dynamics of crowdfunding: An exploratory study,* op. cit. CORDOVA A., DOLCI J., GIANFRATE, G., *The determinants of crowdfunding success: evidence from technology projects,* op. cit.

4.2. Sample and data collection

The dataset was created considering all the projects presented on the Ulule platform, one of the main crowdfunding reward based portals in Europe, examining the projects presented in 2018 (from January to December) in reference to the "technology," "games," "fashion & design" and "crafts & foods," considered identifying different areas and macro-categories present on the platform, and more generally of the main categories supported through crowdfunding. The final sample obtained is 103 successfully funded projects (including 20 in the technology category, 46 in the games category, 20 in the fashion & design category and 17 in the crafts & foods category).

Description of the variables

Dependent variable:

Ln Funding: the logarithmic transformation (natural logarithm) of the total funding raised by the initiatives.

Independent variables:

1. Ln Goal: The logarithm of the amount of funding requested, or the goal to be achieved in order to be financed successfully;
2. Ln Average amount: The logarithm of the average amount of contributions from each lender;
3. Founder Star: The number of founders who previously supported more than one project and have a "badge" (attributed by the platform based on the activity carried out and the role acquired within it);
4. Created by the founder: The number of projects created by the founder before the launch of the campaign;
5. Supported by the founder: The number of projects supported by the founder before the launch of the campaign;
6. Followed by the founder: The number of projects followed by the founder before the launch of the campaign;
7. Funder experts: The number of supporters who previously funded at least one project;
8. Financed by expert funders: The number of projects previously funded by expert funders;
9. Created by funders: The number of projects created by funders previously;

10. Followed by the funder: The number of projects followed by the funder previously;

11. New supporters: The number of newly enrolled supporters who finance a project for the first time;

12. Comments: The number of comments written by the lenders (and to which the founder may or may not have replied);

13. News: The number of updates entered by the founder.

Table 16. Descriptive statistics

Variables	Obs	Mean	Std. Dev.	Min	Max
Ln Funding	103	7.976164	1.06023	5.703782	11.61498
Ln Goal	103	7.655348	1.014757	5.29909	11.51967
Ln Average Amount	103	3.86348	.5626244	2.515147	5.765613
Founder Star	103	.1650485	.3730396	0	1
Created by the founder	103	.4951456	1.798004	0	11
Supported by the founder	103	.9902913	1.629959	0	9
Followed by the founder	103	1.572816	2.435851	0	12
Expert funders	103	14.4466	24.60501	0	181
Funded by expert funders	103	75.27184	86.10484	0	537
Created by funders	103	.3786408	1.103617	0	10
Followed by funders	103	15.02913	21.15603	0	97
New Supporters	103	95.52427	265.3662	4	2646
Comments/Notes	103	63.31068	173.1191	0	1381
News	103	11.1165	11.25141	0	50

Note: This table shows the descriptive statistics regarding the successfully funded reward crowdfunding projects. It shows the mean (mean), the standard deviation (Std. Dev.) and the minimum (min) and maximum (max) values for each variable used.

Table 17. Correlation matrix and VIF

(1-14)															VIF
1.Ln Funding	1.0000														
2.Ln Goal	0.8972	1.0000													2.78
3.Ln Av. Amount	0.5291	0.4815	1.0000												1.78
4.Founder Star	0.0253	-0.0761	0.0125	1.0000											1.92
5.Cr. by founder	0.1616	0.0280	0.0270	0.6224	1.0000										3.13
6.Sup. by founder	0.6437	0.5377	0.2373	0.2284	0.2325	1.0000									3.00
7.Fol. by founder	0.5621	0.5153	0.2336	0.2726	0.2950	0.7323	1.0000								2.81
8.Expert funders	0.5402	0.3289	0.1220	0.3380	0.6405	0.5208	0.4445	1.0000							4.86
9. F. ex. Funders	0.4538	0.3176	0.1393	0.3044	0.4449	0.4984	0.4390	0.7161	1.0000						2.71
10.Cr. By funders	-0.0667	-0.0759	-0.1790	-0.0342	-0.0806	0.0675	0.0753	0.0233	-0.0250	1.0000					1.10
11.Fol. by funders	0.6189	0.5151	0.0459	0.0106	0.2324	0.5371	0.5130	0.5883	0.5454	0.0432	1.0000				2.52
12.New sup.	0.5098	0.5246	-0.0314	-0.0505	-0.0023	0.3567	0.4177	0.2966	0.1104	0.0586	0.5151	1.0000			2.08
13.Com./Notes	0.4591	0.3090	0.1050	0.3235	0.6248	0.5123	0.3680	0.8040	0.5838	-0.0503	0.5171	0.2610	1.0000		3.45
14. News	0.5041	0.3020	0.3352	0.1682	0.2884	0.4700	0.4315	0.5239	0.5373	-0.0060	0.3573	0.1397	0.4626	1.0000	1.77
$p \leq .05$															Mean VIF 2.61
VIF: Variance Inflation Factor															

The average Vif is 2.61 and single values are lower than the critical thresholds (5-6), therefore there are no problems related to multicollinearity.

5. Analysis and results

The OLS Regression method was used for this work, since the dependent variable follows a normal distribution. In the model robust standard errors were used and there are no problems related to multicollinearity, recording an average VIF of 2.61 and the individual values are lower than the critical thresholds,[116] as shown in table 17. The model is statistically significant[117] and the R^2 index is equal 91%.

Table 18. Model 1

Number of obs	=	103
F (14,93)	=	107.35
Prob > F	=	0.0000
R-squared	=	0.9174
Root MSE	=	.32613

	Coef.	Robust Std. Err.	t	P>t	[95% Conf.	Interval]
Ln Goal	.6690645	.0707212	9.46	0.000	.528543	.8095859
Ln Average Amount	.274633	.0707786	3.88	0.000	.1339975	.4152685
Founder Star	.0686498	.1513774	0.45	0.651	-.2321339	.3694336
Created by the founder	-.0180831	.0344826	-0.52	0.601	-.0865992	.050433
Supported by the founder	.0823176	.0316098	2.60	0.011	.0195096	.1451256
Followed by the founder	-.0358209	.0183999	-1.95	0.055	-.0723812	.0007394
Expert funders	.0106837	.0040045	2.67	0.009	.0027269	.0186406
Financing by expert funders	-.0008735	.000578	-1.51	0.134	-.002022	.0002749
Created by the funders	-.0137082	.0153393	-0.89	0.374	-.0441871	.0167707
Followed by the funders	.0063735	.0029483	2.16	0.033	.0005152	.0122318
New supporters	.0001559	.000175	0.89	0.375	-.0001917	.0005036
Comments/ Notes	-.0004534	.0004425	-1.02	0.308	-.0013327	.0004258

116Values above 5 and 6 can highlight problems related to multicollinearity.
117(Prob F > 0.0000).

News	.012639	.0055786	2.27	0.026	.0015544	.0237235
_cons	1.459768	.4530868	3.22	0.002	.5594945	2.360042

$p<0.05$

With reference to the first hypothesis, i.e. the qualities of the founder, the only significant variable is represented by the number of projects previously supported by the founder (coeff. 0.0823 which corresponds to an increase of approximately 8.6% of the funding for an increase of one unit of the projects supported by the founder). It positively affects the amount of funding raised and partially confirms the first hypothesis.

As regards the qualities of the lenders, both the number of projects followed by the funders previously (coeff. 0.0064 corresponding to an increase of approximately 0.65% of the funding for a unitary increase of projects followed by the funders) and the number of expert funders (coeff. 0.0106 or an increase of approximately 1.1% of the funding for an increase of one unit of expert supporters), are positively correlated, albeit with a small impact, on the funding obtained, confirming even if in the second hypothesis is minimal.

This evidence shows how the share capital of the founder and funders constitute relevant elements in the success of the initiative. In fact, the number of expert supporters for example represents a quality element for the project, since the presence of these subjects can somehow attract other financiers, and therefore a greater number of contributions, thanks to the links previously created by the funders (who have already financed more than one project). Even the projects supported by the founders previously are a sign of the bonds that it has previously established, precisely through the support given to other initiatives.

6. Conclusions and implications

This work lends itself to contributing to the current debate on the role of social capital and the factors linked to the success of the initiatives proposed on the crowdfunding portals, showing an analysis that also refers to the social capital of funders, and not only that of the founders. The work represents an extension of the literature on internal social capital in crowdfunding, expanding and implementing the previous considerations proposed by a previous paper with reference to the qualities of the founders, while with reference to the social capital of the funders the contribution presents considerations hitherto absent on theme.

As for the qualities of the founders, this work shows how they, represented by the previously supported projects (variable identified as "internal social capital" by Colombo et al., as an expression of the degree of the supported projects), positively influence the amount of funding raised, and additional elements representative of the qualities of the founder such as the projects created and followed previously have also been taken into consideration (albeit without impact). The results emerged therefore broaden the current knowledge on the topic, which had hitherto highlighted how the internal share capital of the founder favored the success of the initiatives by showing a positive correlation in the initial stages of the launch of the initiative, i.e. on the first financiers involved and therefore the first contributions received.[118]

With reference instead to the qualities of the funders, this contribution highlights the existence of a "stock" of social capital that has been created within the crowdfunding platforms, also considering the funders, who, like the founders, have supported, created or followed previously by crowdfunding campaigns, thus establishing a series of connections with the various users of this funding collection mechanism. In particular, both the number of projects previously followed by the funders and the number of expert funders, that is, who have supported more than one project previously, are positively correlated, albeit to a limited extent, with the funding received.

This work therefore highlights the importance of internal social capital in this crowd funding mechanism, as opposed to previous contributions, such as those of Agrawal et al.[119] and Mollick,[120] which had paid attention with reference to only "external share capital."

Furthermore, this contribution also focuses on the prospects of the funders, through a consideration of the possible business implications of the same deriving from the use of this tool.

The contribution may have interesting implications for the managers of the crowdfunding platforms, which favor the connections between the subjects, but also for the funders and the founders. In particular, the latter receive useful information on the factors that influence the success of the initiatives launched.

118COLOMBO M.G., FRANZONI C., LAMASTRA C.R., *Internal Social Capital and the Attraction of Early Contributions in Crowdfunding,* op. cit.
119AGRAWAL A., CATALINI C., GOLDFARB A., *Some Simple Economics of Crowdfunding,* op. cit.
120MOLLICK E., *The dynamics of crowdfunding: An exploratory study,* op. cit.

A future development of this work consists of an in-depth analysis of the trade-off of new supporters-supporters already present within the community, to analyze whether, under pawns of conditions, one of the two categories has a greater influence on the success of the initiatives.

CHAPTER 4

Empirical analysis of the connections of crowdfunding actors and success factors

1. Introduction

Crowdfunding in recent years has experienced a considerable diffusion on the world scene, becoming a real viral phenomenon, as evidenced by the exponential number of projects proposed on an ever-increasing number of online platforms supported by millions of people. Initially this form of financing did not have a "disruptive" impact and only in recent years has it seen its explosion following the spread of Web 2.0[121]technologies and the increase in difficulties in obtaining post-crisis financing in 2008.[122]

The proliferation of online alternative finance platforms, including crowdfunding ones, with technological innovations increasingly focused on simplicity, speed and transparency, and aimed at satisfying users' needs, have radically changed the way of investing and raising capital from part of the people.[123]

At the base of crowdfunding is the concept of crowdsourcing[124] in

---

121AGRAWAL A., CATALINI C., GOLDFARB A., *Some Simple Economics of Crowdfunding,* op. cit. BELLEFLAMME P., LAMBERT T., SCHWIENBACHER A., *Crowdfunding: Tapping the right crowd,* op. cit.

122COSH A., CUMMING D., HUGHES A., *Outside Enterpreneurial Capital,* in *The Economic Journal,* vol. 119, n. 540, 2009, pp. 1494-1533.

123WARDROP R., ROSENBERG R., ZHANG B., ZIEGLER T., SQUIRE R., BURTON J., HERNADEZ E.A., GARVEY K., *Breaking New Ground. The Americas Alternative Finance Benchmarking Report,* Cambridge Centre for Alternative Finance and Polsky Center for Enterpreneurship and Innovation, University of Cambridge-Judge Business School, 2016.

124KUPPUSWAMY V., BAYUS B.L., *Crowdfunding creative ideas: The dynamics of project backers in Kickstarter*, op. cit. HOWE J., *Crowdsourcing. Why the power of the crowd is driving future of business,* op. cit. KLEEMANN F., VOSS G.G. and RIEDER K., *Un(der)paid innovators: The commercial utilization of consumer work through crowdsourcing,* op. cit.

which the crowd plays the important role of "supplier" of ideas,[125] enhancing their ability to solve problems, based on the concept of "wisdom of the crowd."[126]

In the specific case of crowdfunding, the role played by the crowd is to directly provide financial resources[127] necessary to support the projects proposed by the founders through an open call on the internet.[128]

Although the term crowdfunding appeared a few years ago,[129] its "use" comes from many scholars traced back to practices implemented centuries earlier, particularly in the civic field.[130]

Crowdfunding allows you to raise funds without having to resort to traditional intermediaries, thus allowing those who have an idea to be able to test the validity of the business on the market and the feedback of their products.[131] Crowdfunding, in fact, is an interactive process of collecting money from a large number of people,[132] in which the founder comes into contact with potential supporters with the aim of being able to transform his idea into a business reality.[133]

125HOWE J., *The rise of Crowdfunding,* in *Wired*, 6 January 2006. Available at: https://www.wired.com/2006/06/crowds/ . SCHENK E., GUITTARD C., *Towards a characterization of crowdsourcing practices,* in *Journal of Innovation Economics & Management,* vol. 1, n. 7, 2011, pp. 93-107.

126SUROWIECKI J., *The Wisdom of Crowds: Why the Many Are Smarter Than the Few and How Collective Wisdom Shapes Business, Economies, Societies and Nations,* op. cit.

127BELLEFLAMME P., LAMBERT T., SCHWIENBACHER A., *Crowdfunding: Tapping the right crowd*, op. cit.

128HOWE J., *Crowdsourcing. Why the power of the crowd is driving future of business,* op. cit. KLEEMANN F., VOSS G.G. and RIEDER K., *Un(der)paid innovators: The commercial utilization of consumer work through crowdsourcing,* op. cit.

129Historically, the introduction of the term crowdfunding was traced back to Michael Sullivan in 2006 on the occasion of the launch of Fundavlog, an incubation system for videoblog-related projects in which an online donation collection system was set up.

130At the end of 1800, one of the first funding campaigns by the "reward-based" crowd, by J. Pulitzer in the "World" newspaper of New York with the aim of raising 100 thousand dollars to complete the settlement of the Statue of Liberty by publishing the names of all supporters in the newspaper.

131MOLLICK E., *The dynamics of crowdfunding: An exploratory study,* op. cit. LAMBERT T., SCHWIENBACHER A., *Crowdfunding: Tapping the right crowd*, op. cit.

132BELLEFLAMME P., LAMBERT T., SCHWIENBACHER A., *Crowdfunding: Tapping the right crowd*, op. cit.

133RAMSEY Y.A., *What the Heck is Crowdfunding?,* in *Business People*, vol. 25, n. 11, 2012, pp. 54-57.

This collective "effort" of individuals who provide resources refers, in addition to the collection of money, also to a "social" phenomenon, as it involves a multitude of individuals who create a network.

The potential of this alternative type of financing is closely connected with the interaction of financial, technological and social aspects.[134] The positive outcome of a crowdfunding campaign depends on the founder's ability to relate to groups of individuals who share the same interests and are therefore prepared to make small donations to support the initiatives.[135]

Based on one of the latest crowdfunding definitions provided by Belleflamme et al.,[136] which in turn had integrated the definition of Kleemann et al.,[137] the following crowdfunding definition is suggested in this work: "Crowdfunding is a new concept of funding that provides for the active participation of supporters, from all parts of the world, to a community through the contribution of money in exchange for various rewards, to support and push the projects proposed by the founders, through an online open call, and to so that the latter can undertake the entrepreneurial path and start their own business."

Social networks play a crucial role for the founders, in fact the different personal networks such as Facebook,[138] Linkedin[139] and Twitter[140] represent a particularly useful tool to promote initiatives and attract supporters.

Some specific campaigns have shown an incredibly rapid and viral spread, such as among the most funded campaigns in the history of

134NASRABADI A.G., *Equity Crowdfunding: Beyond Financial Innovation,* Springer International Publishing, 2016.
135LYNN D., SABBAGH H., *The JOBS Act opens door for crowdfunding offerings,* in *Morrison & Forrester Social Media Newsletter,* vol. 2, n. 3, pp. 6-8.
136BELLEFLAMME P., LAMBERT T., SCHWIENBACHER A., *Crowdfunding: Tapping the right crowd,* op. cit.
137KLEEMANN F., VOSS G.G. and RIEDER K., *Un(der)paid innovators: The commercial utilization of consumer work through crowdsourcing,* op. cit.
138MOLLICK E., *The dynamics of crowdfunding: An exploratory study,* op. cit. BECHTER C., JENTZSCH S., FREY M., *From Wisdom of the Crowd to Crowdfunding,* in *Journal of Communication and Computer,* vol. 8, n. 11, 2011, pp. 951-957.
139COLOMBO M.G., FRANZONI C., LAMASTRA C.R., *Internal Social Capital and the Attraction of Early Contributions in Crowdfunding,* op. cit.
140AN J., QUERCIA D., CROWCROFT J. *Recommending investors for crowdfunding projects,* in *WWW' 14: Proceedings of the 23rd international conference on World wide web,* April 2014, pp. 261-270. BECHTER C., JENTZSCH S., FREY M., *From Wisdom of the Crowd to Crowdfunding,* op. cit.

Kickstarter, the interactive book library "Bring Reading Rainbow" with 105,857 supporters and 5,408,916 dollars received, the film "Veronica Mars" with 91.585 and 5.702.153 dollars received, and still other projects concerning games or technological products (Oculus Rifit, Pebble Smartwatch etc.). In these cases the number of supporters became exponential during the course of the campaigns as fans and supporter groups disseminated and shared the initiatives through social networks, and involved and encouraged friends and family to join, to ensure that the project films, products and technologies come to life, as in the case of projects for social purposes.[141]

In recent years, the sharing economy, social finance platforms and marketplaces have spread. According to Goldman Sachs report "The Future of Finance - The Socialization of Finance" of 2015 "Millennials are the agent of change in shifting behaviors." Crowdfunding is a type of financing that attracts Millennials, thanks to the possibility of being involved in the creative process and feeling connected to the effort: According to the report mentioned, they are inclined to participate in the various types of crowdfunding and 47% of the interviewees have supported crowdfunding campaigns or are favorable and will support them shortly.

2. Community

Communities play a considerable role for different categories of subjects such as people and organizations, thanks to their ability to create value. This prompted several authors to analyze them, describe the characteristics of the participants[142] and discuss their types (such as Kozinets et al.,[143] who defined the concept of "Online Creative Consumer Communities"-OCCC).

141The Reading Rainbow project, for example, involved creating a virtual library of interactive books and videos by providing free access to the classrooms that needed them. The campaign included, upon reaching certain targets in terms of funds raised, the free subscription for thousands and thousands of classes as well as free web access to help the classes.

142SCHWIENBACHER A., LARRALDE B., *Crowdfunding of Small Entrepreneurial Ventures,* in *Handbook of Entrepreneurial Finance,* CUMMING D., (ed. by), Oxford, Oxford University Press, 2010, pp. 1-23.

143KOZINETS R., HEMETSBERGER A., SCHAU H.J., *The Wisdom of Consumer Crowds: Collective Innovation in the Age of Networked Marketing,* in *Journal of Macromarketing,* vol. 28, n. 4, 2008, pp. 339-354.

In the specific case of crowdfunding as mentioned above, the online community supports the projects by making sums of money,[144] driven by "emotional" motivations and is sometimes linked by certain values,[145] which differentiates this type from crowdsourcing, and consequently from others types of community.[146]

The community contributes significantly to making a project come to life and crowdfunding is often associated with so-called "community-based experiences" that generate benefits for the participants.[147]

In fact, participation in the funding mechanism through the crowd generates a sense of belonging to a community,[148] and the involvement of the members of the community is fundamental so that there is always continuous participation, and supporters can increase or at least keep the current ones, not doing decrease the number of the community.[149]

The interaction between the promoter of the project and the supporters is fundamental for the dissemination and promotion of the initiative,[150] as demonstrated by several cases that have quickly become "viral."[151] The benefits generated by the communities include the validation of the market and the sponsorship of the project, since the members of the community themselves attract other subjects, and a series of useful information is generated.[152]

144BELLEFLAMME P., LAMBERT T., SCHWIENBACHER A., *Crowdfunding: Tapping the right crowd,* op. cit.

145For example, social, ideological, etc.

146For example, community open source, Community crowdbased microwork, Community production of software or open innovation contests.

147BURTCH G., CHOSE A., WATTAL S., *An Empirical Examination of the Antecedents and Consequences of Contribution Patterns in Crowd-Funded Markets,* in *Information Systems Research,* vol. 24, n. 3, 2013, pp. 499-519.

148GERBER E.M., HUI J.S., HUO P.Y., *Crowdfunding: Why People Are Motivated to Post and Fund Projects on Crowdfunding Platforms,* op. cit.

149LI H., LAI V.S., LUO R., *Understanding the Role of Social Situations on Continuance Participation Intention,* in *Journal of Electronic Commerce Research,* vol. 17, n. 4, 2016, pp. 358-380.

150BEAULIEU T.Y., SARKER S., *Discursive Meaning Creation in Crowdfunding: A socio-material Perspective Research-in-Progress,* in *Thirty Fourth International Conference on Information Systems, ICIS,* 2013.

151It is easy to find projects that have been "pushed" by fans as in the case of films or video games, or by social or cultural initiatives.

152CHENG Y.Q., WANG Q., XIE J., *Online social interactions: A natural experiment on word of mouth versus observational learning,* in *Journal of Marketing Research,* vol. 48, n. 2, 2011, pp. 238-254. SALAMPASIS D., MENTION A.L. (Eds.), *Open Innovation. Unveiling the Power of the Human Element,* Open

In addition, an additional stock of share capital may develop within the community.[153] To give an idea of the size of the communities, consider that for example Kickstarter (one of the most important portals in the world) has 17,466,247 members and Ulule (one of the most important portals in Europe) with 2,854,445 members worldwide.

From what has been said so far on the communities, it is clear that this participatory mechanism implies the involvement of both the founders and funders.

Participation can sometimes also concern specific aspects and issues that are treated in certain forums, blogs or ad hoc areas. For example, the main portals have specific sections in which it is possible to deal with different topics, open debates and receive useful information, for example "Ulule Vox" of the Ulule portal is cited, as are similar areas in the most well-known portals such as Kickstarter, IndieGoGo, etc.

Just starting from the consideration of these aspects, there are a series of interesting reflections on the possible implications for the participants in the community. Those who belong to it, can exchange ideas, contributions and opinions that allow improvements from various points of view, such as the management of a project, the quality of the good/service on which the campaign is centered, the reprogramming of a process, implementation of innovations, feedback, solutions to problems and so on.

Community members therefore become part of a "participatory" and sometimes "cooperative" creative process, since supporters sustain the proposer of the initiative in different ways, primarily financial support, but also a series of information and indications.

So both crowdfunders and founders find themselves in a continuous "innovative" process, finding themselves confronted on different aspects and seeing firsthand the emergence of new needs or new "problems" to be solved or solved with their support. From this continuous interaction, certain trends emerge in the members of the community, such as the possibility that the creative and/or entrepreneurial process takes part in them, and decide to carry out their own project based on what emerged during the participation (and therefore exchanges of information and feedback) within the community and launch an initiative.

Innovation: Bridging Theory and Practice vol. 2, World Scientific Publishing Co., Singapore, 2017.

153COLOMBO M.G., FRANZONI C., LAMASTRA C.R., *Internal Social Capital and the Attraction of Early Contributions in Crowdfunding,* op. cit.

One possible consideration for the community is that participants can implement a spin off process. This process which could be called "community's spin off" can be interpreted as both a "spontaneous" and "planned" pushing process.

In the first case, the decision to implement a project or the maturation of the idea underlying the initiative (if it has not yet emerged), takes place autonomously, for a knowledge of certain needs or needs felt by the community, to example of specific goods or services. Participation in the community has somehow stimulated the creative process of some of its participants, who have decided to create a service or asset that could be successful, given some "gaps" in some projects or the absence of certain goods/services. The same crowdfunders can thus get involved and create their own initiative, highlighting an entrepreneurial capacity that emerges from participation in this mechanism, both by seizing the opportunities presented and by developing ideas that had never been developed so far, despite their intrinsic potential.[154]

In the other case, instead, the process is driven by the users of the community themselves who, manifesting the need for a good/service, request it from users of the community with certain skills (e.g. engineers, developers, etc.). More and more often in ad hoc sections, such as forums or dedicated pages, there are discussions about a specific product or service (in particular think of technologies, software, etc.), which lacks certain requirements and is completely absent in the desired version or with certain characteristics, or even with completely non-existent products/services and for which it would be necessary to design and implement a specific output. In this case, this process was triggered by the users of the community themselves, who for example made requests (or expressed the potential for success given by the need that emerged) to members of the same with certain skills (software developers, designers, web developers, engineers, etc.), who have been driven to launch a specific project with strong support and aware of the feedback from the community. Figure 9 below shows the described mechanism graphically.

154BAID C., ALLISON T., *How crowdfunding deals get done: signaling, communication and social capital perspectives,* in *Handbook of Research on Crowdfunding,* LANDSTRÖM H., PARHANKANGAS A., MASON C. (ed. by), Edward Elgar Publishing, Cheltenham, UK Northampton, MA, USA, 2019, pp. 191 ss.

Figure 9. New projects launched by the community

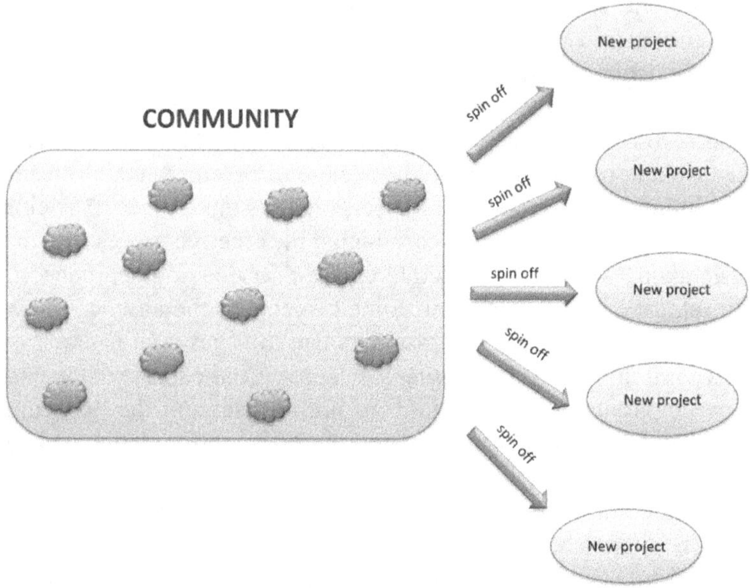

Source: Processing by the author

Figures 10 and 11 present the description of the process. In particular, in figure 10, users who register on a crowdfunding platform enter a "participatory" situation, where they support initiatives through economic donations in different ranges. Participating in a community, in addition to financial support, leads funders to share experiences, ideas and make contributions and feedback, whether they can allow proposers to improve their projects and make them feasible, attractive and suitable for users' needs, whether they can give life to new ideas and future projects.

Figure 10. The participatory community mechanism

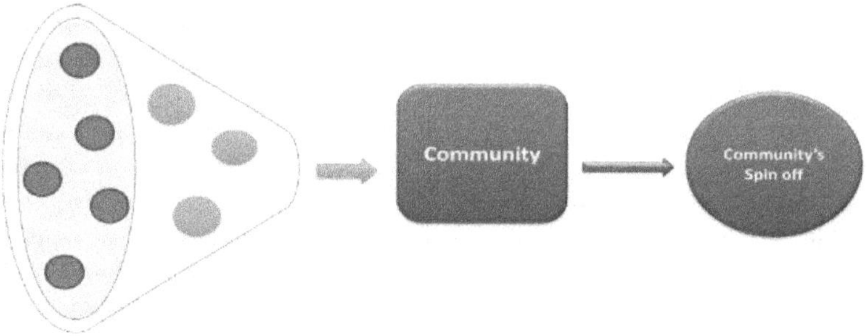

Source: Processing by the author

Figure 11. The process of community's participatory mechanism

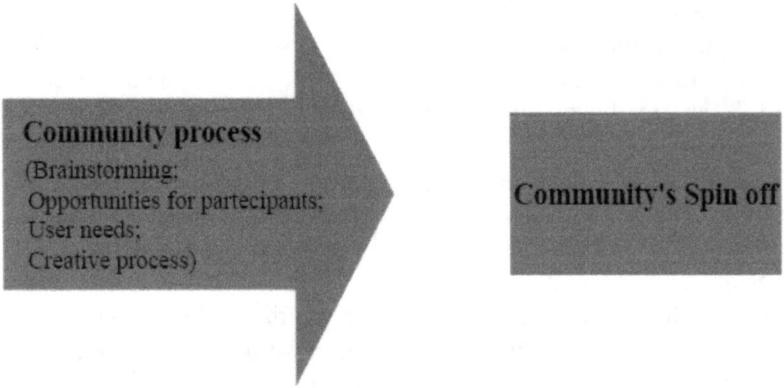

Source: Processing by the author

3. Literature review

In recent years scholars have shown a particular interest in this emerging form of bottom-up financing.

The most significant contributions in literature on the topic of crowdfunding are quite recent, and have shed light, through mainly exploratory studies, on the functioning of the financing mechanism through the crowd, and in particular on the drivers and factors associated with the success of the initiatives, as shown for example by the works of Belleflamme et al. in 2013,[155] by Mollick in 2014,[156] and by Ahlers et al. in 2015.[157] The influence of geographical distribution in crowdfunding projects it can be seen, for example, in the works of Agrawal et al. in 2011[158] and by Mollick in 2014.[159] Finally, the trade-off between the types of crowdfunding and the business models it can be seen in the works of

155BELLEFLAMME P., LAMBERT T., SCHWIENBACHER A., *Crowdfunding: Tapping the right crowd*, op. cit.

156MOLLICK E., *The dynamics of crowdfunding: An exploratory study,* op. cit.

157AHLERS G.K.C., CUMMING D., GÜNTHER C., SCHWEIZER D., *Signaling in Equity Crowdfunding,* op. cit.

158AGRAWAL A., CATALINI C., GOLDFARB A., *Some Simple Economics of Crowdfunding,* op. cit.

159MOLLICK E., *The dynamics of crowdfunding: An exploratory study,* op. cit.

Cholakova and Clarysse in 2014,[160] Belleflamme et al. in 2014,[161] Ahlers et al. in 2015[162] and Cumming et al. in 2015.[163]

Personal networks are associated with the success of crowdfunding initiatives as evidenced by the work of Mollick in 2014,[164] Colombo et al. In 2014,[165] Bechter et al. in 2011,[166] and An et al. in 2014,[167] as are the quality signals underlying the projects and "social information."[168]

Social networks seem to play a crucial role for initiatives, and in literature they are considered as variables that measure relationships, as can be seen, for example, from the works of Stuart and Sorenson in 2005[169] and Shane and Cable in 2002.[170]

With reference to the community, the Belleflamme et al. in 2014[171] show that both in the pre-ordering (reward-based) model, in which the entrepreneur urges lenders to pre-order products, and in the profit sharing (equity-based) model, in which the entrepreneur sells a share of equity, the participants in this system enjoy "community benefits" that increase their usefulness.

160CHOLAKOVA M., CLARYSSE B., *Does the Possibility to Make Equity Investments in Crowdfunding Projects Crowd Out Reward-Based Investments?*, op. cit.

161BELLEFLAMME P., LAMBERT T., SCHWIENBACHER A., *Crowdfunding: Tapping the right crowd*, op. cit.

162AHLERS G.K.C., CUMMING D., GÜNTHER C., SCHWEIZER D., *Signaling in Equity Crowdfunding,* op. cit.

163CUMMING D.J., LEBOEUF G., SCHWIENBACHER A., *Crowdfunding models: Keep-it-All vs. All-Or-Nothing,* op. cit.

164MOLLICK E., *The dynamics of crowdfunding: An exploratory study,* op. cit.

165COLOMBO M.G., FRANZONI C., LAMASTRA C.R., *Internal Social Capital and the Attraction of Early Contributions in Crowdfunding,* op. cit.

166BECHTER C., JENTZSCH S., FREY M., *From Wisdom of the Crowd to Crowdfunding,* op. cit.

167AN J., QUERCIA D., CROWCROFT J. *Recommending investors for crowdfunding projects,* op. cit.

168KUPPUSWAMY V., BAYUS B.L., *Crowdfunding creative ideas: The dynamics of project backers in Kickstarter*, op. cit.

169STUART T.E., SORENSON O., *Social Networks and Entrepreneurship,* in *Handbook of Entrepreneurship Research. Disciplinary Perspectives,* ALVAREZ S.A, AGARWAL R., SORENSON O. (ed. by), Springer, Boston, MA, 2005, pp. 233-252.

170SHANE S., CABLE D., *Networks Ties, Reputation, and the Financing of New Ventures,* in *Management Science,* vol. 48, n. 3, 2002, pp. 313-452.

171BELLEFLAMME P., LAMBERT T., SCHWIENBACHER A., *Crowdfunding: Tapping the right crowd*, op. cit.

In some recent works, the role of social capital was analyzed, in particular highlighting its importance for attracting supporters and raising funds in the early days of crowdfunding campaigns[172] and as signs of quality in the success of companies.[173] Previous works, however, have highlighted the importance of the social capital "external" to the community owned by the founders, with particular reference to the support of family and friends[174] and social networks.[175]

Intrinsic non-financial motivations are a strong determinant of decisions to support reward-based crowdfunding projects rather than extrinsic financial reasons as evidenced by the work of Cholakova and Clarysse in 2014.[176]

Some authors such as Allison et al. in 2015[177] and Cholakova and Clarysse in 2014 used the self-determination (SDT) and cognitive evaluation theory (CET), to explain the intrinsic and extrinsic motivations of individuals, although the use of information asymmetries is more frequent.

Crowdfunding has been interpreted as a collective effort by individuals who network and pool their resources[178] and as an interactive process, through the internet, to raise funds as shown for example by the

---

172COLOMBO M.G., FRANZONI C., LAMASTRA C.R., *Internal Social Capital and the Attraction of Early Contributions in Crowdfunding,* op. cit.

173AHLERS G.K.C., CUMMING D., GÜNTHER C., SCHWEIZER D., *Signaling in Equity Crowdfunding,* op. cit. RYU S., KIM K., *Crowdfunding Success as a Quality Signal to Venture Capital,* in *22nd Americas Conference on Information Systems: Surfing the IT Innovation Wave, AMCIS 2016,* Association for Information Systems, United States, 2016.

174AGRAWAL A., CATALINI C., GOLDFARB A., *Some Simple Economics of Crowdfunding,* op. cit. ORDANINI A., MICELI L., PIZZETTI M. and PARASURAMAN A., *Crowd-Funding: Transforming Customers into Investors through Innovative Service Platforms*, op. cit.

175MOLLICK E., *The dynamics of crowdfunding: An exploratory study,* op. cit.

176CHOLAKOVA M., CLARYSSE B., *Does the Possibility to Make Equity Investments in Crowdfunding Projects Crowd Out Reward-Based Investments?,*op. cit.

177ALLISON T.H., DAVIS B.C., SHORT J.C., WEBB J.W., *Internal Social Capital and the Attraction of Early Contributions in Crowdfunding,* in *Entrepreneurship: Theory & Practice,* vol. 39, 2015, pp. 53-73. LANDSTRÖM H., PARHANKANGAS A., MASON C. (ed. by), *Handbook of Research on Crowdfunding,* Edward Elgar Publishing, Cheltenham, UK Northampton, MA, USA, 2019.

178DE BUYSERE K, GAJDA O, KLEVERLAAN R. and MAROM, D., *A Framework for European Crowdfunding,* op. cit.

works of Belleflamme et al.[179] and Ahlers et al.[180] This mechanism represents a way to establish a link between entrepreneurs who raise capital and new investors.[181] If all sides cooperate, results can be achieved.

Other authors have highlighted founders' practices such as in the work of Belleflamme et al. in 2013 and described what are the determinants of the good results of the campaigns and how the supporters support the initiatives during the funding cycle, as well as the mechanisms that guide to finance.[182]

Crowdfunding platforms represent a place for social connections and in the present work they are identified as a set of networks. In fact, crowdfunding platforms can be understood as a set of many ego-centered networks such as Burt's work in 1995[183] and Borgatti in 1996 and 1997[184] for example. Each project launched by a promoter represents a network in itself stand-alone, consisting of nodes and links. The central node (ego) is represented by the founder, to whom the funders (alters) are connected through funding to support the initiative.

This work intends to provide a contribution that describes how the network of crowdfunding platforms is formed and analyzes the correlation between the funding received and the relational qualities between the funders, expressed through two network indices (redundancy and effective size), and the links established by the founder before the launch of his initiative.

Discussions in the literature on the dynamics and mechanisms underlying the network are absent, as well as empirical analyzes that consider elements of measurement of the relationships between subjects within the network.

179BELLEFLAMME P., LAMBERT T., SCHWIENBACHER A., *Crowdfunding: Tapping the right crowd*, op. cit.

180AHLERS G.K.C., CUMMING D., GÜNTHER C., SCHWEIZER D., *Signaling in Equity Crowdfunding,* op. cit.

181VALANCIENE L., JEGELEVICIUTE S., *Valuation of Crowdfunding: Benefits and Drawbacks,* op. cit., pp. 39-48.

182BELLEFLAMME P., LAMBERT T., SCHWIENBACHER A., *Crowdfunding: Tapping the right crowd*, op. cit. CHOLAKOVA M., CLARYSSE B., *Does the Possibility to Make Equity Investments in Crowdfunding Projects Crowd Out Reward-Based Investments?,* op. cit. KUPPUSWAMY V., BAYUS B.L., *Crowdfunding creative ideas: The dynamics of project backers in Kickstarter*, op. cit.

183BURT R.S., *Structural Holes. The Social Structure of Competition,* Harvard University Press, USA, 1995, pp. 324.

184BORGATTI S.P., JONES C., *A measure of part collaboration,* in *Connections,* vol. 19, n. 1, 1996, pp. 58-60. BORGATTI S.P., EVERETT M.G., FREEMAN L.C., *Ucinet 5.0.*, Natick, MA: Analytic Technologies, 1997.

The work continues with a description of the networks linked to the crowdfunding platforms and in the following paragraph an empirical evidence is made which tests two hypotheses, which will be described below.

4. The crowdfunding networks

A crowdfunding platform contains a series of projects launched on it by the founders, who have received support from the community. Starting from this, it is possible to identify crowdfunding platforms as networks, in which there are a number of actors that make up the ecosystem, such as for example occurred with the American and European thematic platforms.[185]

The "network approach" highlights the actions of the actors, and is a useful tool for analyzing different approaches and strategies.[186]

Several authors have used graph theory as a tool to describe and analyze network evolutions, relationships and actors.[187] The structure of the networks is made up of nodes (vertex), i.e. the subjects participating in the network, and links (edges), represented by the links established between them. So the graph is defined with the following type: G=[N,L] (or G=[V,E]).

By applying this type to crowdfunding, we have as nodes the participants in this type of financing, therefore both founder (promoters) and funder (supporters), and as links the relationships between the various subjects (therefore both funder with founder, and between subjects of the same mechanism).

Each project that is launched through the portal resembles an ego network (or even ego-centered network),[188] or a network characterized by

---

185INTERREG-CENTRAL EUROPE ARTISTIC, *Strategy Handbook for the Crowdfunding network. Deliverable D.T2.2.5. (WP T2, Activity A, T2.2),* ISN-innovation service network GmbH, PP13, Graz, version 2, 2019. Project website: https://www.interreg-central.eu/Content.Node/ARTISTIC.html

186JOHANSON J., MATTSSON L.G., *Interorganizational relations in industrial systems: a network approach compared with the transaction cost approach,* in *International Studies of Management & Organization,* vol. 17, n. 1, 1987, pp. 34-48. BELLEFLAMME P., OMRANI N., PEITZ M., *The economics of crowdfunding platforms,* op. cit.

187ALBERT R., BARABASI A.L., *Statistical mechanics of complex networks,* in *Reviews of Modern Physics,* vol. 74, n. 1, 2002, pp. 47-97.

188BURT R.S., *Structural Holes. The Social Structure of Competition,* op. cit. BORGATTI S.P., JONES C., *A measure of part collaboration,* op. cit. BORGATTI S.P., EVERETT M.G., FREEMAN L.C., *Ucinet 5.0.*, op. cit.

the presence of an ego focal node, in this case the founder who proposes the project, and a series of other, with which the ego has ties, in this case the funders who support the initiative. The alter are all connected with the ego through the financing of certain campaigns, representing an objective identifying data of the established connection.

Then a representation of the ego network is provided with reference to crowdfunding (see Figure 12). The founder represents the ego, and is connected to the funders who funded the initiative. Using undirected link, in which there is no differentiation between the direction of the flows or flows (also definable as bidirectional connections), we have the representation of Figure 12.

Figure 12. The (ego-centered) crowdfunding network

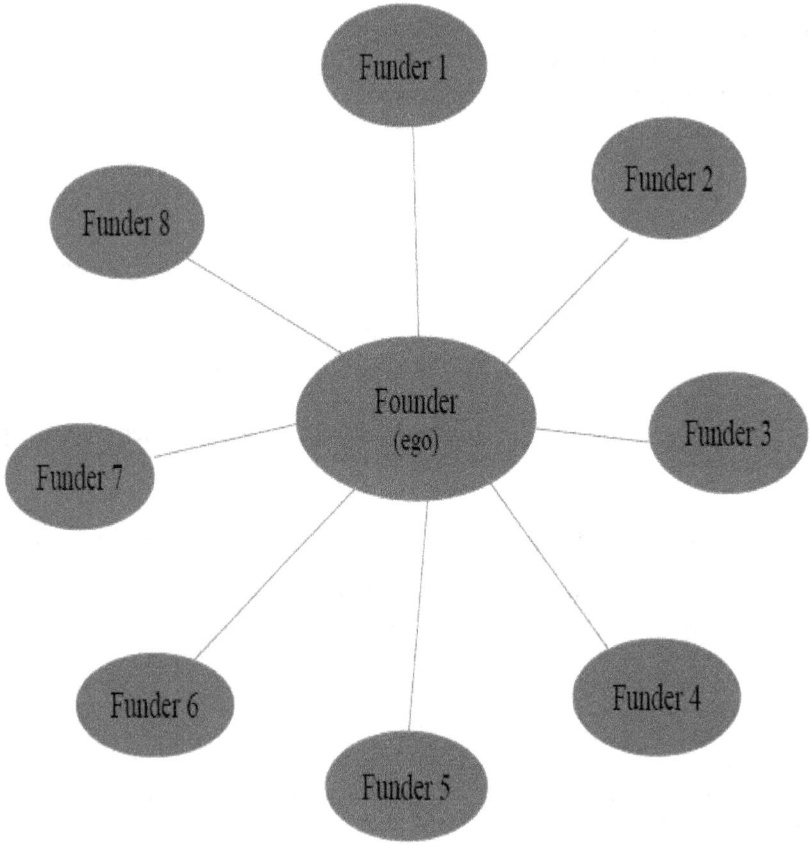

Source: Processing by the author

In the case of crowd funding, the links change according to the type of crowdfunding that is considered, for example in the donation model based there is no type of reward that the proposer will have to pay to supporters, so in this link they could be considered to be of unidirectional type (see Figure 13).

Figure 13. The unidirectional crowdfunding network

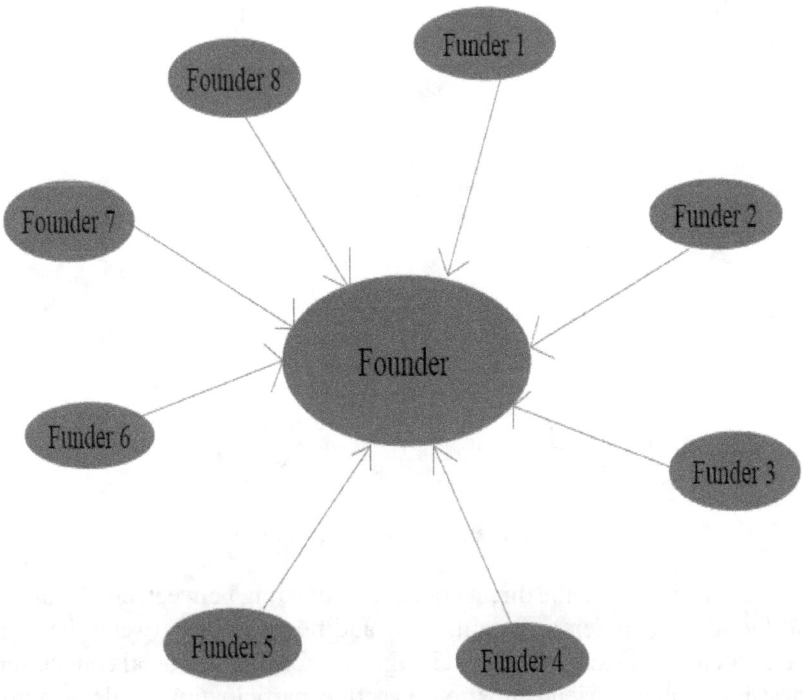

Source: Processed by the author

In the case of the more widespread, reward-based model, the connection between funders and ego can be represented in terms of link directed, since the bidirectional link in this case is expressed both by the donation in monetary terms that the funders do in favor. of the founder, both the rewards that the latter will give to the supporters (Figure 14).

Figure 14. The bidirectional reward-based crowdfunding network

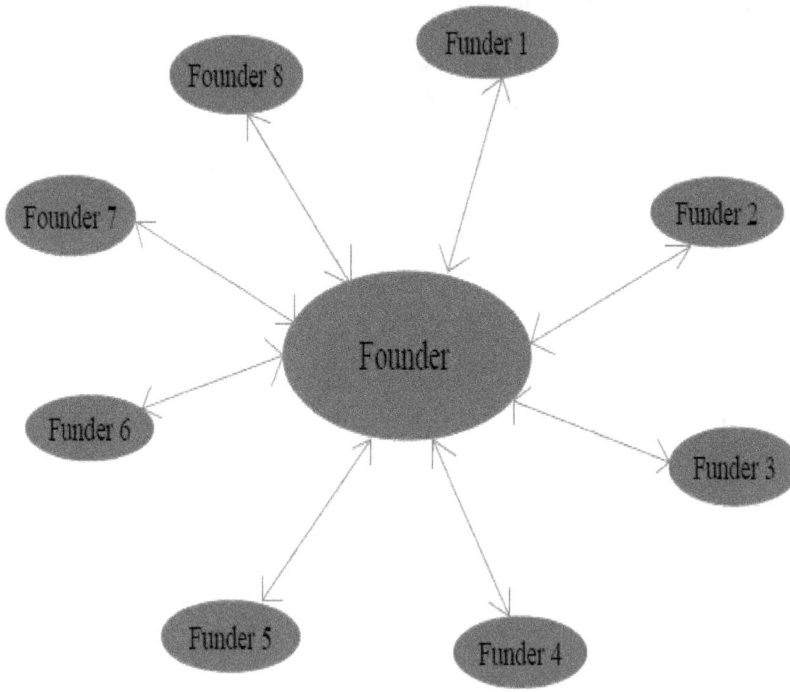

Source: Processed by the author

In addition to the direct connection existing between ego (founder) and the alters (funders), there may be additional links between the same alters, such as for example the exchange of information, social connections (messages, blogs, friendships, etc.), active participation in determining communities, etc.

In the figure below (see Figure 15) an ego network is represented which presents connections between the alter (dashed links).

Figure 15. Ego network with connections between the alter

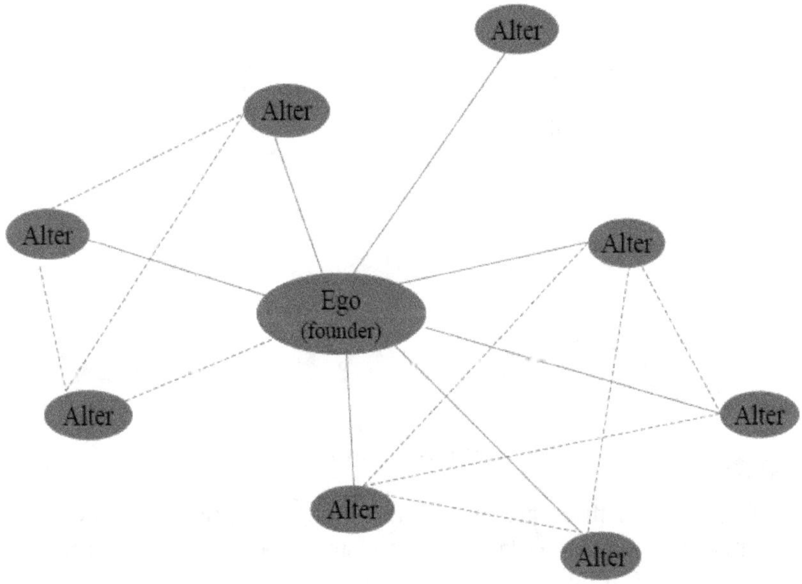

Source: Processing by the author

With regard to crowdfunding, two levels of analysis can be distinguished. The first is represented by individual projects (ego-network) within the platform, the second is given by the network of the entire platform containing the various projects, and in which it is possible to highlight the relationships between the various actors. Among these relationships are funders who can also support multiple projects, thus coming into contact with other founders (see Figure 16).

Figure 16. Funder that finances multiple projects

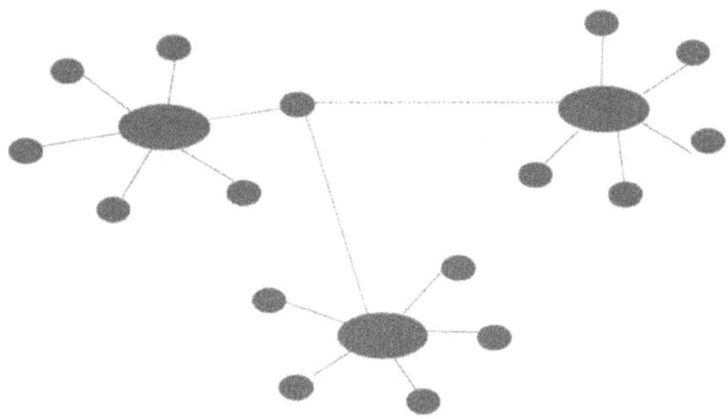

Source: Processing by the author

However, there are also founders who finance other initiatives, thus becoming funders (Figure 17) and in a certain sense returning the support received in turn.

Figure 17. Founder who becomes funder

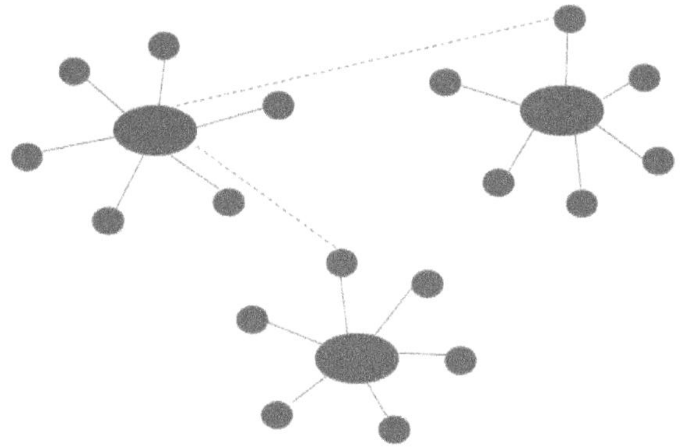

Source: Processing by the author

With reference to the relationships between the actors of the network, it is possible to detect three types of connections (see Figure 18).

Figure 18. The three types of relationships between network actors

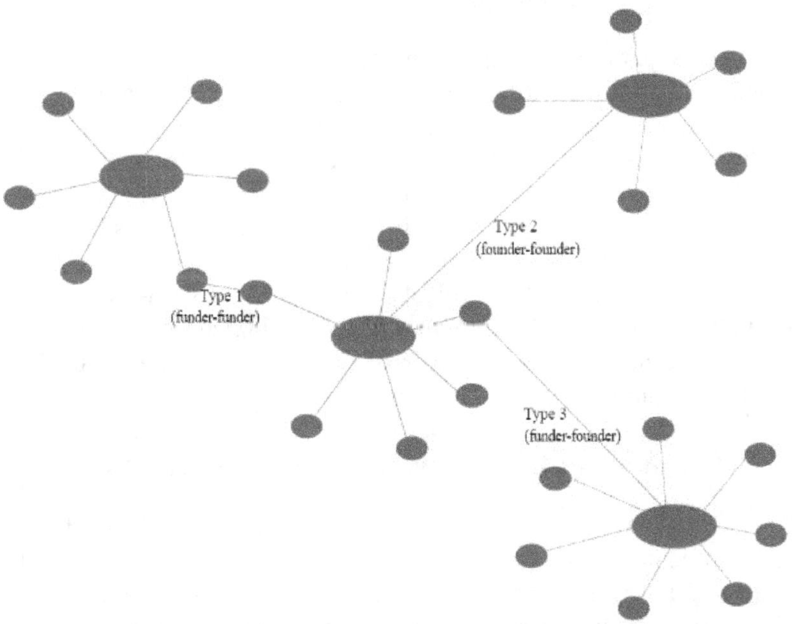

Source: Processing by the author

1. Funder-funder type: The supporters can be connected with each other in real ways, for example links deriving from having financed the same projects and initiatives, or from participation in communities or specific forums on certain topics, or even connections deriving from social networks, such as facebook, twitter, linkedin, etc.

2. Founder-founder type: In this typology, the proposers of the projects can be in contact with each other, either through support or following certain initiatives, or through belonging to the community or social networks.

3. Mixed type (funder-founder: In this case the supporters and promoters of the projects are in contact with each other, both through the funding that the former carry out in favor of the latter, and through links represented by connections on facebook, twitter, friendship, etc. or belonging to certain communities, forums, etc.

5. Methodology

5.1. Research objectives

This paragraph aims to investigate the impact that relational variables have on the success of funding collections. It is argued that in the funded initiatives, the links between the funders (excluding the founder) within the same network, positively affect the amount of funding collected, just as a positive correlation exists between the connections that the founder created in the previous period at the launch of his/her project.

The two hypotheses to be tested are the following:

Hypothesis 1: The level of connections between the funders is positively correlated to the amount of funding obtained.

Hypothesis 2: The number of ties of the founder is positively related to the amount of funding obtained.

5.2. Method analysis and data collection

The data was collected through the Ulule platform, considered the main European reward crowdfunding portal. The projects presented for the entire 2018 were considered in four representative categories of the main areas of interest present in the different crowdfunding platforms: Games, crafts & foods, fashion & design and technology. This resulted in a dataset consisting of 105 successfully funded projects (45 in the games category, 18 in the crafts & foods category, and 21 in both the fashion & design and technology categories). The methodology used is the OLS Regression model (with the only dependent variable considered following a normal distribution) and some tests were carried out on the sample in question (Tables 19 and 20) to exclude the presence of any problems (multicollinearity, autocorrelation, heteroskedasticity).

Description of the variables

Dependent variable:

Ln Funding: the logarithmic transformation (natural logarithm) of the total funding raised by the initiatives.

Independent variables:

1.Ln Average amount: The logarithm of the average amount of contributions from each lender;

2. Founder's Ties: The number of links that the founder established before the launch of the campaign (both supported and followed up projects);

3.Redundancy: The density of the number of bonds between the actors of the network except the founder (ego) (calculated as 2t-n);

4.Effective size: The number of financiers (i.e. nodes except the founder) minus redundancy (calculated as n-2t/n);

5.Comments: The number of comments written by the lenders (and to which the founder may or may not have replied);

6.News: The number of updates entered by the founder.

As for the connection between the funders, it was decided to use two network variables considered in the literature as identifying the links between the actors, namely the effective size and redundancy.[189] Redundancy measures the number of connections that connect actors in a network and the effective size measures how much the alter connected to ego is directly related to each other.[190] In particular, the choice was made to use redundancy and effective size as formulated by Borgatti,[191] which revisited the indices previously proposed by Burt,[192] as reported in the description of the variables.

The other variables present in the model, i.e. average contribution, news and comments, are control variables used frequently in the literature in crowdfunding models, as shown for example by the works of Mollick in 2014[193] and of Cordova et al. in 2015.[194]

Table 19. Descriptive statistics

Variables	Obs	Mean	Std. Dev.	Min	Max
Ln Funding	105	7.976164	1.06023	5.703782	11.61498
Ln Average Amount	105	3.86348	.5626244	2.515147	5.765613
Ties del Founder	105	3.038835	4.669304	0	28
Comments/Notes	105	63.31068	173.1191	0	1381

189BURT R.S., *Structural Holes. The Social Structure of Competition,* op.cit. BORGATTI S.P., JONES C., *A measure of part collaboration,* op. cit. BORGATTI S.P., EVERETT M.G., FREEMAN L.C., *Ucinet 5.0.*, op. cit.
190BURT R.S., *Structural Holes. The Social Structure of Competition,* op. cit.
191BORGATTI S.P., JONES C., *A measure of part collaboration,* op. cit.
192BURT R.S., *Structural Holes. The Social Structure of Competition,* op. cit.
193MOLLICK E., *The dynamics of crowdfunding: An exploratory study,* op. cit.
194CORDOVA A., DOLCI J., GIANFRATE, G., *The determinants of crowdfunding success: evidence from technology projects,* op. cit.

News	105	11.1165	11.25141	0	50
Redundancy	105	.6981127	.5026542	0	3.619048
Effective size	105	109.2728	273.6123	6	2709.323

Note: This table shows the descriptive statistics on successfully funded reward crowdfunding projects. It shows the mean (mean), the standard deviation (Std. Dev.) and the minimum (min) and maximum (max) values for each variable used.

Table 20. Correlation matrix and VIF

		1	2	3	4	5	6	7	VIF
1	Ln Funding	1.0000							
2	Ln Average Amount	0.5291	1.0000						1.17
3	Ties of the Founder	0.5668	0.2129	1.0000					1.91
4	Comments/ Notes	0.4591	0.1050	0.6092	1.0000				1.77
5	News	0.5041	0.3352	0.4978	0.4626	1.0000			1.54
6	Redundancy	0.4368	0.1878	0.2511	0.2878	0.2399	1.0000		1.13
7	Effective size	0.5423	-0.0198	0.3869	0.3249	0.1822	0.1255	1.0000	1.21
	$p \leq .05$							Mean VIF	1.45

VIF, variance inflation factor

Note: The sample has no heteroskedasticity (Breusch Pagan test) and there is no autocorrelation (Durbin Watson test).

The average VIF is 1.45 and the individual values are lower than the critical thresholds (5-6), therefore there are no problems related to multicollinearity.

6. Results

In this paragraph we will highlight the positive effects of both the connections of the funders and the bonds of the founder on the financing obtained. The model shows an R^2 index higher than 70% and is statistically significant.[195] With reference to the first hypothesis, both variables

195(Prob F > 0.0000).

considered, redundancy (coeff. 0.4604 which corresponds to an increase in funding of 58% for unit increases of redundancy of the network) and effective size (coeff. 0.0016 or an increase of 0 ,2% approximately of the funding for unit increases of links between the others), are significant and positively influence the amount of funding received (albeit the second to a small extent).

As for the second hypothesis, this too is confirmed, in fact, the number of bonds (tie) of the founder (coeff. 0.0369 which corresponds to an increase of about 4% of the funding for each additional unit of bonds of the founder) is positively correlated with the amount of funding received.

Table 21. Model 1

Number of observations	=	105
F (6,96)	=	41.99
Prob > F	=	0.000
R-squared	=	0.7241
Adj R-squared	=	0.7068
Root MSE	=	.57405

	Coef.	Std. Err.	T	P>t	[95% Conf.	Interval]
Ln Average Amount	.7767711	.1094436	7.10	0.000	.5595272	.994015
Ties del Founder	.0369364	.0168126	2.20	0.030	.0035636	.0703091
Comments/Notes	.0003568	.0004363	0.82	0.415	-.0005092	.0012229
News	.0122067	.0062603	1.95	0.054	-.0002199	.0246333
Redundancy	.4604073	.1202941	3.83	0.000	.2216255	.6991892
Effective size	.001618	.0002285	7.08	0.000	.0011644	.0020715
_cons	4.206377	.4071156	10.33	0.000	3.398259	5.014495

$p<0.05$

7. Conclusions and future research

This work represents an initial study, conducted with quantitative methods, which provides indications on the networks in the context of financing through crowdfunding platforms and highlights how the relationships of the actors affect the amount of funding obtained from the initiative. With reference to crowdfunding, this contribution is the first that uses network analysis techniques and analyzes projects considering them as ego-centered networks, starting from the consideration of crowdfunding platforms as a set of projects. The purpose of this discussion is to contribute to the current debate on online communities[196] and above all to the debate on crowdfunding, shedding light on the characteristics of the network and its internal dynamics, analyzing the links of the actors, both funders and founders.

In fact, in recent years, communities have played a considerable role in the development of entrepreneurial initiatives, both for their ability to generate useful information for project proponents or business ideas, and for their ability to develop social interactions that allow the dissemination of messages and initiatives that need support to be successful.

This contribution analyzes the role of communities in crowdfunding platforms, providing a consideration regarding the birth of ideas and initiatives that can find their origin thanks to participation in this funding collection mechanism through the active presence and sharing in the crowdfunders community present within the portals.

The empirical analysis carried out shows that the overall funding raised through the crowdfunding campaign is positively correlated both with the connections created by the founder prior to the launch of its initiative, and with the internal links of the networks. With reference to the first aspect, the connections of the founders highlight the importance of the participation of the proposers in previous campaigns (having already followed or supported others previously) which allows them to be known within the community, as well as allowing them to see firsthand the dynamics of this tool. The weight of these links that have been created between the founder and the funder is in fact decisive for the success and the positive result of the initiative, thus allowing the proponent of the project to have adequate support. As for the second aspect, the presence of links within the supporters of the same campaign highlights the importance of the relational aspect in the success of the initiatives.

196KOZINETS R., HEMETSBERGER A., SCHAU H.J., *The Wisdom of Consumer Crowds: Collective Innovation in the Age of Networked Marketing,* op. cit. BORST I., MOSER C., FERGUSON J., *From friend funding to crowdfunding: Relevance of relationships, social media, and platform activities to crowdfunding performance,* in *New Media & Society,* vol. 20, n. 4, 2017, pp. 1396-1414. DEMIRAY M., BURNAZ S., ASLANBAY Y., *The Crowdfunding Market, Models, Platforms, and Projects,* in *Crowdfunding for Sustainable Entrepreneurship and Innovation,* VASSALLO W. (ed. by), IGI Global, 2017, pp. 90-126.

Crowdfunding is in fact a tool that "rewards" projects that manage to involve a greater number of financiers, and in this participatory mechanism crowdfunders are decisive for the success of the initiative thanks to their ability to influence and involve other subjects (through word of mouth, social media, etc.). In this way, "friends of friends" are involved and become part of this system to support entrepreneurs who launch the business idea. This therefore confirms the importance of the links within the same network between the various supporters. Moreover, this consideration is in line with some policies recently implemented by some crowdfunding platforms (in particular reward-based), albeit in a still very limited number (one of these, for example, is Ulule), which provide for a first "check" the goodness of the initiative through the involvement, by the founder, of a small circle of "close" people. After this first "validation," which highlights how the founder was able to convince other people to support him, we move on to the actual launch, then turning to an audience also made up of strangers, who could in turn be users who were involved by the acquaintances themselves.

This work can represent a support to various stakeholders for a better understanding of the phenomenon and is susceptible of further future applications at a wider range. In fact, an upcoming work that we will try to carry out is the expansion of the analysis extended to the networks of other platforms, in order to make comparisons and observe the dynamics of the actors who in some cases could be users of multiple platforms. Furthermore, additional network variables (between centrality, clustering coefficient, density, etc.) which can provide indications on the networks of the platforms will be considered, not only considering the individual projects but their whole. An initial step can be constituted by the analysis of the networks divided by categories, finally arriving at the analysis of the entire platform thus further expanding the field of investigation. In this way it will be possible to reconstruct a complete mapping of the nodes represented by both the founders and the funders, highlighting the connections between all the actors of the system, therefore both promoters of initiatives and supporters who have supported, for example, more than one project (in this case with multiple links), sometimes also belonging to more than one category. The usefulness in particular of this type of analysis lies in the possibility of being able to create a dynamic representation of the phenomenon, thus allowing to highlight the evolution of the network over time.

CHAPTER 5

Effects and implications for the companies used the equity crowdfunding mechanism

1. Equity crowdfunding definitions proposed by the current literature

In this paragraph we will provide a review of the definitions of equity crowdfunding proposed in a literature.

Gerrit, Ahlers et al.[197] define equity crowdfunding as follows: A method of financing whereby an entrepreneur sells equity or equity-like shares in a company to a group of (small) investors through an open call for funding on Internet-based platforms. This definition shows how equity crowdfunding is in all respects a type of crowdfunding and how it maintains its main characteristics. The funding, in fact, comes from a group of small investors (crowds) and through an online platform.

Belleflamme et al. instead give a definition of equity crowdfunding which underlines the differences between this form of financing and the traditional ones: "Entrepreneurs make an open call for funding on a crowdfunding platform, and investors make their decisions based on the information provided therein. Moreover, the crowdfunding platform facilitates the transaction by providing a standardized investment contract and settling the payments."[198] This definition underlines two fundamental points for the functioning of equity crowdfunding: The entrepreneur must commit himself to provide the necessary information so that investors can make their investment decisions, and the platform does not play a passive role, but must contribute to the definition a standard loan agreement and at the same time take care of the transfer of payments.

197AHLERS G.K.C., CUMMING D., GÜNTHER C., SCHWEIZER D., *Signaling in Equity Crowdfunding,* op. cit.

198BELLEFLAMME P., LAMBERT T., SCHWIENBACHER A., *Crowdfunding: Tapping the right crowd*, op. cit.

A final definition that we report is the one provided by Pierrakis and Collins who define equity crowdfunding "as the offering of securities by a privately held business to the general public, usually through the medium of an online platform. The model permits anyone to acquire a share in privately held businesses, i.e. those that have yet to float on the stock exchange, by allowing a business to offer a certain proportion of its equity for a set amount of capital it is aiming to raise. Investors can then, through the platform, buy small parts of this equity stake."[199] This latter definition also includes all the fundamental points that characterize equity crowdfunding as described in the previous ones.

1.2. The actors involved in the equity crowdfunding phenomenon

The equity crowdfunding phenomenon is based on five main actors: The proposer (one or more entrepreneurs), the equity crowdfunding platform, investors (commonly called crowdfunders), the project (or business idea) and regulation. As we will see below, equity is the type of crowdfunding most involved in investor protection issues, so we thought it appropriate to introduce regulation as a fifth player, given the significant impact it has on the phenomenon and in particular on its operating mechanisms.

a) The Proponent (or team of proposers) is the one who launches the project and publishes it on an online platform with the aim of collecting the financial resources necessary for the realization of the business idea. The motivations that push the proposer to start a fundraising campaign can be of various kinds and often have characteristics of strong subjectivity. A survey conducted by Gerber et al.[200] shows that creators are incentivized to participate in crowdfunding mainly to raise money and at the same time show how social dynamics also have a significant impact. Among these, is the intention to increase awareness of their work by making it known to other people and receive feedback to satisfy their desire for approval. Added to this is the possibility of getting in touch with people through a long-term interaction that can also extend beyond the single financial transaction. An additional motivation is linked to experience and learning. The survey shows, in fact, how some creators after having concluded a

---

199PIERRAKIS Y., COLLINS L., *Crowdfunding: A New Innovative Model of Providing Funding to Projects and Business,* op. cit.

200GERBER E.M., HUI J.S., HUO P.Y., *Crowdfunding: Why People Are Motivated to Post and Fund Projects on Crowdfunding Platforms,* op. cit.

campaign, with or without success, are motivated to continue to play an active role in crowdfunding to improve their skills in marketing, management and financial planning with the aim to raise funds later effectively.

b) Equity crowdfunding platforms are online portals that connect creators and potential investors and are the virtual means by which venture capital is raised. The platforms offer the opportunity for proposers to publish their project and for investors to carry out financial transactions to result in the purchase of financial instruments. The remuneration modalities of the platform operators can vary considerably. Typically, a success fee is applied if the outcome of the collection proves to be positive. There are also some platforms that apply management fees regardless of the outcome of the project and others that offer additional service packages to improve their visibility.

In the census carried out on the platforms present on a global level, it emerges how managers choose to operate with business models that differ from each other. The legislation in force in the country to which the platform belongs can also have a significant impact on the methods of operation and the regulations that they must comply with in order to perform their role as intermediary.

Ingram & Taigland[201] in a study conducted on the adoption of crowdfunding in Sweden by young IT companies, say that the role of the platforms is to offer entrepreneurs the opportunity to test the market, attract skills and expertise and create brand awareness.

In this sense, the platforms facilitate the creation of the community and enable entrepreneurs to jointly develop the project with all the members who are part of it.

Finally, Agrawal et al.,[202] state that the goal of the platforms is to maximize the number and size of successful projects, the remuneration being mainly linked to a success fee on the amount collected in the individual campaigns. Consequently, the incentive for the platforms is to involve the greatest number of creators and investors, attract quality projects, reduce the risk of fraud and facilitate the correspondence between business ideas and available capital; for example by increasing the degree

---

201INGRAM C., TEIGLAND R., *Crowdfunding Among IT Entrepreneurs in Sweden: A qualitative Study of the Funding Ecosystem and ICT Entrepreneurs' Adoption of Crowdfunding,* in *SSRN Electronic Journal,* 2013, pp. 1-49.

202AGRAWAL A., CATALINI C., GOLDFARB A., *Some Simple Economics of Crowdfunding,* op. cit.

of dissemination of information on the one hand and on the other allowing for an effective search for investment opportunities by potential investors.

c) Investors (or crowdfunders) are the funders of the project, i.e. those who provide the financial resources for the realization of the latter. The literature deals with the motivations that push individuals to invest and in general to participate in the phenomenon of crowdfunding. As for the proposers, the motivations for the crowdfunders are heterogeneous and with characteristics of strong subjectivity.

d) The project is the business idea that is published on the platform and is the central element around which the phenomenon of equity crowdfunding revolves. Wanting to identify them according to the classification that we proposed in the first chapter, the projects that raise risk capital through the equity-based model are business-type projects, which recognize a monetary return to the lender and are oriented towards the generation of economic value. On some platforms, other non-monetary benefits are also offered to investors, the so-called rewards, with the aim of increasing the expected return on investment. Typically, the reward is the final product (often not yet present on the market) that the proposers intend to make thanks to the funds raised and is offered "at a discount" compared to the target or market sale price; in this case we speak of pre-sales.

Among the characteristics that a project published on a platform must possess in order to attract the greatest number of investors is certainly the description of the idea and the proposers and, at the same time, the clarity of the presentation with which this information is provided to the public of the financiers. The importance of these elements is even more accentuated for equity type projects since, being characterized by investments in risk capital, there is the need to provide potential investors with all the information useful for the purposes of the investment decision. The proposers publish all the documents concerning the offer on the platform: The business plan with a description of the company and the business model, the marketing plan with the market prospects for the product/service offered, the economic and financial projections, the organizational structure, the description of the management and other information relating to the offer.

e) Given the international situation, regulation must also be considered an influential player for the development of the phenomenon. Each country is defining autonomously the rules within which equity crowdfunding can be developed, for this reason, in analyzing the operating dynamics of this new form of financing, one cannot ignore the study of the implications brought about by the regulation in force in each single nation.

In the next paragraphs we will provide an analysis of the current state of regulations in the USA and the European Union.

1.3. The fundraising stages for the proposer

Each equity crowdfunding project is characterized by a series of steps ranging from sending the fundraising proposal to the post-financing relationship with the crowdfunders. Here are five phases common to all projects, but there may be some differences regarding the business ideas of start-ups and the different management models adopted by the individual equity crowdfunding platforms:

(i) Entrepreneur-platform contact: The first step occurs when the entrepreneur sends the fundraising proposal to a platform. The choice of the platform can depend on many factors: The reputation in the community of entrepreneurs, the specialization for a certain sector, the country to which it belongs and the relative legislation and brokerage costs required.

Once the proposal is received, the platform can directly publish the project, or analyze a series of factors before validating the fundraising: The quality of the business idea, the adequacy of the project to the characteristics of financing through equity crowdfunding, the reputation of the entrepreneur and the odds of fraud. The analysis of the offer, therefore, can take place in different time instants depending on the way the different platforms operate. Some platforms such as Crowdcube (www.crowdcube.com) perform this analysis before publishing the project (Crowdcube founder Darren Westlake said that around 75% of requests received are rejected); others, like the German Symbid, only carry out due diligence once the fundraising has reached the required target but at the same time before making the transfer of the funds raised to the start-up.

(ii) Transfer of information to investors: Once the project is published, the platform must provide all the information regarding the business idea in order to guarantee investors the tools necessary to evaluate the investment opportunity. In addition to the presentation of the business model, information is provided on the entrepreneur and on the members of the work team, explanations regarding the use of the capital raised and all other financial details (the percentage of capital offered, the existence of maximum funding limits, etc.). This information is often conveyed with multimedia tools such as images and videos, in order to be better understood even by less experienced investors.

(iii) Connection with the investors: Only a small part of the potential investors will autonomously reach the fundraising page, therefore the entrepreneurs and the platform must exploit the available networks in such a way as to reach with the offer the greatest number of possible investors. During the progress of the campaign it is essential that the entrepreneur remains in contact with potential investors through forums made available by the platform, e-mail, or through social networks, in order to be able to provide all information regarding the progress of the collection and answer questions from potential investors.

(iv) The all-or-nothing model: At the beginning of the fundraiser, the entrepreneur defines in accordance with the platform a "funding window" (usually the platform offers a standard window, or defines a maximum duration limit for the collection). All crowdfunding platforms that offer financial instruments adopt the all-or-nothing model. This model foresees that the entrepreneur will receive the funding collected only if the pre-established minimum funding threshold has been reached at the end of the "funding window." Otherwise, the funds raised by the platform are not transferred to the entrepreneur, but returned to the lenders (generally the platforms provide for a success fee on the amount collected which is withdrawn only if the minimum funding threshold is reached).

(v) Post-financing: The transfer of funds usually involves an external financial institution which, at the end of the funding window, transfers the capital to the start-up if is successful. Post-investment management practices differ from platform to platform. Some, such as Seedrs (seedrs.com), operate through a nominee structure: The individual investor does not appear in the start-up shareholders' register, but all the shares are registered in the name of the platform that collected the funding. This undertakes to maintain relations with the start-up in the interest of the crowdfunders, who have no voting rights, but only obtain the financial flows deriving from the investment. Other platforms such as Crowdcube and Symbid, on the other hand, have not provided for collective management mechanisms, but leave the management of the relationship with the start-up to the individual investor.

These are the steps common to all the platforms operating on the market. Each platform, however, can make small changes to these phases; for example, the steps can be divided into a series of simplified activities, in order to offer a more efficient service to both entrepreneurs and investors.

Here are the fundraising steps for the English Sharein platform: In the preparation phase, the entrepreneur collects the necessary information and, in some cases with the help of the platform, prepares the pitch to be presented to investors. Subsequently, the project is launched after approval by the managers and then the transfer of information to investors. Finally, there is the broadcasting or connection with investors phase, which is fundamental to maximizing the probability of success of the campaign. The management of the collection is done with an all-or-nothing logic, the platform transfers the funds to the start-up at the end of the funding window (in this case set at sixty days) only if the pre-established minimum funding threshold is reached. Sharein does not use nominee structures, but transfers the shares to investors who in all respects become the proprietors of the start-up and, as underlined in the "returns" step, the legal system defined by the platform allows for a simplified relationship with investors.

1.4. The stages of fundraising for crowdfunders

As for crowdfunders, there are no real steps to follow. After registering on the platform, the investor makes investment decisions based on the information collected and, if the collection is successful, receives the shares purchased by becoming a shareholder of the company.

The success of crowdfunding, however, is based on the active participation of all the actors involved. The platform and the entrepreneur ask investors for active support. In order for fundraising to be successful and the crowdfunding market to grow, crowdfunders are asked to advertise the pitch during the collection and, in some cases, investors are called to support the entrepreneur in the development of the project. Making the funder feel a key player in the financing process also allows you to create very strong networks and social networks that certainly increase the probability of success of the campaign.

Sharein also proposes a series of steps for the investor: In particular, the platform facilitates and encourages investors to use the tools available, such as social networks, to promote the visibility of the pitch. If successful, the shares are delivered to the investor who becomes a shareholder of the start-up. The last "returns" phase is the moment when the crowdfunder sees the financial returns from the investment. The figure also warns potential investors that in their investment decisions they must take into account that investing in a start-up is a long-term investment and that, in most cases, a start-up does not pay dividends. because the profits are used to finance the growth of the company.

2. Crowdfunding as an alternative financing channel

In the first chapters we saw how crowdfunding, born under the pressure of donations and commitments from the crowd in social causes, has now become a global multibillion-dollar industry. Crowdfunding allows people and organizations to collect money in the start-up phases of a business for the development of a product/service or for the realization of the aforementioned social causes.

Equity crowdfunding, which has spread late compared to other types, has emerged as an alternative to traditional financing instruments (bank loans, Business Angel, Venture Capital etc.) used mainly by start-ups and small and medium-sized enterprises. The large-scale adoption of information and communication technologies, together with the wide acceptance of social networks, have allowed the birth and use of online platforms by an increasing number of people. In fact, these are able to offer scale and purpose and can help overcome the countless challenges that corporate finance is facing in these times and which have prevented business growth and economic development in many regions of the world. These challenges include:

a) provide small and medium-sized enterprises with access to capital;

b) cultivate the growth of high-potential entrepreneurs in developing countries;

c) supporting access to export markets;

d)concentrate capital flows within and between communities, regardless of the physical distance that divides them.

The investment through equity crowdfunding is suitable for different types of companies but especially for high growth start-ups (often belonging to the technological sectors), research institutes but also for more traditional small and medium-sized enterprises. Start-ups that use incubator and business accelerator ecosystems in the early stages of the life cycle are particularly suitable for benefiting from investments through equity crowdfunding. In fact, they find broad understanding and acceptance by the market, they can take advantage of the high skills and structures made available by the incubator ecosystems and subsequently access the capital market to collect the funds necessary for the subsequent growth phases. Even the most traditional companies not belonging to sectors with high technological content or high growth, generally do not have access to bank loans and other forms of debt since they have few guarantees to offer; for which crowdfunding, and in particular the equity-based model, can offer them the opportunity to convert customers into investors, providing the necessary financing for growth. Of course, equity crowdfunding is not suitable for companies with very high structure costs and with business models that require too long payback times, or that require a large contribution of initial capital such as large-scale infrastructure projects. The limits for these companies in the use of equity crowdfunding are primarily the amount of money that can be collected which is unable to reach the necessary critical mass; in secundis, the investment recovery time horizon too far in the future, not in line with the preferences of crowdfunders who are geared to return in a shorter period.

2.1. Crowdfunding against micro funding

Alternative sources of financing can be of various kinds, but they all share one fundamental characteristic, that of providing access to capital to a segment of the population that cannot access it through traditional forms. However, there are significant differences between crowdfunding and another common financing mechanism, micro funding, which includes microfinance and social lending (peer-to-peer lending). These models differ profoundly, including their goals and objectives.

Microfinance provides loans and other basic financial services for the poorest population, i.e. people with little or even no income. This form of financing is widespread in third world countries and the main service offered by specialized institutes, often called "banks of the poor" or "ethical banks," consists of microcredit, that is, the granting of small loans to small entrepreneurs, typically artisan traders and farmers, who need to start or expand their small business. There are also other services and financial instruments offered such as the collection of savings, insurance (microinsurance) and microleasing. To date, one of the major operators in this market is the Grameen Bank, which deals with microfinance in Bangladesh and India, granting micro loans to very poor local populations without requiring collateral and thus guaranteeing their access to credit.

Social lending is a sub-category of microfinance and constitutes a personal loan granted by private individuals to other private individuals on the internet. Kiva Microfund, an American non-governmental organization, inspired by the experience of the Grameen Bank, promotes microcredit actions in less well-off countries through a fundraiser that takes place through the internet channel and with the help of field partners. who make deals directly with local small business owners.

The equity and lending-based crowdfunding models are the most recent asset class in the private capital market and fill the void left between microfinance and institutional investors (business angel, venture capital). These forms of financing are potentially able to provide greater amounts of capital both compared to microfinance and to institutional investors given their scarcity of capital. They can also be seen as an extension of the social mechanisms of microfinance to help start-ups with high growth potential and in some cases allow expansion for existing businesses.

2.2. Equity crowdfunding and business life cycle

The growth path of a company, commonly called life cycle, is divided into several phases:

1.Seed stage: It is the very first step in which the entrepreneur conceived the business idea, which however has yet to be developed and tested. In this phase the focus is on product development and the drafting of the business plan.

2.Start-up stage: The idea was developed to the point of allowing the marketing of the product/service. This phase lasts on average less than a year.

3.Early stage: The production and distribution of the product/service takes place. This phase can have a duration of five years and the company may also not be profitable throughout the period.

4.Later stage: The business is already mature and profitable. In this phase it generates positive cash flows and if it continues in its growth path it can reach great popularity in a period between six and twelve months.

In general, companies that face the initial stages of their life cycle face difficulties in attracting external financing.[203] As we have already seen, start-ups do not have the possibility of accessing debt both because of the risky nature of their business and due to the lack of sufficient collateral to be able to receive a bank loan. For this reason, in order to start their business and start generating profits, start-ups must rely on alternative forms of financing that allow them to finance growth and in particular the initial early stage. Typically, the first lenders of a start-up, in addition to the entrepreneurs who often use their savings, are friends and relatives.[204]

The start-ups in fact, not generating cash flow in the first years of activity, are not able to repay financial charges or even reimbursement portions of the capital possibly loaned. Jeff Lynn, founder of Seedrs, underlined how this phenomenon actually means that only those with wealthy friends or family members can obtain the financial resources necessary for the development of the business idea. This translates into the

---

203COSH A., CUMMING D., HUGHES A., *Outside Entrepreneurial Capital,* op. cit.
204For further details see: AGRAWAL A., CATALINI C., GOLDFARB A., *Some Simple Economics of Crowdfunding,* op. cit.

fact that there will be many cases in which funding from friends and family will be insufficient. For all these reasons, the demand for access to risk capital through equity crowdfunding in these cases is potentially very high.

In recent years, moreover, we are witnessing a shift in investments by business angel and venture capitalists towards companies that are in more advanced stages of their life cycle. Venture capitalists in particular have started to exclude investments in the seed phase also due to the increase in transaction costs in relation to the amount of investments required in these embryonic phases of the life cycle.

This trend therefore constitutes an opportunity for equity crowdfunding to play a valuable role within two markets: The first is seed financing, i.e. investment in the very early stages of experimentation with the business idea, where the contribution of financial resources from friends and relatives may not be sufficient and, at the same time, the amount of money required may prove too small to attract the investment from a business angel. The second is the market space between the level of investments typically made by a business angel, where the required amount is too small for a venture capitalist, and the level of investments characterizing the venture capitalist's activity.

To date most of the capital raised through crowdfunding has gone to occupy the lower part of the market space but this does not exclude the possibility that it may in all respects constitute an alternative to the business angel and the venture capitalist, especially if in a future increase the amount of capital raised thanks to the participation of "more sophisticated" investors who tend to have a greater availability of financial resources to invest.

2.3. Factors affecting fundraising through equity crowdfunding platforms

Which companies are best suited to financing through equity crowdfunding is still under discussion and probably only time will reveal it. To date, in fact, there are not enough elements to be able to determine it. However, there are some factors to consider and which can affect fundraising through equity crowdfunding:

a) The ability of the instrument to provide funding in different rounds. Generally, companies resort to numerous steps and in some cases it happens that the source of funding is always the same; in others it happens that there are different for each round of financing (Chemmanur and Chan, 2006).[205] Some companies prefer traditional sources of finance because they can take advantage of the relationships established with the venture capitalist or with the business angel precisely to obtain funding in subsequent rounds.

b) companies belonging to certain sectors and operating with certain business models, for example those where customer company contact is a fundamental component in the use of the product, are particularly suitable for collection through equity crowdfunding. This is because consumers themselves can also act as lenders. Furthermore, for the company, the extent of this relationship with potential investors and customers at the same time can be considered a confirmation of the profitability of the project or business idea.

c)companies with a focus on creating value for the social sector could benefit more from funding opportunities through equity crowdfunding. In these cases, the non-financial motivations that push people to invest are predominant. Supporters in particular will have an incentive to involve other people and are more likely to advertise the funded company.

d) equity crowdfunding does not seem to be suitable for those companies that do not want to disclose information on their business idea or other confidential product/service information to the market;

e) in the same way, it may be unsuitable for those companies that need the contribution of managerial skills and specific networks that only institutional investors are able to provide.

2.4. Business angel and venture capital

According to Radamani[206] the "business angels represent private investors who, during their active work, have gained wealth and experience and are ready to invest them in new small and medium enterprises in order to help the young entrepreneurs and receive profit simultaneously."

From the above definitions it is possible to deduce what are the peculiar characteristics of business angels:

1. it has personal financial wealth and/or wealth;

205CHEMMANUR T.J., CHEN Z., *Venture Capitalists Versus Angels: The Dynamics of Private Frim Financing Contracts,* in *Review of Corporate Finance Studies,* vol. 3, n. 1-2, 2014, pp. 39-86.

206RAMADANI V., *Business Angels-Who They Really Are?,* in *Strategic Change,* vol. 18, n. 7-8, 2009, pp. 249-258.

2. is a private investor, that it finances companies with equity capital;

3. prefers to invest in unlisted companies that face the early stages of their life cycle, in particular seeds and start-ups;

4. makes investments with a high level of risk;

5.investments typically in local businesses in order to be able to visit them and closely monitor their progress.

The companies subject to investment are often newly created companies but there are some cases in which there is only the business idea shown on a business plan.

The literature deals with the reasons that push business angels to invest in young businesses and, from a study carried out by Newcastle Business School,[207] it emerges that the opportunity to make monetary returns is not the only determining factor. In fact, it is highlighted how many business angels benefit in supporting entrepreneurs through their skills and their network of knowledge. Similar results were obtained in a survey carried out by France angels[208] among the main reasons emerged: The opportunity to create value both for themselves and for the company being invested in by helping entrepreneurs in realizing their business idea, the opportunity to have fun in living a new adventure and, finally, to contribute to the economic development of local communities thanks also to the creation of new jobs.

The investment process of business angels is divided into several phases:

1. initial assessment (pre-screening), which consists of a preliminary analysis of the business plan in which the business potential of the project is verified;

2. screening, in which the business angel meets the entrepreneur or the team of entrepreneurs in order to acquire more confidential information on both the project and the proposers;

3. due diligence, in which detailed assessments are made on the technology, the reference business and the legal aspects;

4. investment, in which all the contracts are prepared, the corporate vehicle used to make the investment and the "closing" of the operation;

5. post-investment, which consists of active participation in the management of the company.

207MACHT S., *Business angels offer more than money*, 2007. Available at: www.growingbusiness.co.uk.

208OECD, *OECD Economic Surveys 2002-2003: France*, *OECD*, vol. 2003/11-July.

Venture capital and private equity funds from the other part are investment funds that aim to achieve capital gain over a few years, typically between five and seven years.

According to the European Private Equity and Venture Capital Association the "venture capital is a type of private equity focused on start-up companies. Venture capital funds often back entrepreneurs who have just the germ of a business idea."[209]

Two characteristics of venture capital emerge from the definition: The first is that venture capital funds typically invest in companies already born but still in the start-up expansion phase. The second is that from a terminological point of view, venture capital falls into the broader category of private equity which generally identifies the contribution of risk capital by a private entity.

EVCA itself defines private equity as follows: "Private equity is a form of equity investment into private companies that are not quoted on a stock exchange. Private equity is distinguished by its active investment model, in which it seeks to deliver operational improvements in its companies, over several years."

In the latter definition, a further characteristic of the investment model of private equity and at the same time of venture capital emerges, that is, active participation in the management of the company with the contribution of managerial skills in order to improve its performance.

Indeed, there is evidence that venture capital companies have higher economic performance and a higher growth rate than other entrepreneurial realities,[210] which means that the active monitoring activity of managers and involvement in management are able to increase their value.

The venture capital investment process is divided into several phases:

1. Research of investors and collection of subscriptions to the fund;

2. Research and selection of companies in which to invest the capital raised, which in turn includes the due diligence, business plan evaluation and negotiation and closing activities;

209For further details on venture capital visit the official site of EVCA: www.evca.com/

210KEUSCHNIGG C., *Venture Capital Backed Growth,* CESifo Working Paper n. 664(5), 2002, pp. 1-27. BOTAZZI L., DA RIN M., *Venture Capital and the Growth of innovative Firms in Europe,* in *Crossroads of Entrepreneurship,* 2004, pp. 83-97.

3. Enhancement of the companies in the portfolio, which consists of the activities carried out by venture capital aimed at increasing their performance;

4. Exit, i.e. the phase of exit from the investment that venture capital makes with the aim of achieving a capital gain through the sale or listing on the Stock Exchange.

Metrick and Yasuda[211] attribute five distinctive characteristics to venture capital:

1. Is a financial intermediary that invests capital raised by investors directly into a portfolio of companies;

2. Invest exclusively in unlisted companies;

3. Plays an active role in monitoring and supporting the companies in the portfolio;

4. Has the primary objective of maximizing the financial return with the exit from the investment through the sale or the listing on the stock exchange (IPO);

5. Makes investments to finance the internal growth of businesses.

From the characteristics listed above it is possible to make a comparison between business angels and venture capital which are similar in some respects but differ in others. A first substantial difference is that venture capital, compared to business angels, is not a private investor, i.e. it does not invest equity capital. Generally, a venture capital fund is structured as a limited partnership with two different actors: The general partners who deal with the establishment and management of the fund, the limited partners, that is, the investors who provide the financial resources. The fact that the business angel invests with its own financial resources significantly changes the economy of investment decisions compared to venture capital. In fact, since the business angel is entitled to the total returns expected from the investment, it has a proportionally lower cost of capital than venture capital and this means that there are companies in which the business angel invests but in which venture capital does not find convenience in investing.

A second difference that impacts on the different investment logics of these two financial operators concerns the motivations and objectives with which they make their investment choices. On the part of venture capital, the selection of the investment is much more tied to financial considerations while, as mentioned above, it is known that for the business angel, profitability is not the only determinant that drives

211METRICK A., YASUDA A., *Venture Capital & the Finance of Innovation*, 2nd edition, Wiley, USA, 2007.

them to invest. In fact, an accurate due diligence, that is the stipulation of contractual conditions with any clauses aimed at ensuring a favorable exit and an accurate analysis of the projections of future cash flows are indispensable elements in the selection of venture capital investments; these do not occupy the same relevance in the decision making model of a business angel. In this regard, Van Osnabrugge,[212] on the basis of the theory of agency costs, highlights how business angels and venture capital adopt different approaches to reduce the information asymmetries in the main agent relationship with the entrepreneur and, in the case of venture capital, also with the lenders of the fund. Venture capital uses the principal-agent approach, in which we try to reduce the ex ante information asymmetries (before the investment) and this translates into high screening costs and due diligence to have a thorough knowledge of the company object of the investment. The business angel, on the other hand, is not obliged to bear the costs related to a detailed due diligence, since it invests its own money, so the approach used to reduce information asymmetries with the sole entrepreneur is the incomplete contracts approach, i.e. the direct control carried out ex post (after the investment) which translates into a greater participation of the business angel in the management dynamics of the company.

A further distinctive element is the different degree of liquidity of the investments linked above all to the different ways of way out of the investment. In the case of venture capital investing in companies in more advanced stages of the life cycle, often with prospects for listing on the stock exchange, the disposal of the investment can prove to be much less difficult. On the contrary, for the business angel the most frequent way-out is the sale to third parties, who can be strategic buyers or the founders of the company; in this case, the disposal of equity investments is on average more complicated.

Ultimately we can say that the business angel has a greater propensity to invest in companies in the very early seed and start-up phases since in these phases the financial needs and skills required, not only managerial but also specific on technology and product, they are more in line both with the amount of capital that the business angel is willing to invest and with its natural predisposition to provide the skills necessary to start the company's growth path.

212VAN OSNABRUGGE M., *A comparison of business angel and venture capitalist investment procedures: An agency theory-based analysis,* in *Venture Capital. An International Journal of Entrepreneurial Finance,* vol. 2, n. 2, 2000, pp. 91-109.

Venture capital has no convenience in intervening in these phases since the modest amount of the investment often does not justify the screening and due diligence costs that must be incurred. For this reason, venture capital tends to invest in the most advanced stages of the life cycle and therefore assumes a position of complementarity with respect to the business angel.

2.5. Business angel against venture capital and their relationship with crowdfunding

From the considerations made in the previous paragraphs on the peculiarities of equity crowdfunding and on the characteristics of the business angel and venture capital, it is possible to deduce what are the main similarities and differences between these different forms of financing.

The first factor to be taken into consideration is related to the "level of maturity" of the companies involved in the investment. All these three forms of financing take into consideration companies that are facing life cycle growth stages. In this respect there is a greater commonality between crowdfunding and business angels since both are mainly concentrated in the seed phase, unlike venture capital which typically intervenes in the start-up and early stage phases.

Another factor is related to the type of companies financed, i.e. those with high growth prospects. In the Italian legislation and in the prospectus of the American one, for example, it is clear that equity crowdfunding is aimed at companies operating in sectors with a high technological content and who invest heavily in research and development.

Finally, we can assert that as well as business angels and venture capital, crowdfunders also invest with the aim of obtaining a capital gain from the future sale of the investments and therefore have no interest in maintaining control of the company in the long run.

As for the differences, a first consideration can be made regarding the average investment cut which, in the case of venture capital, is significantly higher than the business angel and equity crowdfunding.

The second is about the reasons that push these different subjects to invest. Crowdfunders and business angels, as mentioned above, are motivated not only by the possibility of obtaining a monetary return but also by the emotional involvement and interest in the specific project or business idea in which they invest. On the contrary, venture capital is driven by the sole desire to make profits.

The other substantial difference lies in the fact that, once the investment is made, business angels and venture capital actively participate in the management of the company through the contribution of technical and managerial skills. Crowdfunders, unlike them, may not have any specific skills in the sector, in technology and especially in business management. Literature speaks of wisdom of the crowd in reference to the fact that the crowd, equipped with collective intelligence, can sometimes be more efficient than few investors (such as business angels and venture capital) to solve some business problems.[213] In agreement with Gerber et al.[214] what drives the crowd to invest is also the desire for participation and support in the product development phases. However, the activity of monitoring and active participation in the management dynamics of the company by business angels and venture capital, cannot in any way be compared with the exchange of ideas or the collection of feedback and preferences on products that typically take place within the crowdfunders community.

Hornuf and Schwienbacher[215] point out that a substantial difference between business angels and crowdfunders also lies in the type of financial contracts stipulated with the financed company. In equity crowdfunding, the investment takes place through an online platform and the offer of financial instruments is aimed at an indistinct audience of potential investors, for which the contracts are standardized and there is no possibility of making negotiations to make any changes. On the contrary, one of the elements that characterize the investment activities of the business angel and venture capital is the use of customized contracts and financial instruments, often the subject of long negotiations with the group of entrepreneurs.

An advantage of equity crowdfunding compared to traditional forms of financing is the value of the information conveyed. If the interest of crowdfunders is correlated with market demand, the entrepreneur would be able to make an estimate of the appreciation of the product by the public and therefore of the market potential.[216] This would reduce the uncertainty

---

213SCHWIENBACHER A., LARRALDE B., *Crowdfunding of Small Entrepreneurial Ventures,* op. cit.

214GERBER E.M., HUI J.S., HUO P.Y., *Crowdfunding: Why People Are Motivated to Post and Fund Projects on Crowdfunding Platforms,* op. cit.

215HORNUF L., SCHWIENBACHER A., *Crowdinvesting-Angel Investing for the Masses?,* op. cit.

216SCHWIENBACHER A., *Crowdfunding: Tapping the right crowd,* op. cit.

about the validity of the product and the entrepreneur can decide to interrupt or continue the project based on the information collected during the financing campaign. In this regard, the case of Pebble is emblematic with the creator Eric Migicovsky who, after receiving refusals from a series of institutional investors, raised $ 10.2 million on Kickstarter and the information conveyed through the campaign fully validated the success of the device and its market potential.

As previously mentioned, due diligence represents a fundamental activity for business angels and venture capital in the process of selecting the companies subject to investment. With equity crowdfunding, this does not happen, except in a limited way by the platforms, so crowdfunders are subject to a higher operational risk. This also applies in relation to the fact that the business plan and in particular the estimates contained therein may not be true since it does not have any "certification," unlike what happens with professional investors such as business angels and venture capital.

Finally, there is empirical evidence that venture capital requires a well-developed stock market since venture capitalists greatly appreciate the possibility of an exit through IPO which tends to guarantee a higher capital gain than other forms of way-out. Companies financed through equity crowdfunding are still premature and too small so the chances of exiting the investment with a stock exchange listing are very low. However, some platforms, including the Australian Assob and the German Bergfürst, are equipping themselves with a secondary market where crowdfunders can exchange the shares of the companies purchased on their respective platforms.

2.6. The risk-return generated by equity crowdfunding

To date, there is no study carried out on the returns generated by equity crowdfunding and the same applies to the riskiness of investments. The reason is mainly related to the lack of data and therefore to the sample size which does not allow for meaningful analyzes. However, some qualitative considerations can also be made regarding the differences with respect to the risk-return profiles of traditional sources of financing.

Venture capital, as well as business angels, are looking for companies with high return risk profiles and high growth prospects. This could prove to be a limit since it means that for companies that do not reflect these characteristics, there is no possibility of raising capital.

Equity crowdfunding, on the other hand, could allow the financing of those projects with lower potential returns but which in any case justify a long-term investment. In addition, social and non-monetary benefits such as rewards and product discounts (pre-sales) offered in addition to the company's shares, can contribute to lowering the capital cost.[217] This is why crowdfunders are willing to accept lower monetary returns for the same risk. Similarly, through equity crowdfunding, companies characterized by very high risk levels compared to the potential monetary returns they are able to offer can be financed.

Equity crowdfunding can therefore constitute an alternative or in some cases a complementary source of financing for companies characterized by risk return profiles not in line with business angel and venture capital preferences. Therefore, it can offer them the opportunity to finance the early stages of product development and market growth.

An explanatory example of complementarity between business angels and crowdfunding is the case of Antabio, a start-up born with the aim of discovering new drugs to treat and prevent antibiotics resistant to bacterial infections. The start-up was founded in Toulouse, France, in 2009. Through the equity crowdfunding platform, WiSeed raised € 300,000 in less than two months. Antabio started the selection process on the WiSeed platform in August 2010. Actually there was an initial evaluation phase and a second due diligence phase. The first round of financing started in October 2010 and ended in December of the same year, after raising € 300,000 from 207 investors. A second round of financing took place after about a year, in December 2011, and was fully subscribed by a business angel who, in June of the same, took over the entire participation shares held by the crowdfunders. As stated by one of the founders of the start-up, the role of the crowdfunders has proved to be of fundamental importance because thanks to their contribution Antabio has managed to finance its research and development activities, which have allowed it to achieve the first results and to implement the new technology to arouse the interest of large investors.

The phenomenon of equity crowdfunding is expanding, but today it is still configured as a financing model suitable for small amounts. This is partly due to the still too small size of the investor crowd and, in relation to this, the regulatory factor has certainly had a significant impact. Secondly, it is due to the modest amounts of money that crowdfunders are willing to invest. On the other hand, however, a factor that can make equity

---

217AGRAWAL A., CATALINI C., GOLDFARB A., *Some Simple Economics of Crowdfunding*, in *Innovation Policy and the Economy*, op. cit.

crowdfunding particularly suitable for seed financing and in the start-up phases, which tends to be very risky, is precisely the fact that allows investors to engage with small amounts in different projects or initiatives, allowing them to spread the risk effectively.

2.7. Co-investment between crowdfunders and professional investors

Questions about the possibilities of cooperating between crowdfunders and professional investors, especially business angels, is one of the most heated debates today. The authorities, platform managers and investor associations involved in the equity crowdfunding phenomenon are trying to understand whether crowdfunders and business angels replace or complement each other. In the interviews published by the Venture Crowd (Crowdfunding equity investment into business, 2012)[218] to some institutional investors operating in the UK it is underlined how the collaboration between sophisticated and not investors is considered of fundamental importance as it is able to guarantee greater protection for the crowd. The reason for this is due to the fact that professional investors, given their specific skills in the field of investment decisions, would fill the knowledge gap in the crowd. Italian legislation on equity crowdfunding has, for example, introduced the 5% rule, understood as the minimum percentage of equity subscribed by a professional investor, in order to protect other investors and encourage their co-investment. However, in Italy the opinions on this rule are divergent and, some experts and platform owners, believe it may constitute a brake on the development of the equity crowdfunding market.

The challenges that this model of cooperation still faces are still many and one of these concerns precisely the investment conditions for professional investors who probably want to be rewarded for the efforts and costs incurred for the evaluation of the company (e.g. costs of due diligence). According to Agrawal et al.[219] one of the risks related to crowdfunding is the fraud risk since, given the small size of the money invested, even if they were able to carry out the due diligence, crowdfunders would not be incentivized. This would lead to free ride behavior on investment decisions made by other individuals.

218COLLINS L., PIERRAKIS Y., *The Venture Crowd. Crowdfunding equity investment into business,* NESTA, 2012.

219AGRAWAL A., CATALINI C., GOLDFARB A., *Some Simple Economics of Crowdfunding,* in *Innovation Policy and the Economy,* op. cit.

Beyond these aspects, the fact remains that equity crowdfunding offers an investment alternative also to professional investors who could take advantage of both the low transaction costs and the possibility of liquidating their holdings by addressing the crowd. Furthermore, it should be remembered that the non-monetary benefits received from crowdfunders and the value of the information conveyed, could be used by the professional investors themselves to obtain answers on the quality of the project in which they invested.

Today we are witnessing the birth of new equity-based platforms and some of these, including the Belgian MyMicroInvest, give the opportunity to the crowd to co-invest with traditional financial operators such as business angels. This testifies how the platforms are moving more and more towards an integrated financing model where the crowd can count on the financial and monitoring skills of the business angel and at the same time the business angels can count on the ability of the crowd to bridge the gap of financial resources necessary to start the project.

3. Incentives and disincentives for investors and entrepreneurs

The potential of equity crowdfunding is closely connected to the unique characteristics that this new form of financing has compared to traditional forms of financing. These characteristics translate into the fact that equity crowdfunding has different incentives and disincentives compared to other forms of financing, both for the entrepreneur and the investor. Below we list these factors by analyzing specifically which incentives and disincentives influence the choice of the entrepreneur and which the choice of the lender.

3.1. Incentives and disincentives for the investor

The incentives concern the social and relational sphere which is very accentuated in this form of financing and implies that the lender perceives an added value from the investment that goes beyond the expected financial return. These factors impact the individual investor's willingness to pay and allow the entrepreneur to obtain financing with a lower cost of capital than other forms of financing.

The investment through crowdfunding involves a series of social implications that do not intervene in other forms of financing. The social implications are relevant in the investment decisions of the crowdfunders and under some hypotheses they contribute to increase the perceived value deriving from the investment and, therefore, to increase the willingness to pay of the investor. The entrepreneur and the platform for presenting successful collections must try to “amplify” the social value linked to the investment by promoting it with the appropriate tools. The main components of social value are: a) Self-expressiveness: Means the ability of a product/service to create an image of the investor in the eyes of others. Crowdfunders prefer to finance products/services that can help create an image of themselves. This component is very important in crowdfunding as it is a financing method closely linked to social networks. In many cases, investors advertise their investment decisions on personal online pages to obtain social approval or try to create a representation of themselves in the eyes of others (for example, an individual who is very attentive to ecological issues could invest in a start- up that defines itself as green and decides to advertise the investment through social networks to promote itself as a person involved in the cause). In most cases, crowdfunding platforms give the possibility to publish the fundraising page through the most common social networks in a simple and direct way. This contributes to facilitating the increase in the social value of the investment perceived by crowdfunders. b) Community participation: Many projects create web communities where crowdfunders can communicate with each other and maintain relationships with entrepreneurs. These peer investor communities contribute to increasing the social value of the investment as the investor can build relationships with people who probably have common interests. The web communities also contribute to increasing the sense of involvement that impacts the emotional value perceived by the crowdfunder. Furthermore, building a close proposing-investor relationship allows a joint project development. In fact, investors may be asked to take part in the output development process. For example, the entrepreneur can ask investors for advice on the design and functions that the product must have. This form of participation allows you to increase the value perceived by the investment as the crowdfunder not only feels part of a peer investor community, but also feels useful in business development.[220]

The emotional value is the utility acquired from the sensations or affective states generated by an investment or a product. There are a number of dimensions that affect emotional value such as the sense of participation. However, these dimensions are presumed to intervene in all

---

220AGRAWAL A., CATALINI C., GOLDFARB A., *Some Simple Economics of Crowdfunding,* in *Innovation Policy and the Economy,* op. cit.

forms of investment. A dimension that hardly impacts on other forms of investment is the fun, which instead seems to influence the behavior of investors in crowdfunding: a) Fun: an analysis of the discussions between crowdfunders in online newsgroups, carried out by Harms,[221] showed how many lenders have underlined how they had invested online in fun. The results of this analysis can be read in the light of research by Koufaris et al.[222] which examined the relationship between the fun of shopping and the intentions of shopping online. The conclusion they reached with their research is that the feeling of fun deriving from shopping is an important determinant of consumer behavior also online. These conclusions could therefore also apply to crowdfunding, which is why it can be assumed that the feelings of fun have a positive effect in the investment decisions of crowdfunders.

Many start-ups allow investors an early access to the project output (product/service) compared to the rest of the market. For some individuals, this translates into an increase in the perceived value of the investment as they feel part of a selected group of early adopters.[223]

Since the determinants of willingness to pay are issues related to the personal sphere of the investor, they impact differently on individuals (social issues deemed important for one person may not have any perceived value for another). This is why the size of the network is relevant for the success of a fundraiser: The larger the network, the more likely it is to find individuals who associate positive values with the determinants of willingness to pay, and therefore the more likely is that the entrepreneur will be able to collect loans with a lower cost of capital.

Let's now analyze the disincentives for the investor that are related to the risks that characterize online investments in start-ups.

In particular, equity crowdfunding allows platforms to offer start-up shares to the market which by definition are subject to high risks. The investment in innovative start-ups is characterized by higher risk profiles on average compared to investments in traditional financial instruments. The start-up in fact, given its nature, can be defined as a company that offers an idea and a project to carry it out and hardly presents characteristics similar to mature or consolidated companies, which at least

221HARMS M., *What drives Motivation to Participate Financially in a Crowdfunding Community?,* in *SSRN Electronic Journal*, 2007.

222KOUFARIS M., KAMBIL A., LABARBERA P.A., *Consumer Behavior in Web-Based Commerce: An empirical Study,* in *International Journal of Electronic Commerce,* vol. 6, n. 2, 2001, pp. 115-138.

223AGRAWAL A., CATALINI C., GOLDFARB A., *Some Simple Economics of Crowdfunding,* in *Innovation Policy and the Economy,* op. cit.

theoretically have a lower risk profile. Consequently, investment decisions do not always occur by evaluating on the basis of rational economic elements (start-ups do not have results to present, do not distribute profits and typically do not have guarantees to offer) for which reason it is often linked to subjective assessments based on instinct and emotions perceived by the investor.

Precisely for this reason one of the distinctive elements of the offers published on the online portals is the presence of images, videos and other objects that have the purpose of attracting emotions in the visitor (potential investor), and can therefore influence the decision to invest or less by the latter. In essence, the inevitably emotional approach with which the investment is assessed and the intrinsic risk associated with the activity of a newly created company are the basis of the main risks of investing in a start-up. To these is added the risk of fraud related to the transaction which is performed directly online. In summary, the main risks are: a) Risk of loss of capital; b) risk of illiquidity; c) risk of fraud.

The risk of loss of capital is linked to the nature of the financial instruments subject to the offers, or "venture capital securities" with which you become a partner in the start-up and therefore participate in the economic risk characterizing the business activity. As previously said, since the startups are "young" companies and moreover operating in innovative sectors, the risk that the business idea is not implemented is very high and this translates into the real possibility of losing the entire invested capital.

As regards the risk of illiquidity (or liquidity), in the case of investment in start-ups it is also higher than traditional financial instruments, such as for example those traded on stock exchanges which are "organized markets" where it is more easy to sell stocks quickly and at a price that reflects their value. Being instruments that are not traded in these markets, it can be difficult to liquidate them or understand their actual value and, consequently, the associated liquidity risk is high. Nonetheless, the possibility of buying and selling between private individuals remains in compliance with the rules established for individual cases and at the same time the possibility for platform managers to facilitate the creation of a real secondary market where members can buy and sell their own financial instruments.

Finally, the risk of fraud is strictly connected to the use of the internet channel to carry out transactions. In this regard, many regulators have imposed the obligation of management of payments by banks or investment firms for which the amounts invested can be paid only and exclusively to the account in the name of the issuer, opened at a bank or a brokerage company.

For this reason, the financial authorities of the various countries are trying to define a regulatory framework that enables the development of the market on one hand, facilitating access to capital for small businesses, and on the other that protects investors, in particular retail unlike institutional investors, they do not have the means to protect themselves from the risks associated with the investment.

In literature, reference is made to two conditions necessary for the investor to be adequately protected. The first condition is transparency of information: The supervisory authority can oblige market players to disclose all the information necessary for the market to function properly even in the absence of a rigid regulatory framework. The lack of transparency of information can cause the market to fail as occurred in the US in the 1990s with the rule n. 504, a law that allowed small businesses to issue financial instruments without particular disclosure obligations. This has led to numerous problems on the functioning of the market; more experienced investors were able to alter the price of the securities issued, given the low capitalization of the operations, and this allowed them to sell the overpriced securities to less experienced investors.

This example testifies to the importance of information for the functioning of the market, but the approach does not seem to be suitable for a still immature market such as that of equity crowdfunding in which both professional and retail investors operate. Basing investor protection solely on information transparency could cause an "overload" of information and curb investments by less experienced investors and, consequently, compromise one of the fundamental components of the crowdfunding phenomenon, that is the crowd.

The second solution provides for the "merit-review" approach: The protection of the investor is guaranteed, as well as by information obligations, by a tighter control of the legislator who undertakes to evaluate the quality of the financial instruments. This approach is more expensive, but it is necessary in developing markets where investors with different experience levels operate. This solution therefore seems to adapt better to the equity crowdfunding market.

Given the difficulties in defining a regulation that on the one hand facilitates access to capital for small and medium-sized enterprises and on the other protects the investor, many regulators have chosen to prudently and gradually open this form of financing which in the future could be expanded to more businesses. This is because to date many questions remain open, in particular, what are the difficulties for companies in managing a large number of shareholders and how to deal with the strong information asymmetries between business and investors.

3.2. Incentives and disincentives for the entrepreneur

If the entrepreneur chooses to finance himself through equity crowdfunding, he presents his project on an authorized platform according to the methods previously seen and obtains the loan only if the amount of the investments received exceeds the pre-established threshold value.

This form of financing involves a series of costs and disincentives for the entrepreneur who can influence the choice of the financing channel:

a) Fee and costs for using the online platform: The platforms require a remuneration for the service offered. The platforms usually require a success fee calculated on a percentage basis on the amount of the collection if this is successful. Furthermore, some platforms require the payment of additional fees which may vary according to the services requested by the proposer. These costs are typical of this form of financing, and do not impact (if not differently) on traditional forms of financing, so they can be considered a disincentive to financing through equity crowdfunding.

b) Image damage: A fundamental characteristic of financing through equity crowdfunding is that the trend in fundraising is visible to the indistinct public. This means that in the event that the fundraising fails, the start-up can suffer an image damage. In fact, not obtaining funding from the crowd can mean that the value of the proposed product/service is not recognized by the company's future customers, or that the business plan or the characteristics of the team proposed/manager are not considered suitable for business development.

This means that in the event of a failure to raise funds, the company's assessment can be revised downwards by the market.

c) disclosure: An important disincentive for entrepreneurs is the disclosure of information relating to the business idea to the public and at the same time also to potential competitors.

To obtain the necessary funding, the entrepreneur must provide information on the strategy, key human resources, customers, costs, etc.

Disclosure of this information may also result in a devaluation of the intangible assets of the start-up as it may compromise the protection of intellectual property.

This disincentive can be mediated with the adoption of strategies for the protection of sensitive information such as patents or non-disclosure agreements, in order to reduce the risk of spill over, but these actions involve additional costs for the promoter.

d) Investor management costs: Managing a large number of investors can be complicated and expensive. A series of best practices developed by promoters and platforms, however, have made it possible to reduce the impact of these factors.

On the other hand, the choice to finance oneself through the web entails a series of advantages for the entrepreneur:

a) Extraction of benefits for individuals: Obtaining funding through equity crowdfunding makes it possible to create a strong separation between ownership and control. This separation encourages the entrepreneur to extract private benefits from the company at the expense of small financiers, who cannot implement adequate control action unless they incur high costs.

The extraction of private benefits is an advantage for the entrepreneur who can extract value for personal purposes from the company's coffers. This obviously affects the value of the company which is reduced by an amount equal to the private benefits extracted.

b) bundling: Many equity crowdfunding platforms allow you to have a hybrid approach regarding the type of investment remuneration, allowing you to combine the sale of shares with different types of reward. The rewards offered can be very varied depending on the project, a fairly common practice is to offer the outcome of the activity to lenders for free or with a discount proportional to the number of shares purchased. This practice makes it possible to attract financing from "product enthusiasts" who will be willing to recognize a price premium for the shares purchased in order to have the possibility of obtaining the product before it is marketed on the market.

c) Network and value of information: The social nature of this form of financing allows promoters to use the lender community as a vehicle for information to and from the market. For example, lenders may arouse the interest of new crowdfunders, advertise the company, attract new customers and bring ideas for the development of the project. In this perspective, the success of a collection has a double value: On the one hand it allows you to create a community of investors in contact with each other and with the company that can contribute by bringing information from the market useful for strategic decisions, on the other hand, the fact that a number of investors have financed the project and therefore recognized the value of the product/service that the company wants to develop, allows to reduce the variance on the estimates of the future market for the project output.

This aspect is also confirmed by Ingram and Teigland[224] who claim that the success of fundraising can increase the value of the start-up since being able to obtain funding from the crowd means that the market appreciates the product/service, therefore the entrepreneur gets more certainties about the future market that will have its own creation. This means that the corporate business plan gains greater credibility in the eyes of future investors, who attach greater value to the company in their assessments.

d) better matches: Choosing crowdfuding means seeking capital from the "crowd" where the offer is presented to a global pool of investors (to date, start-ups have only been able to target a highly limited local market). Therefore, crowdfunding allows the start-up to find financing at more favorable conditions than the possibilities offered by traditional forms of financing. The most favorable conditions are guaranteed by the fact that it will be more likely to find lenders with a greater willingness to pay for their shareholdings and therefore willing to pay a higher price for the capital offered by the company. As evidence of this, the data collected by Agrawal et al.[225] which showed how the funders of the Sellaband platform were on average 3,000 miles from the creator, while the average distance between entrepreneur and lenders in traditional financing channels (venture capital) can be taken as an example it is only 70 miles.[226]

The ability to find investors with greater willingness to pay can be considered proportional to the number of people reachable by the offer, and therefore proportional to the network of people built by the entrepreneur and the platform on which the project is published.

It is therefore reasonable to assume that the entrepreneur, if through the crowdfunding platforms he manages to reach a sufficient number of investors with high willingness to pay, he manages to obtain a price premium compared to the case in which he turns to a local market for financing.

The differences in willingness to pay between investors can be justified with a series of reasons related to the perceived value of the offer

---

224INGRAM C., TEIGLAND R., *Crowdfunding Among IT Entrepreneurs in Sweden: A qualitative Study of the Funding Ecosystem and ICT Entrepreneurs' Adoption of Crowdfunding,* op. cit.
225AGRAWAL A., CATALINI C., GOLDFARB A., *Some Simple Economics of Crowdfunding,* in *Innovation Policy and the Economy,* op. cit.
226STUART T.E., SORENSON O., *Social Networks and Entrepreneurship,* op. cit.

that goes beyond the financial value and is proportional to social and behavioral factors that differ from investor to investor (we analyze these factors in the investor section).

e) Lottery effect: As described in Kahneman and Tversky's Prospect Theory,[227] investors can behave irrationally due to the influences of the context and some perceptual phenomena that occur when making investment decisions. The prospect theory was formulated by Kahneman and Tversky by conducting experiments with the aim of studying the dynamics that guide an investor in situations similar to gambling. With these experiments they have shown that investors are risk adverse for positive pay-offs, while they are risk seekers for negative pay-offs (this means that statistically an individual prefers to have a prize of € 100 instead of having a 50% probability of having it one for € 200, while he prefers to have a 50% probability of paying a fine of € 200 instead of paying a € 100 fine). Prospect theory also demonstrates that there are situations in which, in the presence of low chances of obtaining large profits, investors behave as risk seekers and are willing to "bet" on small amounts of money (lottery effect).

The latter consequence of prospect theory has interesting implications for the phenomenon of crowdfunding. In crowdfunding, investments are made in start-ups which by definition are characterized by high risks, but also by large potential returns, therefore due to the phenomenon of the "lottery effect" crowdfunders are led to make investments even in cases where the expected return is negative, unlike venture capital.[228]

The lottery effect, therefore, occurs when the expected return on investment is negative. In this case, prospect theory suggests that some investors are still willing to invest small amounts of money if very large potential returns exist.

Gerber et al.[229] carried out a series of interviews with entrepreneurs who obtained funding through equity crowdfunding and collected a series of comments that present other advantages deriving from financing via the web: Some entrepreneurs underlined how crowdfunding can allow to raise capital in horizons shorter timeframes than other forms

---

227KAHNEMAN D., TVERSKY A., *Prospect Theory: An Analysis of Decision under Risk,* in *Econometrica,* vol. 47, n. 2, 1979, pp. 263-291.

228HARMS M., *What drives Motivation to Participate Financially in a Crowdfunding Community?,* op. cit.

229GERBER E.M., HUI J.S., HUO P.Y., *Crowdfunding: Why People Are Motivated to Post and Fund Projects on Crowdfunding Platforms,* op. cit.

of financing. Fundraising through the internet takes less time to prepare the necessary documentation and does not require long due diligence times as in the case in which it is decided to finance itself through professional investors.

Other creators have underlined how the start-up can obtain added value thanks to the visibility obtained from the online project. Presenting the project on a platform on the one hand allows to obtain visibility towards potential future customers and on the other hand allows to confirm the value of the business idea in case the fundraising is successful.

A final factor that emerged from the research is that entrepreneurs recognize great value by creating a long-term relationship with the "crowd" that allows you to initiate collaborative business development. This consists in exploiting this relationship to make the changes required by the community to the output in such a way that it best meets the needs of consumers.

The characteristics of the financing channel listed show how the entrepreneur can obtain an advantage by financing through equity crowdfunding if he can take advantage of the incentives to reduce the cost of capital obtained and if he can limit the impact of disincentives on funding.

4. The challenges of equity crowdfunding

The success of equity crowdfunding depends on the ability of the actors involved to efficiently solve a series of challenges with which they must face.

4.1. The evaluation of start-ups

The correct evaluation of the company is a fundamental part of the success of fundraising. In order for the market to develop efficiently, the platform must ensure that the assessments proposed by entrepreneurs have been carried out correctly and that the actions offered are not excessively overpriced.

However, the task of the platforms is not simple. In fact, the evaluation of a start-up can be very complicated being, in most cases, almost all of the intellectual assets and therefore intangible and not having consolidated data available, but only estimated data.

The platforms operating in the market have chosen different ways to reduce the risk of incorrectly evaluating the companies presented: The most common practice is to leave the burden of the initial evaluation to the entrepreneur and to be flexible on the percentage of ownership offered so that, given the reactions of the market, the entrepreneur can vary the offer in the race.[230] Another practice adopted by some platforms is to make sure that entrepreneurs are educated on how to evaluate their company. For example, the Bank To The Future platform offers courses to entrepreneurs taught by business valuation experts.

The management of funding with the all-or-nothing model can also help ensure that the assessment is correct. Granting funding only when the minimum threshold is reached means raising the number of lenders necessary for fundraising to be successful. Therefore, having a high number of lenders who can interact with each other and who have assessed the offer fair, can be read as confirmation of the correct assessment of the company.

4.2. Equity crowdfunding and institutional investors

As we have already analyzed, the adhesion of an institutional investor can be read as a guarantee of the goodness of the investment because thanks to their professional skills they can reduce information asymmetries.

For this reason, some platforms study methods to attract investments also from this class of investors in order to reduce the risks for small investors and the burden on the platform itself.

4.3 The differences with the traditional business plan

A start-up that finances itself through equity crowdfunding can develop different business models than those of companies that finance themselves through traditional channels.

In traditional forms of financing, start-ups to obtain financing must demonstrate that the product/service is commercially viable. A company that finances itself online, however, often advertises an idea through social media, without having developed the product/service in practice. The proposers then check online if the idea is supported by the crowd and if there are potential investors who could finance the project.

230PIERRAKIS Y., COLLINS L., *Crowdfunding: A New Innovative Model of Providing Funding to Projects and Business,* op. cit.

The business model of these companies, therefore, is developed through the digital economy, that is, through a continuous comparison with potential investors. This financing model, therefore, can allow the development of companies that otherwise would not be able to overcome the embryonic state because they would not be able to obtain the necessary funds or because they would not be able to demonstrate that their idea could have a market. If on the one hand the development of companies that otherwise would not be able to overcome the embryonic phase is allowed, on the other hand investors are exposed to greater risks as they can finance companies that have not yet developed a concrete business model.

4.4. Corporate control and collcctive management methods

The promoters generally try to maintain corporate control even after the capital increase. To facilitate the achievement of this goal many platforms allow them to offer different classes of shares including those without voting rights. This possibility offered by equity crowfunding is difficult to obtain with financing from professional investors who instead have the possibility of monitoring the work of the entrepreneur in much more extensive way.

The separation of ownership and control is seen as a value by the entrepreneur, but contributes to increasing the risks for small investors who have no way of intervening in strategic decisions and who therefore cannot defend their interests (for example in the case of new capital increases which would lead to a dilution effect on their shares). In addition, the inability of small shareholders to have careful monitoring of the entrepreneur's work allows the extraction of private benefits that negatively impact the value of the start-up.

For these reasons, some platforms have developed collective stock management models so that the entrepreneur is forced to deal with a representative who protects the interests of small investors. The Crowdcube platform allows the proposer to set an investment threshold above which he must request permission from the crowd. Some platforms such as Seeders and TheCrowdAngel, on the other hand, maintain control of the shares subscribed by investors through a nominee structure: The individual investor does not have voting rights in practice, but his right is transferred to a single representative for all investors. In this way, the representative has the power to protect the interests of small shareholders who can, with online voting, decide on a common line, voted by the majority, which will be implemented by the representative of the nominee structure.

4.5 Opening of the markets

Creating a global market is one of the main challenges of equity crowdfunding. The possibility of operating in a regulatory framework that allows platforms to raise capital and projects from all over the world is one of the fundamental points required of European regulators by the European Crowdfunding Network, an association that is committed to representing the interests of all the parties involved in the equity crowdfunding. Today there are still many obstacles to creating a global market as pointed out by Luke Lang, co-founder of Crowdcube, who in a interview with growthbusiness.co.uk website (in November 2013) underlined how the process of entering new markets is very complex: "From our experience of setting up Crowdcube in the UK we know it is vital to have a strong presence at a local level. Darren [Westlake, co-founder] has been the envy of the office travelling to Rio de Janeiro, Dubai, Madrid and Milan to ensure we partner with the right people who understand the regulatory environment, and are immersed in the start-up and investment scene. It is not sufficient simply to build a website and hope that people come, life just isn't that simple." At this moment, therefore, operating at an international level is a difficult challenge to face, but the main platforms have started to work in this direction. The opening of markets and the creation of an "international" market could favor the development of crowdfunding as:

a) Operating in multiple countries means being able to create larger networks. The network is a fundamental factor for a platform and allows entrepreneurs to reach a greater number of potential investors and therefore to lower the cost of capital (better matches);

b) the opening of markets leads to greater competition between platforms. Competition translates into a reduction in the commission costs required by the platforms and therefore to a further cut in the cost of financing for start-ups;

c) the possibility for the investor to diversify its portfolio thanks to the investment in platforms and start-ups with offices in different countries allows to reduce the risks deriving from the loan.

5. Equity crowdfunding regulations in US and EU

The growth of crowdfunding and the successes through the first platforms have attracted the attention of world institutions. Equity crowdfunding is considered a financial innovation,[231] which the main governments have decided to introduce to revive businesses and encourage investment.[232]

A recent definition by Ahlers et al., resulting from the combination of descriptions by different authors, states that "equity crowdfunding is a method of financing, whereby an entrepreneur sells a specific amount of equity or equity-bonds in a company to a group of (small) investors through an open call to obtain funding on internet platforms."[233]

The process of purchasing equity securities is a regulated process with the aim of mitigating the risk for investors and preventing fraud. Equity crowdfunding, at least theoretically, has the aim of exploiting all the potential of the so-called "long tail," bringing into play all those who otherwise would not be involved, being the requirements characterizing traditional markets too stringent (for example the stock market).

Therefore, it is configured as a financing model based on participation as broad as possible and whose central engine is the spirit of social participation that unites investors and more generally all participants in the community. In this sense, equity crowdfunding is a tool capable of enabling investors to actively participate in the development of a project, precisely because the lenders do not limit themselves only and exclusively to the economic contribution, but take part personally in the evaluation of the project, to the creation of social ties with the team of entrepreneurs, with the other financiers and all those who have an interest in the realization of the business idea.

In other words, the companies that resort to financing through equity crowdfunding are those that are facing the early stages of the life cycle (seed, start-up) and that precisely in recent years, starting from the

---

231HAGEDORN A., *The Financing Process of Equity-Based Crowdfunding: An Empirical Analysis,* in *Crowdfunding in Europe. State of the Art in Theory and Practice,* BRÜNTJE D., GAJDA O., (eds), Springer, 2016, pp. 71-85.

232BRADLEY D.B., LUONG C., *Crowdfunding: A new opportunity for small business and entrepreneurship,* op. cit.

233AHLERS G.K.C., CUMMING D., GÜNTHER C., SCHWEIZER D., *Signaling in Equity Crowdfunding,* op. cit., pp. 4-5.

crisis of 2008, they had difficulty finding financial resources through the more traditional forms of fundraising.

Equity however, unlike other types of crowdfunding, is a phenomenon of still limited dimensions in terms of market and grows at a less sustained pace than reward and donation-based. One of the main factors that still hinder its growth and, in some countries even its birth, is certainly the regulatory aspect that necessarily intervenes in the mechanisms of operation of the phenomenon.

In relation to this it is the fact that the regulation on equity crowdfunding is not present in all states and in fact in many it is not yet legal and therefore its use is not allowed.[234]

The JOBS ACT (Jumpstart Our Business Startups) was introduced in the United States in April 2012, with the aim of legalizing equity crowdfunding (Title III) and reducing regulation on small businesses. This intervention by the United States government represents a new frontier in startup financing, proving to be an important opportunity for businesses and entrepreneurs to receive financial support, allowing the middle class to invest in the growth of emerging businesses through crowdfunding.[235]

At European level, for example, a dedicated and harmonized set of rules for equity crowdfunding does not yet exist. The direct consequence of this non-harmonized situation is the imposition of territorial limitation to equity crowdfunding usage across Europe, with clear limitation also for its development. On the contrary, US was the first country in the world to formally regulate crowdfunding with the JOBS Act signed on 5 April 2012, dedicating its title II to equity crowdfunding. Unfortunately, the regulation was not incisive enough for launching equity crowdfunding, for at least two main reasons: first, it was not applicable to the crowd but only to accredited investors who can fend for themselves;[236] second, the $ 5 million exemption from the SEC's regime did not avoid state-by-state registration. In this way, equity crowdfunding was both

---

234MANCHANDA K., MURALIDHARAN P., *Crowdfunding: a new paradigm in start-up financing,* op. cit. CUMMING D.J., LEBOEUF G., SCHWIENBACHER A., *Crowdfunding models: Keep-it-All vs. All-Or-Nothing,* op. cit.

235DORFF M.B., *The Siren Call of Equity Crowdfunding,* op. cit. BRADLEY D.B., LUONG C., *Crowdfunding: A new opportunity for small business and entrepreneurship,* op. cit. YAMEN S., GOLDFEDER Y., *Equity Crowdfunding. A Wolf in Sheep's Clothing: The implications of crowdfunding legislation under the JOBS Act,* op. cit.

236HORNUF L, SCHWIENBACHER A., *Market Mechanisms and Funding Dynamics in Equity Crowdfunding,* in *Journal of Corporate Finance,* vol. 50, n. C, 2018, pp. 556-574.

personally and geographically limited or too expensive, involving compliance with each state blue sky's law.[237]

6. Market analysis in US and EU

During the last few years, the equity crowdfunding market has developed considerably, in fact it has shown a constant growth, from 400 million dollars in 2013 to 1.1 billion in 2014 up to, reaching some form of stability only from 2015, and reaching a value of around 2.5 billion of dollars in 2019.

American equity crowdfunding industry is bigger than in European. The United Kingdom is the undiscussed leader of European equity crowdfunding market. It represents the 72% of all the European alternative finance market in 2017. Notwithstanding the UK crowdfunding market volume, represents only the 15% of the amount collected in US in 2016, proportionally, equity crowdfunding market has more relevance in the UK than in the US.[238]

However, the most important data that need be highlighted is the fact that after a rapid growth in previous years, from 2015 to 2019 the growth rate of equity crowdfunding in US and in Europe is now quite stable and in some cases even decreasing. This clearly means that in those countries equity crowdfunding ended its developing phase.

The research providing data on the most funded sectors, given to the platform the possibility to rank the top sectors funded through equity crowdfunding. Although data on the specific volumes are not available, those research provide still precious information. Equity crowdfunding is a financing instrument used mostly by ICT companies both in the US and in Europe. Additionally, although the second place is occupied by different sectors in US and Europe (Internet and E-commerce, as well as Community and Social Enterprise respectively), also the finance sector represent one of the top common field for financing through equity crowdfunding.[239]

237Is a state law in the US that regulates the offering and sale of securities to protect the public from fraud. Though the specific provisions of these laws vary among states, they all require the registration of all securities offerings and sales, as well as of stockbrokers and brokerage firms.

238Cambridge Centre For Alternative Finance, *Entrenching Innovation-The 4th UK Alternative Finance Industry Report, 2017.* The comparison has been made converting the UK collected amount in dollars at the exchange rate of the 01.03.2020.

239Cambridge Centre For Alternative Finance, *Entrenching Innovation-The 4th UK Alternative Finance Industry Report,* op. cit., pag. 17.

In terms of equity crowdfunding platforms, equity crowdfunding market is still an oligopoly with only few companies controlling a wide part of the market. The last years, in UK the most famous crowdfunding platform is Crowdcube, that is also one of the most successful equity crowdfunding platforms in the world, controlling the 48% of the equity market in UK, followed by Seedrs with the 26% and SyndacateRoom with the 18% (see Figure 19).

Figure 19. Equity crowdfunding market in UK

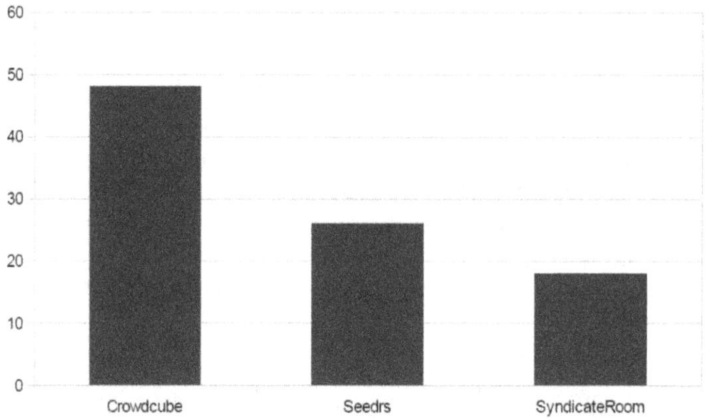

Source: Processed by the author on Beauhurst data

In US, instead, it is possible to find a higher number of platforms than in UK or in other European countries. This could be the result of at least two factors: the less stringent authorization in US and the higher market volume that gives the possibility to more operators to enter the market. In this way, US equity crowdfunding market is less concentrated than the European. If concentration is calculated on the base of the market share owned by the three bigger platforms, US concentration is 68% than 92% of the UK one. The biggest US equity crowdfunding platform, in terms of money collects is EquityNet controlling the 40% followed by the CircleUP with the 15% of the market, and by Crowdfunder and Seedinvest both with the 13% of the market (see Figure 20).

Figure 20. Equity crowdfunding market in US

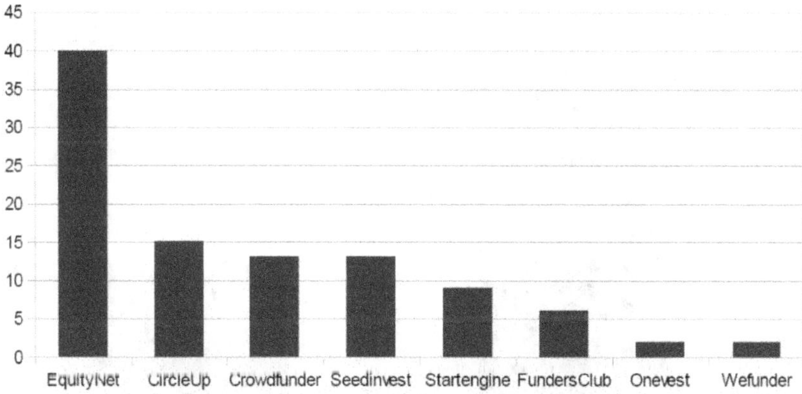

Source: Processing by the author on Crowdexpert data

Differences in financial market dimensions may have created different grounds or frameworks causing the wide spread in terms of development of equity crowdfunding market between US and Europe. At this point, it should be useful consider volumes instead of growth rates. The main reason of this is that development of financial markets, considering also data from the financial literacy, constitutes the basic framework on which equity crowdfunding market may develop.

The US financial market is the biggest, both in terms of number of listed companies and in terms of stock market capitalization to GDP (on average around 139%). UK financial market instead is smaller than the US, although still important. Indeed, UK number of listed companies is just less than half the number of the US and, especially, their average value of stocks traded to GDP differs only less than 20% being the UK around 112%. This results are impressive considering that UK's GDP is 6 times smaller than then US according to World Bank report of 2018 (see Figures 21, 22).[240]

240WORLD BANK, *Global Financial Development Report 2017/2018: Bankers without Borders*, Washington , DC, 2018. Available at: https://openknowledge.world bank.org/handle/10986/28482.

Figure 21. Averaged number of listed companies in US and UK

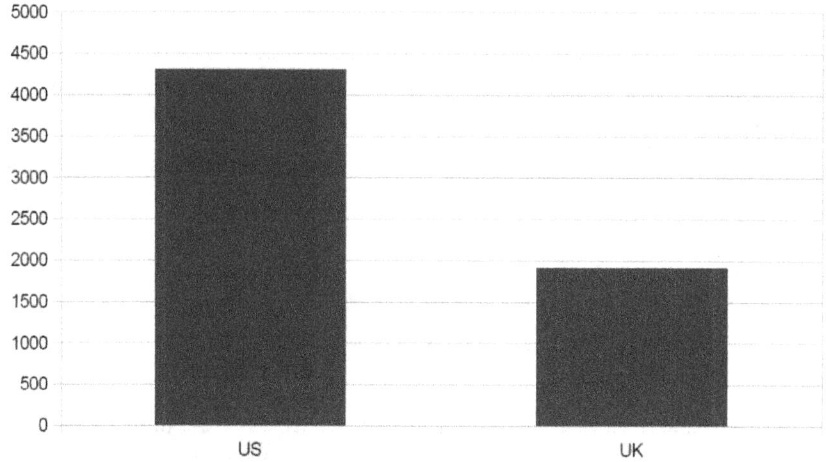

Source: Processing by the author on World Bank data, 2018

Figure 22. Averaged stock market capitalization to GDP (%) in US and UK

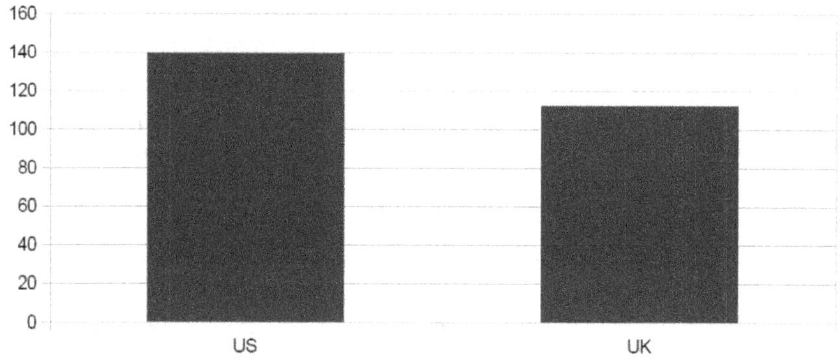

Source: Processing by the author on World Bank data, 2018

Moreover, the UK equity crowdfunding market volume, on average is only 4.5 times smaller than the US ($78 million of the UK, against $318 million of the US) according to data of teh World Bank report of 2018 (see Figure 23).

Figure 23. Averaged US and UK equity crowdfunding volume

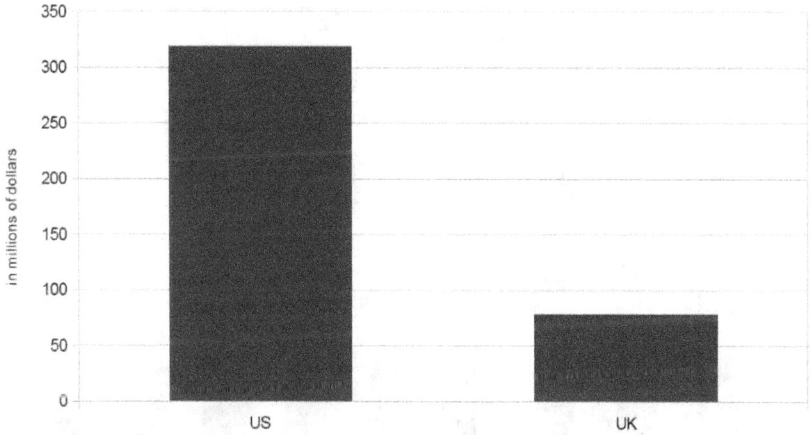

Source: Processing by the author on World Bank report data, 2018

The relation between equity crowdfunding and financial market could be justified by the fact that the former is a financing instrument based on the subscription and trading of companies shares, i.e. the common factor between financial markets and equity crowdfunding. Equity crowdfunding could be considered as a premature initial public offering. Thus, countries with bigger financial markets, such as UK and US have also bigger equity crowdfunding market.

However, different financial market developments could be observed by the investors. Strictly linked with the level of development of financial markets and particularly with those of equity crowdfunding, is the different level of investors' financial literacy of those countries. With this regard, in a research conducted by Standard & Poor's[241] studying the level of financial literacy, i.e. financial decision making in respect of inflation, basic numeracy, interest including and risk diversification, around the world, US and European Union in average display a percentage of adults capable of taking well-informed financial decisions, that is comprised between 55-75%. However, financial literacy rates across European countries vary. For example, Germany, Sweden, Denmark and Netherlands have the highest literacy rates in the European Union reaching the 65%, instead, in Spain and Greece the literacy rated are 49% and 45%

241KLAPPER L., LUSARDI A.,VAN OUDHEUSDEN P., *Financial Literacy Around the World. Insights from the Standard & Poor's ratings services global financial literacy survey,* Washington DC, 2015, pp. 1-28.

respectively. Finally, Romania, with 22% financial literacy, presents the lowest rate in the European Union (see Figure 24).

Figure 24. Financial literacy rates in US and European Union

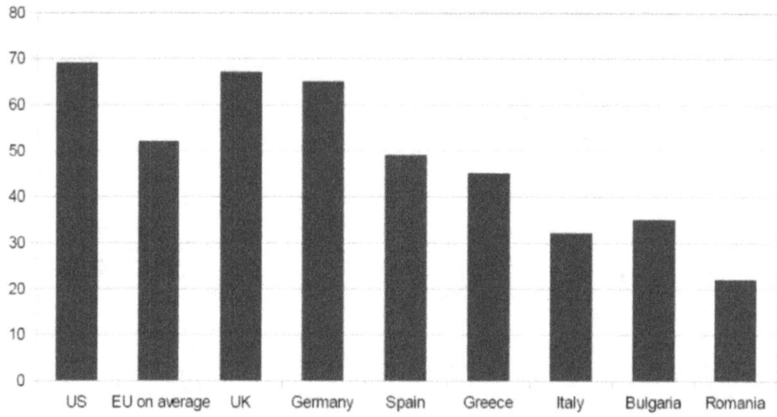

Source: Processing by the author on Standard and Poor's data

Lack or low financial literacy rates is an element with strong influence on equity crowdfunding development. People who are financially literate have the ability to make informed financial choices regarding saving, investing, and more. Without an understanding of basic financial concept, however, people are not well equipped to make decisions related to financial management. The higher is the number of people understanding basic financial concepts, the more are the ones that may decide to invest through equity crowdfunding. On the other hand, in countries such as Bulgaria, Romania, ecc. that traditional financial instruments are not understood (and so not subscribed), is less probable that an alternative financial market could well develop.

7. Literature on equity crowdfunding

Equity crowdfunding is an innovative type of financing that has made its "entrance" only in recent years in the world context therefore the literature on this topic is still in an embryonic phase, unlike the reward-based type. It has been used by most of the authors who have written on crowdfunding, although it has already aroused relevant considerations from various scholars, as reported below.

Cumming and Johan, through a survey conducted on data collected by a 2013 portal in Canada, presented three alternative hypotheses that refer to the regulation of equity crowdfunding, according to the preferences of entrepreneurs, investors and portals: race to the bottom (deregulation or less rigorous regulation); neutrality or uniformity; race to the top (stricter and risk-reducing regulation).

Cumming and Johan,[242] through a survey conducted on data collected by a 2013 portal in Canada, presented three alternative hypotheses that refer to the regulation of equity crowdfunding, according to the preferences of entrepreneurs, investors and portals: Race to the bottom (deregulation or less rigorous regulation); neutrality or uniformity; race to the top (stricter and risk-reducing regulation).

Several authors have dealt with the topic of equity crowdfunding focusing on the regulatory aspects, the legal scenarios and the news from the point of view of the introduction of new rules, securities law, and future prospects such as can be seen from the works of Bradley and Luong in 2014, Yamen and Goldfeder in 2015, Dorff in 2014, Freedman and Nutting in 2015, Bradford in 2012, Figliomeni in 2014, Hogan in 2014 and Hopkins and Hopkins in 2013.[243]

Recent studies on this topic have analyzed the effectiveness of the signals used by entrepreneurs, or "venture quality" (human, social and intellectual capital), to induce investors to commit financial resources in equity crowdfunding as shown by the work of Ahlers et al. in 2015,[244] and the motivations and incentives (financial and non-financial) underlying the decisions to invest in equity, of which financial returns play a primary role.[245]

242CUMMING D., JOHAN S., *Demand-driven securities regulation: evidence from crowdfunding,* op. cit.

243BRADLEY D.B., LUONG C., *Crowdfunding: A new opportunity for small business and entrepreneurship,* op. cit. YAMEN S., GOLDFEDER Y., *Equity Crowdfunding. A Wolf in Sheep's Clothing: The implications of crowdfunding legislation under the JOBS Act,* op. cit. DORFF M.B., *The Siren Call of Equity Crowdfunding,* op. cit. FREEDMAN D.M., NUTTING M.R., *The growth of equity crowdfunding,* op. cit. BRADFORD C.S., *Crowdfunding and the Federal Securities Laws,* in *Columbia Business Law Review,* n. 1, 2012, pp. 1-150. FIGLIOMENI M., *Grassroots capitalism or: how I learned to stop worrying about financial risk in the exempt market and love equity crowdfunding,* op. cit. HOGAN J., *Like oil and water: equity crowdfunding and securities regulation,* op. cit. HOPKINS J., HOPKINS K., *Not all that glitters is gold-Limitations of equity crowdfunding regulations,* op. cit.

244AHLERS G.K.C., CUMMING D., GÜNTHER C., SCHWEIZER D., *Signaling in Equity Crowdfunding,* op. cit.

245See: CHOLAKOVA M., CLARYSSE B., *Does the Possibility to Make Equity Investments in Crowdfunding Projects Crowd Out Reward-Based Investments?,* op. cit.

Also several scholars have compared the different types of crowdfunding as seen in the works of Belleflamme et al. in 2014,[246] by Cholakova and Clarysse in 2014[247] and by Pierrakis and Collins in 2013,[248] highlighting the differences, the benefits (e.g. Bellflamme compares the pre-ordering and the profit-sharing model, analyzing the benefits for the actors) and the incentives/disincentives for founders, funders and platforms in the work of Agrawal et al. In 2014.[249]

Finally, a final point, that the literature on equity crowdfunding by relevance, is the recognition of certain factors that influence the success of equity crowdfunding campaigns, which will be developed in the next paragraph.

8. Success drivers of equity crowdfunding

The current literature proposes the following equity crowdfunding success drivers:[250]

1. Minimum investment: The higher is the minimum amount needed to participate in an equity based campaign, the fewer are the number of investors and the amount raised. This happens, because requiring potential investors to use a higher amount of liquid funds may discourage investment decision together with increasing difficulties for diversification of one's portfolio.

246BELLEFLAMME P., LAMBERT T., SCHWIENBACHER A., *Crowdfunding: Tapping the right crowd*, op. cit.

247CHOLAKOVA M., CLARYSSE B., *Does the Possibility to Make Equity Investments in Crowdfunding Projects Crowd Out Reward-Based Investments?*, op. cit.

248PIERRAKIS Y., COLLINS L., *Crowdfunding: A New Innovative Model of Providing Funding to Projects and Business,* op. cit.

249AGRAWAL A., CATALINI C., GOLDFARB A., *Some Simple Economics of Crowdfunding,* in *Innovation Policy and the Economy,* op. cit.

250For further details about the works analyzing success drivers of equity crowdfunding see: AHLERS G.K.C., CUMMING D., GÜNTHER C., SCHWEIZER D., *Signaling in Equity Crowdfunding,* op. cit., concentrated their research on the Australian crowdfunding platform ASSOB. LUKKARINEN A., TEICH J.E., WALLENIUS H., WALLENIUS J., *Success drivers of online equity crowdfunding campaigns,* in *Decision Support System*, vol. 87, 2016, pp. 26-38, analyzed sixty campaigns published in the Finland platform Investdor between May 2012 and September 2014. RALCHEVA A., ROOSENBOOM P., *On the Road to Success in Equity Crowdfunding,* in *SSRN Working Paper,* 2016, concentrated their work on 541 campaigns launched between January 2012 and March 2015 on the UK platform Crowdcube.

2. Provisions of financial: Showing financial data in the pitch of the crowdfunding campaign is positively correlated with the number of investors attracted. This, may be a signal of credibility and capability, while their lack as unprofessional and dubious. The majority of European and not only regulations do not require the issuer to expose those data. For this reason, they are easily available only if they are disclosed by the issuers. Particularly, some platforms show in a clear way only the pre-money valuation of the company. Usually, this is calculated on the basis of the percentage of the share offered and on the target amount, while the data and the procedure followed to made the calculation are not always made available by the issuer.

3. Funding target: The amount of money that issuers want to collect, is positively correlated with the number of investors participating in the campaign although it is not significantly related with the amount raised. The reason could be that investors will be more attracted by companies with higher target, because the more is the amount collected, the more are the possibility for the company to grow and to increase in value. Moreover, high funding target attracts investors because, this increases their trust in the fact that the project presented will be successfully developed.

4. Presence of institutional investors: Participation in an equity campaign of an institutional investor increases the success possibility of the equity crowdfunding campaign. Retail investors, thus, could consider this as a signal of the value of the presented project and infer positive information acquired by the institutional investor.

5. Equity participation offered: The higher is the participation offered, the lower is the potential investor. This situation reduces attractiveness and trust of investors which may think that the issuer do not strongly believe in its success. Actually, according to the traditional principles of the agency theory, the higher is the participation retained by the promoter, the easier will be to align the interests of the crowd with the interest of the promoter itself.

6. Social media networks: The ability to post and share a campaign on social network is strongly associated with a higher number of investors and of the amount raised by the issuer.

7. Campaign duration: The number of days necessary to complete and fund collection is negatively associated with the number of investors, although not significantly associated to the amount raised. Actually the shorter is the duration the more the issuer could appear determined in carrying on the project and the more the investors will act fast, instead of postponing investment decision.

8. Presence of early investors: Is positively associated with the number of participant and the amount raised. Investors that do not want or that are not able to perform a due diligence may take investment decisions basing on at least some of the other has already verified the published information. This is enhanced, considering the number of investors that only after few days from the launching of the crowdfunding campaign decide to participate in the collection.

9. Intellectual property protection: Patents, trademarks, copyright etc., participate in incrementing the possibility of success of an equity crowdfunding campaign. Actually, one of the risk of going public is that the product and the business idea could be stolen and then developed by better financed firms. Protection, however, participates in transmitting the idea that the business presented has higher possibility of success.

10. Team composition: Past experience, education and age of the people composing the operating team of the issuer are considered by potential investors. Team composition is thus strongly related with the campaign success. Particularly, education and past experience of the team will be a clear signal of success of the present project.

The previous enlisted determinants applied by investors and determing the percentage of success of the major equity crowdfunding campaign realized in most European countries and in US.

The predominance of such drivers may cause, however, some risks for investors. Such mechanisms could bring for example misallocation of funds. In absence of frauds of incoherencies, such drivers makes investors choose the more profitable project. However, this will be impossible if detained financial information are not available.

Thus, our purpose in the following paragraphs is to analyze the the impact that this new form of financing has had for companies that have used this tool.

9. Survey on equity crowdfunding

9.1. Data and method

This section analyzes effects and implications for companies that have resorted to financing from investors through equity crowdfunding.

The reference platform used for this survey is Crowdcube (UK), one of the best known and most important portals on a global level.

Some successful (or funded) campaigns from 2011 to 2019 were studied, in total 290.

Several of these campaigns (just under a quarter) refer to calls re-proposed by the same companies. In total, 30 companies have launched more than one equity crowdfunding campaign on the Crowdcube platform (of which 25, or 5/6 equal to 83.33%, have launched 2 campaigns, while only 5 have launched more than two campaigns, or 3 or 4). The focus is placed on them.

In the following table (see Table 21), these latter companies are reported, with an indication of the total capital raised through equity crowdfunding during the campaigns carried out on the portal over the years.

Below is the list of companies with reference to the individual years and the total funding collected (Table 21).

Table 22. Company and funding raised

Company name	Total capital raised with equity crowdfunding in £
Kamm & Sons	£ 505.000,00 (total amount)
The Rushmore Group	£2.000.000,00 (2011)
Commercial and Northen Ltd	£2.135.456,00 (2019)
Magway Limited	£ 1.360.000,00 (2019)
Charge Box	£ 505.940,00 (2015)
Cadence Performance	£ 594.780,00 (2015)
Crowdcube limited	£ 13.516.110,00 total amount (2011,2013,2014,2016)
Universal Fuels	£ 150.000,00 (2012)
Red Advertising	£ 886.840,00 total amount (2012,2013,2014)
Righteous	£ 216.460,00 total amount (2012, 2013)
Front Up Rugby	£ 227.160,00 total amount (2012,2013)
iNeed	£ 143.400,00 total amount (2012, 2013)
Empiribox	£ 170.310,00 total amount (2014, 2016)
My Mate Your Date	£ 231.380,00 total amount (2014,2015)
Earlybird	£ 429.890,00 total amount (2014,2015)

Crowdfunder	£ 1.804.170,00 total amount (2014, 2015)
Crowd Mortgage Limited	£ 182.980,00 total amount (2013,2014)
East End Manufacturing	£ 399.270,00 total amount (2013,2014)
Powered Now	£ 1.147.330,00 total amount (2014,2015)
Innovation Makers	£ 618.750,00 total amount (2014, 2015)
Earwig Academic Timelines	£ 381.200,00 total amount (2014, 2015)
Workabode	£ 277.510,00 total amount (2014,2015)
Hybrid Air Vehicles Limited	£ 3.420.240,00 total amount (2015, 2016)
Health-Connected	£ 303.860,00 total amount (2014, 2015)
Powervault	£ 2.295.630,00 total amount (2014,2015,2016)
Compare and Share	£ 274.120,00 total amount (2013, 2015)
One Rebel	£ 4.458.680,00 total amount (2014, 2015)
Cauli-Rice	£ 2.005.820,00 total amount (2014, 2015)
Carbonlights Solutions	£ 299.950,00 total amount (2013, 2015)
Pizza Rossa	£ 599.250,00 total amount (2013, 2015)
AutoTrip	£ 581.400,00 total amount (2015, 2016)
Luxtripper	£ 753.430,00 total amount (2015, 2016)
Gamesgrabr	£ 628.314,00 total amount (2013, 2015)
GF Foods	£ 345.400,00 total amount (2013, 2015)
Monzo	£ 2.392.020,00 (2017)

Source: Processing by the author on Crowdube data

Taking these companies into consideration, we investigated the effect that crowdfunding campaigns had on them and the evolution over the years of the companies themselves.

The main reference element that has been considered is the value of the companies, information present in each company that has voluntarily decided to sell a percentage of equity (without going into the merits of the calculation of the value, which certainly reflects the market value, but which does not is part of the purpose of this work), considered a relevant proxy capable of providing useful indications on the status of post-crowdfunding companies.

The verification of the growth (or not) of the companies was carried out by analyzing the value of the individual start-ups during the equity crowdfunding campaigns, whose increases in percentage terms are shown in the table below (Table 23).

To calculate the increase or not of the value of the companies, the initial value with which the company launched its first campaign, and the value in the last round of financing on the platform (in the majority of cases it is two campaigns as we said). This comparison expresses the measure of the "development" or extension of society, through an objective measurement which reflects a true representation of the companies about their status.

The following table (see Table 23) shows the companies indicated, with the respective targets required (in terms of the capital to be obtained) and the share of equity offered (in% terms) through the crowdfunding platform.

Table 23. Target and equity quotas sold by the companies

Company	Year	Corporate value in £	Money Raised in £	Equity on offer	Increase %
Kamm & Sons	2011	782.608,70	180.000,00	0,23	
	2012	1.625.000,00	325.000,00	0,2	107,6389
The Rushmore Group	2011	10.000.000,00	1.000.000,00	0,1	
	2011	10.000.000,00	500.000,00	0,05	0,0000
	2013	10.845.986,98	500.000,00	0,05	8,4599
Commercial and Northen Ltd	2019	16.423.637,76	2.140.000,00	0,13	

Magway limited	2019	28.936.170,21	1.360.000,00	0,05	
Charge Box	2015	4.549.820,14	505.940,00	0,11	
Cadence Performance	2015	2.994864,04	594.780,00	0,19	
Crowdcube limited	2011	3.555.000,00	319.950,00	0,0900	
	2013	4.761.904,76	1.000.000,00	0,2100	33,9495
	2014	19.500.780,03	5.000.000,00	0,2564	309,5164
	2016	53.533.190,58	5.000.000,00	0,0934	174,5182
Universal Fuels	2012	714.285,71	100.000,00	0,1400	
	2012	1.250.000,00	50.000,00	0,0400	75,0000
Red Advertising	2012	1.136.363,64	125.000,00	0,1100	
	2012	1.000.000,00	100.000,00	0,1000	-12,0000
	2013	1.800.000,00	180.000,00	0,1000	80,0000
	2014	2.202.643,17	400.000,00	0,1816	22,3691
Righteous	2012	500.000,00	75.000,00	0,1500	
	2013	753.050,00	150.610,00	0,2000	50,6100
Front Up Rugby	2012	500.000,00	100.000,00	0,2000	
	2012	460.000,00	23.000,00	0,0500	-8,0000
	2013	720.461,10	100.000,00	0,1388	56,6220
iNeed	2012	416.666,67	50.000,00	0,1200	
	2013	682.593,86	60.000,00	0,0879	63,8225
	2013	769.230,77	40.000,00	0,0520	12,6923
Empiribox	2014	865.051,90	50.000,00	0,0578	
	2016	865.051,90	50.000,00	0,0578	0,0000

My Mate Your Date	2014	594.421,58	130.000,00	0,2187	
	2015	917.992,66	75.000,00	0,0817	54,4346
Earlybird	2014	326.939,84	75.000,00	0,2294	
	2015	1.486.620,42	300.000,00	0,2018	354,7076
Crowdfunder	2014	5.000.000,00	500.000,00	0,1000	
	2015	11.627.906,98	1.000.000,00	0,0860	132,5581
Crowd Mortgage Limited	2013	247.418,24	57.500,00	0,2324	
	2013	500.000,00	94.500,00	0,1890	102,0870
	2014	1.332.196,97	35.170,00	0,0264	166,4394
East End Manufacturing	2013	750.000,00	150.000,00	0,2000	
	2014	436.893,20	108.000,00	0,2472	-41,7476
Powered Now	2014	1.157.790,27	350.000,00	0,3023	
	2015	2.155.172,41	350.000,00	0,1624	86,1453
Innovation Makers	2014	650.759,22	150.000,00	0,2305	
	2015	1.857.872,74	400.000,00	0,2153	185,4931
Earwig Academic Timelines	2014	1.000.000,00	140.000,00	0,1400	
	2015	1.220.883,53	152.000,00	0,1245	22,0884
Workabode	2014	825.471,70	70.000,00	0,0848	
	2015	2.840.909,09	150.000,00	0,0528	244,1558
Hybrid Air Vehicles Limited	2015	33.333.333,33	2.000.000,00	0,0600	
	2016	24.154.589,37	500.000,00	0,0207	-27,5362
Health-Connected	2014	942.211,06	150.000,00	0,1592	
Monzo	2017	84.523674,91	2.392.020,00	0,03	

	2015	910.194,17	75.000,00	0,0824	-3,3981
Powervault	2014	400.000,00	100.000,00	0,2500	
	2015	844.594,59	350.000,00	0,4144	111,1486
	2016	2.275.485,44	750.000,00	0,3296	169,4175
Compare and Share	2013	263.852,24	50.000,00	0,1895	
	2015	1.733.102,25	100.000,00	0,0577	556,8458
One Rebel	2014	3.403.373,78	1.150.000,00	0,3379	
	2015	6.643.046,94	1.500.000,00	0,2258	95,1900
Cauli-Rice	2014	1.198.083,07	300.000,00	0,2504	
	2015	1.675.041,88	200.000,00	0,1194	39,8102
	2015	3.295.978,91	500.000,00	0,1517	96,7699
Carbonlights Solutions	2013	1.428.571,43	100.000,00	0,0700	
	2015	918.367,35	180.000,00	0,1960	-35,7143
Pizza Rossa	2013	685.266,76	280.000,00	0,4086	
	2015	1.404.494,38	150.000,00	0,1068	104,9559
AutoTrip	2015	510.725,23	100.000,00	0,1958	
	2016	1.475.548,06	350.000,00	0,2372	188,9123
Luxtripper	2015	2.202.643,17	150.000,00	0,0681	
	2016	3.062.787,14	400.000,00	0,1306	39,0505
Gamesgrabr	2013	1.851.851,85	150.000,00	0,0810	
	2015	2.173.913,04	250.000,00	0,1150	17,3913
GF Foods	2013	426.039,54	125.000,00	0,2934	
	2015	1.734.605,38	200.000,00	0,1153	307,1466

Source: Processing by the author on Crowdube data

9.2. Results

Companies that have resorted to equity crowdfunding show very significant numbers, which give an idea of the effects over time.

The total value of the companies that used more than one crowdfunding campaign increased by 93.24% corresponding to 70,554,445.99 pounds from an initial total of 75,668,728.94 pounds to 146,223,174.94 pounds.

The representation below (Figure 25) compares the total initial value, i.e. referred to the moment of the first crowdfunding campaign, and the total final value, i.e. referred to the moment of the last crowdfunding campaign (considering the increases in intermediate rounds), of the companies in question.[251]

Figure 25. Value growth of companies that have resorted to equity crowdfunding (in absolute numbers)

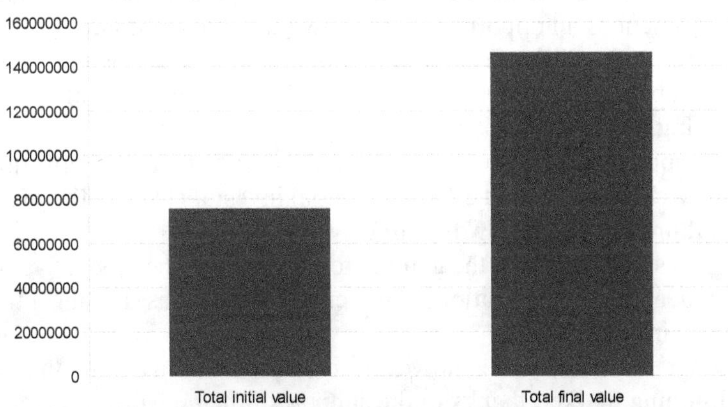

Source: Processing by the author

These numbers are particularly significant for real start-ups, if we consider that some companies that do not fall into this category are included in the sample as they have not been recently established, (such as Carbon Solutions founded in 2008, Hybrid Air Vehicles of the 2007 and The Rushmore Group of 2001) and are in an already maturing phase and not in an initial phase like the others (most born in 2013). At the same

251For further details see the previous paragraph.

time, these numbers mark both the growth of companies and the creation of value for shareholders.

10. Conclusions and future research prospects

Crowdfunding has a strong impact on the global economy and has generated a series of considerable spillover effects, such as the increase in jobs,[252] in projects submitted, in the funds that circulate and are used to finance initiatives, of platforms etc.

The dimensions now taken on by crowdfunding have led to numerous reflections and considerations. The crowdfunding economy has generated unexpected effects and implications for stakeholders, especially entrepreneurs, investors, businesses and the market. This source of funding has had a significant impact on traditional businesses and has brought numerous benefits for users as well as for the community.

For example, companies that have decided to use this financing mechanism have sometimes redefined their internal policies, recognizing this instrument as an opportunity for growth and innovation.

Since the birth of the equity crowdfunding phenomenon, there has been a debate on the real possibility of this new form of financing functioning.

Opponents of the phenomenon argue that the information asymmetries on the market expose potential investors to risks that will lead to the failure of equity crowdfunding.

In support of this, the general formulation of the model has shown that, under certain conditions, the entrepreneur has an incentive to "deceive" investors.

At the same time, however, it has proven as if in the equity crowdfunding market, thanks to the support of the network, investors can interpret the fact that due diligence was carried out as a positive signal and that it was not carried out as a negative signal. The only possible choice for the entrepreneur is not to deceive the market. So if the market worked as described, the entrepreneur should try to propose the project to a large network where investors are incentivized to carry out due diligence and in such a way as to maximize the expected pay-off.

In light of the conclusions we have reached, this financing method must be developed in order to reduce the information asymmetries, thanks

252In the United States, for example, start-ups produce 50% of GDP and create new jobs thanks to the raising of funding from the crowd that allowed the creation of numerous start-ups.

to the interpretation of the signals deriving from the performance of the due diligence, present between creators and crowdfunders. This result, given the conclusions of the model and as discussed in the previous paragraphs, can be achieved in two ways:

a) Market opening: opening markets means allowing platforms to collect projects and funding from a global market. This would lead to the creation of very large networks and therefore to an increase in the probability that the peer-investor community will have the tools necessary to carry out due diligence efficiently and with reduced costs. In conclusion, opening the markets and creating large networks of peer investors would not allow entrepreneurs to "lie" on the value of the start-up and therefore would also reduce the risks for investors.

b) Regulation: Another way that can be followed is to regulate the market in order to discourage fraudulent behavior by entrepreneurs.

This ensures that due diligence is carried out before the funds are transferred to the start-up, in fact, thanks to the tools available, the professional investor can perform a start-up analysis more efficiently than retail investors. However, this solution seems the least suitable for equity crowdfunding, sector experts underline how this choice goes against the founding principles of this instrument: Financing from below (from the crowd) and that it is not a real solution to the problem, but only a tool to get around it.

Furthermore, in the case of equity crowdfunding, companies financed through this model have shown an increase in their value over the years, as well as for shareholders. For this reason there is no clear evidence nor enough studies dealing with the direct and concrete determinants of equity crowdfunding development. The present work represents only a first attempt to highlight possible equity crowdfunding relation with financial market, regulation and entrepreneurship level in US and EU.

Findings suggest that equity crowdfunding is directly correlated with development of financial market. Financial market has been analyzed in terms of its development and population financial literacy. Moreover, direct relation exists with the entrepreneurship level of each interested country. From this point of view, these variables may be considered as the ground on which equity crowdfunding have to develop. Actually, these variables are conditions that pre-existed the common use of this innovative financial instrument by companies.

Diverserly, this is not the case for equity crowdfunding regulation. New rules has been introduced or old rules has been adapted in order to address equity crowdfunding functioning. This means that each country regulator has more power to intervene, trying to enhance equity crowdfunding development. When it is too hard, or even impossible, to intervene in all the other variables, equity crowdfunding regulation amendments could be considered as valid resource to enhance its usage and development.

Having done a crowdfunding campaign can therefore contribute to various purposes including the success and progress of the initiatives.

This research shows some innovative aspects of crowdfunding and that generate a series of reflections, which may lead to further developments. An upcoming work that will be attempted is to analyze the value of the companies taking into consideration also the rounds of financing by other investors, such as venture capitalists and business angels. In fact, this investigation concerned the value of the companies of the Crowdcube platform, but a limit is certainly represented by having limited the sample to the companies that have presented a campaign more than once, therefore not knowing the possible evolution of the companies that have presented a single call, and not considering any subsequent rounds of financing from other investors, which could have changed the status of the companies. A possible development of this work consists in the expansion of the sample and the application of the study also to other platforms, to verify if the same “phenomenon” is repeated also in other realities, and also possibly to other types of crowdfunding (for example to companies that use reward crowdfunding, for example to sell technology products).

In the various types of crowdfunding it is extremely important to have well-defined and contractual relationships between the parties, despite the nature of this particular financing mechanism, which give adequate protection to users.

In the current panorama there are perhaps too many crowdfunding platforms, many of which are almost “deserted” with the presence of very few projects (and in some cases the total absence), which inevitably leads to the closure in a short time of the less used portals and constitutes a high risk of dispersion of resources.

The regulation on the topic, with reference to equity crowdfunding, still highlights application problems and there is no uniform trend at a global level. There are many states without specific regulations, and the countries in which they are present, are showing slowdowns and complications in the use of crowdfunding by project proponents and investors, due to bureaucracy. The risk of over regulation is therefore that it makes the mechanism more cumbersome and slow.

Due to the substantial differences that distinguish the various platforms and market dynamics, a general criterion to be followed in the process of drawing up a regulatory framework is to avoid a so-called "Digital One Size Fits All,"[253] approach, appropriately enhancing the characteristics of each platform and analyzing case by case the competitive conditions (with for example antitrust interventions). An approach based on the analysis of the individual case should be preferred. Intervening in the sectors of the digital economy through forms of regulation that provide for behavioral and/or price obligations, appears to be particularly risky. It is possible, in fact, that the regulator acts "too early," stifling the emergence of more innovative competitive platforms (creating entry limits) and imposing excessive costs on incumbent platforms.

253CHISHOLM A., NELSON J., *Platform regulation — Ex-ante versus ex-post intervention: evolving our antitrust tools and practices to meet the challenges*, in *Competition Policy International*, vol. 11, n. 1, 2015.

CHAPTER 6

The post-crowdfunding scenarios

1. Introduction

Crowdfunding began to assert itself and receive the attention of the institutions in the years following the crisis and the growing difficulty in obtaining credit.[254] This mechanism represents a possible response to the lack of funding by small and medium-sized enterprises, as well as entrepreneurs.

In particular, following the 2008 economic and financial crisis, the difficulties in obtaining financing not only from banks, but also from venture capitalists and business angels, have increased considerably, and the difficulties for nascent or newly-established start-ups are greater.[255]

In this difficult situation, crowdfinance represents an option, especially for growth, for private companies and secondary markets for investors.[256]

Crowdfunding is a type of financing for initiatives, through online

254For further details see: DE BUYSERE K, GAJDA O, KLEVERLAAN R. and MAROM, D., *A Framework for European Crowdfunding.* op. cit. GIUDICI G., NAVA R., ROSSI-LAMASTRA C., VERECONDO C, *Crowdfunding: the new frontier for financing entrepreneurship?,* in *SSRN Working Paper Series*, 2012, doi: 10.2139/ssrn.2157429

255COSH A., CUMMING D., HUGHES A., *Outside Entrepreneurial Capital,* op. cit. MÜLLERLEILE T., JOENSSEN D.W., MÜLLERLEILE A., *Crisis, Co-Financing, and Crowdfunding: Igniting Regional Development,* in *Proceedings of the 7th international conference for entrepreneurship and regional development, ICEIRD 2014,* PAPADOPOULOS G., KETIKIDIS P., KOFTEROS S. (eds.), SEERC, 2014, pp. 277-285.

256FREEDMAN D.M., NUTTING M.R., *The growth of equity crowdfunding,* in *Value Examiner,* 2015, pp. 6-10.

platforms, by a group of interested lenders, or the crowd, who awaits a payoff.[257]

This establishes a link between entrepreneurs who raise capital and new investors who support risks and in return receive a return on monetary or non-monetary investments.[258]

The increase in opportunities for new investments and the availability of risk capital grows thanks to the success of the number of connections and the results cannot be achieved if there is no cooperation between the parties (investors, intermediaries and entrepreneurs).

Relevant for the functioning of the mechanism is the information that the entrepreneur provides to lenders[259] and the role of the crowdfunding platform that allows match.[260]

This mechanism is breaking traditional funding patterns and distorting the traditional approach to finance. In fact, it is gaining popularity as a new form of investment opportunity and source of risk capital,[261] and is finding more and more success and credibility after the JOBS ACT (signed by President Obama).

257ORDANINI A., MICELI L., PIZZETTI M. and PARASURAMAN A., *Crowd-Funding: Transforming Customers into Investors through Innovative Service Platforms*, op. cit.

258VALANCIENE L., JEGELEVICIUTE S., *Valuation of crowdfunding: Benefits and drawbacks,* op. cit. VOORBRAAK K.J.M., *Crowdfunding for Financing New Ventures: Consequences of the Financial Model on Operational Decisions,* op. cit.

259CHOLAKOVA M., CLARYSSE B., *Does the Possibility to Make Equity Investments in Crowdfunding Projects Crowd Out Reward-Based Investments?,* op. cit. BELLEFLAMME P., LAMBERT T., SCHWIENBACHER A., *Crowdfunding: Tapping the right crowd,* op. cit.

260COLOMBO M.G., FRANZONI C., LAMASTRA C.R., *Internal Social Capital and the Attraction of Early Contributions in Crowdfunding,* op. cit. BELLEFLAMME P., LAMBERT T., SCHWIENBACHER A., *Crowdfunding: Tapping the right crowd,* op. cit. BRAET O., SPEK S., PAUWELS C., *Crowdfunding The Movies: A Business Analysis of Crowdfinanced Moviemaking in Small Geographical Markets,* in *Journal of Media Business Studies,* vol. 10, n. 1, 2015, pp. 1-23.

261TOMCZAK A., BREM A., *A conceptualized investment model of crowdfunding,* op. cit.

In fact, there is a funding gap for the initial stages of small and young start-ups.[262] In fact, one of the main problems is the raising of capital for the seed stage and several innovative ideas risk being lost.[263]

The entrepreneur or simply those who intend to promote a project, with the potential of the internet and the network, have a different impulse than in the past, seeing in crowdfunding an important option that can allow them to test the business idea as evidenced by the work of Kuppuswamy and Bayus in 2015[264] and of Colombo et al. in 2014[265] and collect the first contributions, without having to resort to traditional financing methods also for "fear" of being rejected.

In this context, funding from the crowd turns out to be for startuppers or aspirants such, a concrete and valid alternative to external sources, traditionally represented by bank loans, venture capital and business angels as can be seen from the works of Macht and Weatherston in 2014,[266] by MacMillan et al. in 1989[267] of Cumming and Johan in 2013[268] and of Caldbeck in 2013,[269] and internal, traditionally represented

---

262For further details on funding gap of start-up, small and medium companies see: BORELLO G., DE CRESCENZO V., *The Funding Gap and The Role of Financial Return Crowdfunding: Some Evidence From European Platforms,* in *Journal of Internet Banking and Commerce,* vol. 20, n. 1, 2015, pp. 2 ss. LEY A., WEAVEN S., *Exploring agency dynamics of crowdfunding in start-up capital financing,* op. cit. MACHT S.A., WEATHERSTON J., *The Benefits of Online Crowdfunding for Fund-Seeking Business Ventures,* op. cit.

263Cfr. LEY A., WEAVEN S., *Exploring agency dynamics of crowdfunding in start-up capital financing,* op. cit. MANCHANDA K., MURALIDHARAN P, *Crowdfunding: A new paradigm in startup financing. Global Conference on Business & Finance proceedings,* vol. 9, n. 1, 2014, pp. 369-374. LAVINSKY D., *Funding Fathers,* available online at: http://www.sbnonline.com/Local/Article /20471/65 /0/Funding_fathers.aspx

264KUPPUSWAMY V., BAYUS B.L., *Crowdfunding creative ideas: The dynamics of project backers in Kickstarter*, op. cit.

265COLOMBO M.G., FRANZONI C., LAMASTRA C.R., *Internal Social Capital and the Attraction of Early Contributions in Crowdfunding,* op. cit.

266MACHT S.A., WEATHERSTON J., *The Benefits of Online Crowdfunding for Fund-Seeking Business Ventures,* op. cit.

267MACMILLAN I.C., KULOW D.M., KHOYLIAN R., *Venture capitalists' involvement in their investments: Extent and performance,* in *Journal of Business Venturing,* vol. 4, n. 1, 1989, pp. 27-47.

268CUMMING D., JOHAN S., *Demand-driven securities regulation: evidence from crowdfunding,* op. cit.

269CALDBECK R., *Crowdfunding Won't Solve the Venture Capital Series A Crunch,* available at: http://www.forbes.com/sites/ryancaldbeck/2013/01/23/ crownfunding-wont-solve-the-venture-capital-series-a-crunch/

by funds provided by family members or friends (so-called FFF - friends, family and fools) or own capital).[270]

The collection of funding is often particularly complex given the high intrinsic risks of potential new businesses, since they are considered uncertain activities, potentially at high risk of failure, in which to invest and for which a residual part of an investment portfolio.

The emotional impact on a given initiative often leads to an evaluation that is not rational and not based on economic parameters. The risks of an investment in start-ups are mainly that of the loss of the invested capital and illiquidity.

The strong information asymmetries also often lead to "hidden action" and "hidden information" conditions, since the entrepreneur has information on the project that may not be external to the crowd, creating problems of adverse selection and moral hazard.[271]

This work aims to provide support for the understanding of "post-crowdfunding" and the possible options and different scenarios that can occur for founders and funders. In fact, there is little knowledge of what happens after a crowdfunding campaign, whether it has been successful (or has reached or exceeded the set target) or not (goal not reached and therefore not funded). In fact, very few are the contributions that refer to this area, and limited to some cases, such as the fulfillment of the promises as evidenced by the work of Mollick in 2014.[272] The analysis of the phenomenon is carried out through the option theory, interpreting crowdfunding as a "real option," and aims to present a framework on the

---

270AGRAWAL A., CATALINI C., GOLDFARB A., *Some Simple Economics of Crowdfunding,* in *Innovation Policy and the Economy,* op. cit. MOLLICK E., *The dynamics of crowdfunding: An exploratory study,* op. cit. BURKETT E., *A Crowdfunding Exemption? Online Investment Crowdfunding and U.S. Securities Regulation,* op. cit.

271BELLEFLAMME P., LAMBERT T., SCHWIENBACHER A., *Crowdfunding: Tapping the right crowd,* op. cit. WESSEL M., *Crowdfunding: Platform Dynamics under Asymmetric Information,* Darmstadt, Technische Universität Darmstadt, 2016, pp. 1-125. MIGLO A., *Asymmetric Information and Crowdfunding,* 2017, available at SSRN: https://ssrn.com/abstract=3068682. TORABI O., MIRAKHOR A., *Controlling information asymmetry in equity crowdfunding,* in *Journal of Economic and Social Thought,* vol. 5, n. 2018, pp. 32-41. BEBCZUK N.R., *Asymmetric Information in Financial Markets. Introduction and Applications,* op. cit. DAVIES W.E., GIOVANNETTI E., *Signaling experience & reciprocity to temper asymmetric information in crowdfunding evidence from 10,000 projects,* in *Technological Forecasting and Social Change,* Elsevier, vol. 133, n. C, 2018, pp. 118-131.

272MOLLICK E., *The dynamics of crowdfunding: An exploratory study,* op. cit.

opportunities and situations that may arise for both promoters and lenders, analyzing in particular the reward and equity-based models.

Through the decision trees, we will try to explain the possible alternatives and options for the actors, and the possible evolutions of the projects (both in case of success and failure), as well as the role played by crowdfunding in the founder and funder strategies.

2. Representative cases

There are several emblematic cases in the history, albeit short, of crowdfunding, which lend themselves to being significant to improve the discussion in this work. Below are three examples of cases proposed on the Kickstarter platform that have aroused reflections and particular attention for the crowdfunding phenomenon:

a) Pebble Smartwatch;

b) Oculus Rift;

c) Coolest Cooler.

a) Pebble, a company that developed smartwatch technologies initially raised $375,000 from some investors (Silicon Valley Angels) to finance the innovative display watch project that allows interaction with IOS or Android devices.

Once the development phase and the positive results obtained by the prototypes had been completed, the company needed an additional budget of $100,000 to acquire the essential tools for starting the production phase. The founder of Pebble, Eric Migicovsky, despite the support of the incubator/accelerator for start-ups, Y Combinator, and a previous experience in the field of capital raising and production,[273] not finding interested investors decided to use the crowdfunding tool, launching their campaign in 2012 on Kickstarter with the goal of $100,000 and offering various rewards (including smartwatches). The goal was reached in a few hours, and the campaign ended with impressive numbers: 68,929 supporters and raising 10,266,845 dollars. This led the company to have to manufacture over 85,000 smartwatches to fulfill its promises and deliver them within the year.

This typical example of a pre-ordering model highlights how Pebble decided to take the opportunity represented by crowdfunding. This option has allowed the company to have direct contact with the market, experiencing a very high demand, and at the same time to raise the necessary funds for production. Thanks to crowdfunding, the company

273The founder of Pebble had previously created a watch model for the Blackberry.

managed to test its creation and, above all, this allowed it to stand out and acquire reputation. After this successful campaign, Pebble was funded by an early-stage venture capital firm (CRV) in 2013 with $15 million, followed by two other crowdfunding campaigns, one in 2015[274] with 78,471 supporters and raising 20,338,986 of dollars, and one in 2016 with 66,673 supporters and raising 12,779,843 dollars.[275] In total, over 58 million dollars were raised in the Funding Rounds and the company was thus able to develop and implement the smartwatch thus offering new versions, as in the last two Kickstarter campaigns.

For Pebble, therefore, crowdfunding represented an opportunity, given the absence of investors, and was an option to obtain subsequent rounds of financing and further growth.

b) The second case to be analyzed is another company "rejected" by traditional financing systems, Oculus. The company founded in 2012, which made a virtual reality viewer (Oculus rift) (used mainly for video games), launched a crowdfunding campaign on Kickstarter with a goal of $ 250,000 (offering the viewer among the rewards), to develop the Rift kit and implement prototypes.[276] The funding ended with a figure almost ten times the initial target (2,437,429 dollars) and 9,522 financiers, who therefore "supported innovation." Subsequently Oculus obtained over 90 million dollars by 2013 from various Venture Capital funds (including one of 75 million dollars), and was sold to Facebook in 2014 for over 2 billion dollars.

c) A further case of interest is Coolest Cooler, a cooler designed by Ryan Grepper. The first Kickstarter campaign, which ended at the beginning of 2014, failed by failing to obtain the set goal (102.188 dollars out of 125.000 dollars).[277] The founder decided to make changes to the previously proposed version and lowered the goal ($ 50,000). So he launched, after a few months, a new campaign on Kickstarter obtaining $ 13,285,226 from 62,642 supporters.[278] Two years after the campaign, it

---

274For further details see: https://www.kickstarter.com/projects/getpebble/ pebble-e-paper-watch-for-iphone-and-android and https://www.kickstarter. com/projects/get pebble/pebble-time-awesome-smartwatch-no-compromises.

275See: https://www.kickstarter.com/projects/getpebble/pebble-2-time-2-and-core-an-entirely-new-3g-ultra.

276For further details see: https://www.kickstarter.com/projects/1523379957/ oculus-rift-step-into-the-game?ref=most_funded.

277For further details see: https://www.kickstarter.com/projects/ryangrepper/the-coolest-cooler-with-blender-music-and-so-much.

278For further details see: https://www.kickstarter.com/projects/ryangrepper /coolest-cooler-21st-century-cooler-thats-actually.

appeared that about 1/3 of the supporters (about 20 thousand) had received the promised device, while about 36 thousand had not yet received it. The company had not calculated the huge shipping costs (in all countries) and above all the risk of "underproduction" due to the overfunded initiative, since the number of customers to be met was much higher than expected and production had to be changed already programmed, considerably less than the required quantity. Meanwhile, the founder had launched the sale of the devices on Amazon at a price more than doubled compared to that of the crowdfunding campaign, to try to obtain profits capable of covering the shipping costs of campaign supporters who still had to have the products (and who had been asked, as an alternative to waiting, a supplement of 97 dollars to get them in a few months).[279]

The Coolest Cooler case highlights two interesting aspects that generate reflections: The lack of demand may seem like a "wake-up call" and lead to labeling a project as a failure, but this is not always the case, in fact this example shows that re-proposing the call can be successful if improvements are made to the project. Secondly, the aforementioned case highlights the risks due to the overfunded, since the funding of the supporters is certainly an important source for the company, but nevertheless it may not be sufficient if you do not have adequate planning and ability to modify the plans.

3. Literature review

In recent years, more and more academics have shown a greater interest in the so-called "alternative" forms of financing.

Crowdfunding is a particularly complex phenomenon of great interest especially for economics and entrepreneurship scholars.

The literature on it is at the beginning and refers to the four main types of crowdfunding: The donation-based model (donations); the reward-based model (rewards); the equity based model (equity) and; the lending based model (loans).

Crowdfunding has been interpreted as a new innovative model for financing projects and business.[280]

In addition to the comparison between the aforementioned types, some of the works also involved the models implemented by the

279Coolest Cooler devices were offered as a reward against $ 165 funding.

280PIERRAKIS Y., COLLINS L., *Crowdfunding: A New Innovative Model of Providing Funding to Projects and Business,* op. cit.

crowdfunding platforms, namely KIA (Keep it All) or AOT (All or Nothing) model.[281]

The main contributions are exploratory studies and have shown the first evidence of the phenomenon and the elements that determine the success of the projects.[282]

Cordova et al. in 2015 they conducted an analysis on the determinants of success by focusing exclusively on technological projects, identified as initiatives that over time have the potential to become businesses.[283]

Many authors have highlighted the strategies and decisions in the use of this tool,[284] still others have placed the focus on the advantages and disadvantages deriving from crowdfunding for the actors involved.[285]

The risks related to the required disclosure and the capital thresholds to be requested represent potential limits for the founders,[286] while the main advantages are represented by reduced costs[287] and the test

---

281CHOLAKOVA M., CLARYSSE B., *Does the Possibility to Make Equity Investments in Crowdfunding Projects Crowd Out Reward-Based Investments?,* op .cit. CUMMING D.J., LEBOEUF G., SCHWIENBACHER A., *Crowdfunding models:Keep-it-All vs. All-Or-Nothing,* op. cit.

282AHLERS G.K.C., CUMMING D., GÜNTHER C., SCHWEIZER D., *Signaling in Equity Crowdfunding,* op. cit. AGRAWAL A., CATALINI C., GOLDFARB A., *Some Simple Economics of Crowdfunding,* in *Innovation Policy and the Economy,* op. cit.

283CORDOVA A., DOLCI J., GIANFRATE, G., *The determinants of crowdfunding success: evidence from technology projects,* op. cit.

284KRAUS S., RICHTER C., BREM A., CHENG C.F., CHANG M.L., *Strategies for reward-based crowdfunding,* op. cit, pp. 13-23. Doi:10.1016 /j.jik.2016.01.010. BELLEFLAMME P, OMRANI N., PEITZ M., *Understanding the strategies of crowdfunding platforms,* in CESIfo DICE Report, 2, 2016, pp. 6-10. SCHWIENBACHER A., LARRALDE B., *Crowdfunding of Small Entrepreneurial Ventures,* op. cit. GERBER E.M., HUI J.S., HUO P.Y., *Crowdfunding: Why People Are Motivated to Post and Fund Projects on Crowdfunding Platforms,* op. cit.

285JENIK I., LYMAN T., NAVA A., *Crowdfunding and Financial Inclusion,* op. cit. MANCHANDA K., MURALIDHARAN P., *Crowdfunding: a new paradigm in start-up financing,* op. cit. GOLIC Z., *Advantages of crowdfunding as an alternative source of financing of small and medium-sized enterprises,* in *Proceedings of the Faculty of Economics in East Sarajevo,* vol. 8, 2014, pp. 39-48.

286In some cases, there are limits in terms of maximum capital, as in the case of equity crowdfunding as reported by the JOBS ACT in the United States. MANCHANDA K., MURALIDHARAN P., *Crowdfunding: a new paradigm in start-up financing,* op. cit.

287SCHWIENBACHER A., LARRALDE B., *Crowdfunding of Small Entrepreneurial Ventures,* op. cit.

on the market.[288] For funders, on the other hand, the main risks are related to possible fraud[289] and defaults of rewards,[290] while the incentives are represented by access to new products,[291] new investment opportunities[292] and participation in a community.[293]

Belleflamme et al. in 2014[294] and Shneor and Munim in 2019[295] analyzed pre-ordering models (i.e. reward based through product pre-order) and Kuti et al. in 2017[296] and Schwienbacher in 2019[297] profit-sharing (equity crowdfunding), the two forms of crowdfunding most used on the world stage.

Recent contributions have paid attention to the importance that crowdfunding is assuming for start-ups in the initial phase, representing a new paradigm in start-up financing as can be seen from the works of

---

288ORDANINI A., MICELI L., PIZZETTI M. and PARASURAMAN A., *Crowd-Funding: Transforming Customers into Investors through Innovative Service Platforms*, op. cit.

289For further details see: HAZEN T.L., *Crowdfunding or Fraudfunding-Social Networks and the Securities Laws-Why the Specially Tailored Exemption Must Be Conditioned on Meaningful Disclosure,* in *North Carolina Law Review,* vol. 90, n. 5, 2012, p. 1757 ss. CARNI U.S., *Protecting the Crowd through Escrow: Three Ways That the Sec Can Protect Crowdfunding Investors,* in *Fordham Journal of Corporate & Financial Law,* vol. 19, n. 3, 2014, pp. 681-706. GRELLA S., *Fraudulent Crowdfunding Campaign Sets Precedent,* op. cit.

290SCHWIENBACHER A., LARRALDE B., *Crowdfunding of Small Entrepreneurial Ventures,* op. cit. MOLLICK E., *The dynamics of crowdfunding: An exploratory study,* op. cit.

291AGRAWAL A., CATALINI C., GOLDFARB A., *Some Simple Economics of Crowdfunding,* op. cit.

292GUBLER Z.J., *Inventive Funding Deserves Creative Regulation. The SEC should tread lightly regarding the social-media approach to venture capital,* in *WSJ Opinion,* 31 January 2013. Available at: wsj.com/articles/SB100014241 27887323468604578251938686 17572

293COLOMBO M.G., FRANZONI C., LAMASTRA C.R., *Internal Social Capital and the Attraction of Early Contributions in Crowdfunding,* op. cit.

294BELLEFLAMME P., LAMBERT T., SCHWIENBACHER A., *Crowdfunding: Tapping the right crowd,* op. cit.

295SHNEOR R., MUNIM Z.H., *Reward crowdfunding contribution as planned behavior: An extended framework,* in *Journal of Business Research,* vol. 103, 2019, pp. 56-70.

296KUTI M., BEDO Z., GEISZL D., *Equity -based Crowdfunding,* in *Financial and Economic Review,* vol. 16, n. 4, 2017, pp. 187-200.

297SCHWIENBACHER A., *Equity crowdfunding: anything to celebrate?,* in *Venture Capital,* vol. 21, n. 1, 2019, pp. 65-74.

Manchanda and Muralidhara in 2014[298] and of Ley and Weaven in 2011[299] and a modality to create value according to Meyskens and Bird in 2015.[300]

There are some areas that have not been explored in the literature, such as the implications and possible options for founders and funders, after using this alternative form of funding.

Contributions that pay attention to what happens after using this alternative form of financing are limited. Mollick in 2014,[301] for example, analyzed if and when the rewards are delivered, finding that most of the founders fulfill them, but about 75% of which deliver the products with delay compared to expectations. Other authors, however, such as Tomczak and Brem in 2013[302] provide considerations regarding crowdfunding as a replacement or addition to traditional sources of financing in the initial stages of new businesses.

This discussion is based on an in-depth review of the literature on crowd funding and is intended to fit into the current debate on crowdfunding, providing a framework for crowd funding. The purpose of this contribution is to provide a vision of the phenomenon that represents the possible options deriving from crowdfunding, and taking into account the different possible scenarios for the actors involved. Some questions to which this analysis intends to answer are for example "crowdfunded and then?" and "failure and then?." It is interesting for those who approach this mechanism to have an idea of the possible scenarios and future situations that may occur, and an analysis of this type can improve the understanding of the phenomenon for the various interpreters concerned, both for entrepreneurs, funders, platforms and policy makers.

4. Crowdfunding real option

An aspect of absolute importance that emerges from the study of crowdfunding is its ability to present itself as an option that affects the economy and strategies of both entrepreneurs and lenders, making it

---

298 MANCHANDA K., MURALIDHARAN P., *Crowdfunding: a new paradigm in start-up financing,* op. cit

299LEY A., WEAVEN S., *Exploring agency dynamics of crowdfunding in start-up capital financing,* op. cit.

300MEYSKENS M., BIRD L., *Crowdfunding and Value Creation,* in *Entrepreneurship Research Journal,* vol. 5, n. 2, 2015, pp. 155-166.

301MOLLICK E., *The dynamics of crowdfunding: An exploratory study,* op. cit.

302TOMCZAK A., BREM A., *A conceptualized investment model of crowdfunding,* op. cit.

possible to interpret this mechanism as a "real option," in light of option theory.

To analyze this mechanism, characterized by information asymmetries, the logic of real options lends itself well, since we are in the presence of a phenomenon characterized by high uncertainty. The chain of options according to Bowman and Harry[303] in 1993 and of Mcgrath e Macmillan 1996[304] allows an understanding of the opportunities for crowdfundes (shadow options), which create an option. Based on the information generated by this initial phase, uncertainty can be reduced and new opportunities can be generated.

Crowdfunding represents a direct access to the market (Ordanini et al., 2009) and offers the possibility of being able to propose projects to both traditional and non founders (Mollick, 2014).[305]

This alternative type of financing, in fact, is a particularly useful tool, capable of "shaking" and making different subjects seize the opportunity represented by the intrinsic potential of many individuals who, otherwise, would have remained hidden, since in many would not have tried to launch their business idea given a series of objective problems, such as risk aversion, lack of funds, impossibility/inability to turn to banks or venture capitalists, and poor economic/financial knowledge.

Crowdfunding therefore can represent an opportunity for users of this tool in an era characterized by uncertainty,[306] in particular to bring out the entrepreneurial potential of the subjects. Especially those who decide to "get involved" and try to start their own business can benefit from crowdfunding the necessary financial support to finance their project and test their business idea.

Those who decide to use the financing tool through the crowd are faced with the trade-off between the reward (or "pre-ordering") and equity (or "profit-sharing") models. It is appropriate to focus on two key players

---

303BOWMAN E.H., HURRY D., *Strategy through the Option Lens: An Integrated View of Resource Investments and the Incremental-Choice Process,* in *The Academy of Management Review,* vol. 18, n. 4, 1993, pp. 760-782.

304MCGRATH R.G., MACMILLAN I.C., *The Entrepreneurial Mindset: Strategies for Continuously Creating Opportunity in an Age of Uncertainty,* Boston Mass, Harvard Business School Press, 2000.

305See: ORDANINI A., MICELI L., PIZZETTI M. and PARASURAMAN A., *Crowd-Funding: Transforming Customers into Investors through Innovative Service Platforms,* op. cit. MOLLICK E., *The dynamics of crowdfunding: An exploratory study,* op. cit.

306MCGRATH R.G., MACMILLAN I.C., *The Entrepreneurial Mindset: Strategies for Continuously Creating Opportunity in an Age of Uncertainty,* op. cit.

in this system (neglecting the discussion of the third actor involved or the platforms that act as intermediaries), namely the "founders" (or even entrepreneurs) and the "funders" (or even investors), which are treated below.

5. Option for founders

The founders can carry out an "exploratory" project, being able to experiment and test the business idea and the validity of the project at no cost (try and see logic), simultaneously receiving both the first funds, in a fragmented way by a multitude of funders, and important feedback and useful information to reduce uncertainty (learning logic). This first step represents an option of a strategic nature since it opens up further possible opportunities that can only be seized by exploiting the first option (chain of options).

With reference to reward-based projects, the promoter can then launch its initiative through the crowdfunding campaign or carry out a pre-sale of its products.

This first market test can serve to "measure" in a certain sense the size of the public, according to supporters, and attract the attention of other categories of investors.

One of the possible risks related to the success of the initiative is related to the overfunded (overcoming of the objective) in the event that this involved a reprogramming of the production that had been planned due to the high number of rewards to be delivered, as for example in the previously cited case of Coolest Cooler.

In the equity model, the company can sell part of equity or pre-production rights (a classic example is biotech or pharmaceutical companies that study new molecules and then have to start producing drugs) thus finding new finance, useful for example in the case expansion of the company.

The possible risks deriving from this typology mainly derive from the potential governance changes and the dilution in the participation.

In both types, in the event of failure, or of a goal not achieved, the proposer will have the opportunity to propose the campaign again later, making any necessary improvements to the project in light of the information obtained (as in the case of Coolest Cooler).

An interesting consideration about non-funded projects is that failure in some cases may have represented an opportunity for learning and subsequent developments.

In case of failure, the founder also has the opportunity, for example, to change the crowdfunding platform (for example, the Italian startup Kanesis first failed the crowdfunding campaign launched on IndieGoGo, to then be successful with the subsequent campaign launched on Kickstarter).

Furthermore, crowdfunding, for projects that have been successful and reached the goal (but in rare cases even in the case of failure), can represent an option, for the acquisition of credibility and the consequent opportunity to be financed (such as the already mentioned Oculus) also by other institutions such as venture capitalists or business angels, looking for projects with high potential (for example the case of JIBO, a robot, whose campaign launched on IndieGoGo was successful and subsequently received 4 rounds of venture capital financing), and that previously would not have financed them or have not financed them in the past (which is why the proposers have tried with crowdfunding). Having therefore carried out a crowdfunding campaign can represent an important opportunity for investors to “reduce” the risk (banks, venture capital, iban) and sometimes the possibility of acquiring better credit and terms/conditions towards them.

Success can also lead to reproposing other crowdfunding campaigns (such as Pebble for example), or then proposing the campaign using another type of crowdfunding, for example moving from reward-model to equity model or vice versa (for example Panono, which first launched the campaign with reward-model on IndieGoGo in 2014 and in 2015 on Companisto with equity model).

Even in the case of equity crowdfunding, this mechanism can represent an option that leads to other campaigns or to receiving funding from other sources. Taking for example the Crowdcube platform (UK), there are more and more companies, which propose the call again, such as the successful cases of Red Advertising with 4 proposed campaigns (2 in 2012, 1 in 2013 and 1 in 2014), The Rushmore Group with 3 campaigns (2 in 2011 and 1 in 2013) and Compare and Share with 2 campaigns (1 in 2013 and 1 in 2015). Again with reference to the same portal, there is evidence of companies that have obtained successive rounds of financing from other investors after the equity crowdfunding campaign, for example, the cases of E-Car Club are mentioned, which after a campaign in 2012 subsequently obtained 2 rounds of financing with Venture capitalist (1 in 2013 and 1 in 2014), Sole Trader, who after a campaign in 2012 subsequently obtained another 4 rounds of financing (1 in 2012, 1 in 2013 and 2 in 2014).

The entrepreneur can choose to use crowdfunding according to the reward scheme, if the necessary initial capital is small, or equity if the initial capital is larger.[307] With this in mind, it is possible to find that the initiative's ability to succeed and survive (and possibly expand) could be influenced by the resources it seeks to obtain through investors.

Entrepreneurs and companies could then find themselves, following the success through crowdfunding, in an incubation mechanism, by incubators/accelerators or science parks, or even large sector operators, who would develop and support the continuation of their projects, such as for example a subsequent beta prototype or launch on the market (an example of this constitutes the absorption of App-creating start-ups by large companies, such as Google, Facebook, Apple, etc., or operators in the TLC field, like Vodafone which incubated and allowed several start-ups to develop).[308]

For those who have an innovative business idea that is successful, there is often the trade-off between selling the idea or business to a large company or setting up a start up.

The failed project or the failed start up can change and restart with a new project with a view to fail fast.[309]

The main objectives of the equity and reward crowdfunding types for founders are summarized on the next page (see Table 24)

307BELLEFLAMME P., LAMBERT T., SCHWIENBACHER A., *Crowdfunding: Tapping the right crowd*, op. cit.

308See for example Vodafone with the Floome case, a start-up that has created an application with its breathalyzer mountable via USB on your mobile phone. Floome is an elegant and accurate breathalyzer for smartphones that, thanks to the dedicated application, will estimate your blood alcohol concentration and give you access to a large number of other useful features.

309Fail fast or fail forward and fail better are phrases used by entrepreneurs and investors to describe the process of rapidly identifying bad ideas and interactions as a way to ultimately arrive at a successful solution. According to the venture capitalist Andreessen M., "fail fast makes sense for tactics - if a tactic doesn't work, find another tactic. But not so much for longer term goals. I think fail fast is catastrophic if it is applied to strategy and goals (…). A lot of founders talk themselves out of what are going to be good ideas in the long run because they aren't getting immediate traction." SOPER T., *Why venture capitalist Marc Andreessen is critical of the "fail fast" startup mentality*, in *GeekWire*, 13 September 2016.

Table 24.

Founders	
Equity model	Reward model
Equity shares Pre re-production Company development Expansion	Start up capital Business idea test (feedback) Learning or - relationality Pre-sale

Source: Processing by the author

6. Option for funders

As for lenders, in the case of equity crowdfunding, they acquire shares in the capital of the business initiative and, in the case of subsequent corporate events, such as the capital increase, the right to exercise the option to subscribe new shares or quotas issued by the company. If the option is not exercised, there is a risk that the investment will suffer a "dilution" effect due to the entry of new shareholders and consequently that the investment in the company will weigh less in percentage terms (in terms of value, expected dividends, votes etc).

Funders may find themselves holding stakes and therefore be part of a successful start-up, which could gain market notoriety (scalability potential). Their investment would therefore be an option, in which they believe and which could prove to be a possibility of pre-emption in the event of an expansion of the company or a substantial economic response from the future sale of the investment, respecting the parameters of the law.[310]

310Some countries have taken very liberal approaches to equity crowdfunding while others are very protectionist. In UK, for example, the Financial Conduct Authority has taken a relaxed touch regulations, however, equity crowdfunding platforms strongly screen the companies that come through their doors. The progress of the UK's crowdfunding market has also been bolstered by the highly attractive tax incentives offered through the Enterprise Investment Scheme for the more mature start-ups and through the Seed Enterprise Investment Scheme for seed stage early companies. In the US, instead, regulations were coming into force only in 2016, with Title III equity crowdfunding. US based companies can use equity crowdfunding portals to raise up to 1.07 million dollars in twelve month period. This means the se of equity crowdfunding to very early stage companies. On the contrary Canada's rules are more restrictive. There is no single one regulation at a national level. Having 13 sets of rules, has significantly impeded the growth of Canada's equity crowdfunding market. The crowdfunding exemption of 2016, imposes too much cost and disclosure burden for

In the case of the reward model, the funder will receive rewards, or acquire an option for future products, at a lower cost than other consumers and, in case of changes, has the pre-emption (discriminated price).

One of the main reasons that lead funders to support initiatives, in fact, can be represented by the possibility of being able to have innovative products not yet on the market, and to share the process of "innovation."

In the event that the project does not achieve its goal (in terms of budget), the financing will be returned, while in the event that the project reaches the goal and the promises are not kept, the cost for the financing will represent the loss incurred.

The main risk for funders is the loss of invested capital. In the case of the equity model, there is also the risk of lack of dividends (in many regulations, for example, the ban on distributing profits in the early years on innovative start-ups has been introduced), and the risk of illiquidity (i.e. not to be able to sell the financial instruments issued by the start-ups subscribed through equity crowdfunding platforms).

The main objectives of the equity and reward crowdfunding types for funders are summarized below (see Table 25).

Table 25.

Funders	
Equity model	Reward model
Investment	Rewards
Participation in capital	Preemption
Subscription for new shares	Innovative products not on the market
Dividends	Future purchase option

Source: Processed by the author

the start-ups and its real effect was to kill the industry altogether. Finally, in Australia, in the latter part of 2018, equity crowdfunding sites have been making up for lost time by listing offers across many different sectors. In other words, crowdfunding companies are needing to transfer to a less than desirable company structure in order to use equity crowdfunding in Australia. Overall, the equity crowdfunding model is compelling, as it allows starts ups and growing companies to fill the funding gap.

7. Decision trees

In this paragraph a series of decision trees will be developed which represent the different scenarios that are configured for users of this form of financing. The decision trees are the graphic demonstration of the choices made and/or of the possible options for the actors, in this case the promoters of projects who have decided to participate in the financing process through the crowd through a fundraising campaign on special platforms. In the course of the discussion a series of best and worst cases will be developed. For these types of analysis it is also possible to attribute weights to possible events, using for example conditional probabilities (Bayers), or qualifying the possibilities.

Founders who intend to carry out a crowdfunding campaign can either be successful, or reach the goal in terms of money (goal), or fail, or do not reach the goal in terms of money (goal) (see Figure 26).

Figure 26. Crowdfunding outcomes

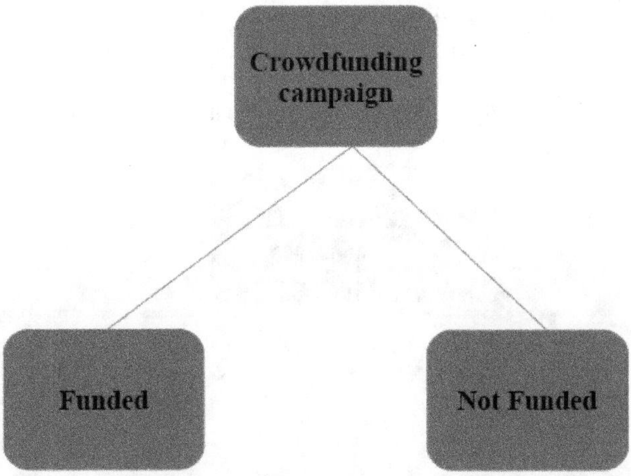

Source: Processing by the author

As for the reward-based model, the Kickstarter platform is considered, for example, in which the average success rate of the campaigns within the platform is equal to 37, 56% in 2019 (see Figure 27).

Figure 27. Success and failure rate on Kickstarter

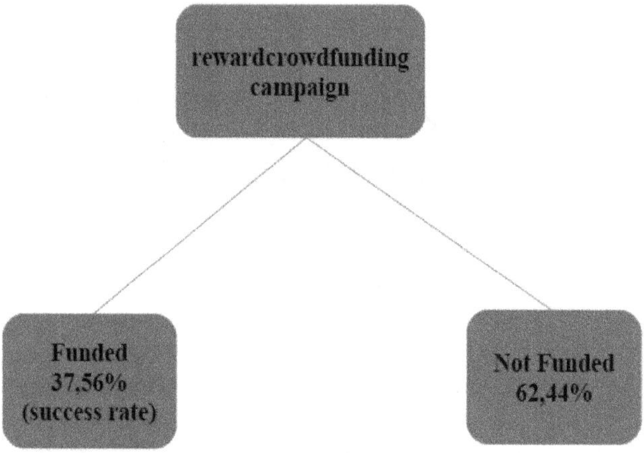

Source: Processing by the author on Kickstarter data

With reference to the equity-based model, the Seedrs[311] (UK) platform is instead taken into consideration. The average success rate of campaigns within the platform is 49% in 2019 (see Figure 28).

Figure 28. Success and failure rate on Seedrs

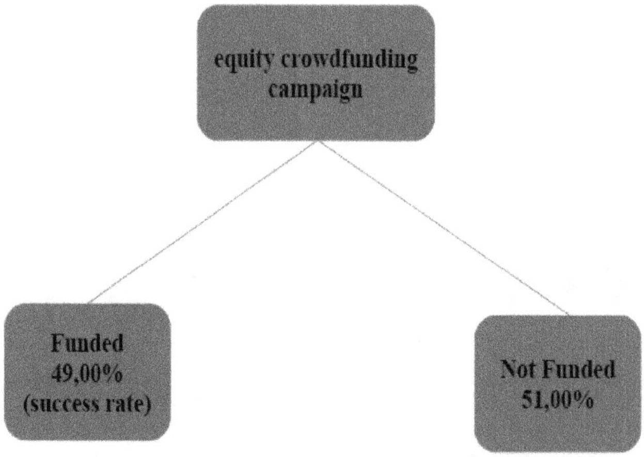

Source: Processing by the author of Seedrs data

311Seedrs is the second largest equity crowdfunding platform in Europe. Seedrs specializes in investments in start-ups and subsequent activities in Europe. It was the first equity crowdfunding platform to receive regulatory approval from a financial regulator, the Financial Conduct Authority in May 2012.

What are the scenarios for successfully funded projects?

Knowledge of after taking part in the crowdfunding mechanism is very limited. Here are some possible post-crowdfunding scenarios in case of success of the campaign. In the case of equity crowdfunding, the following representation is proposed (see Figure: 29).

Figure 29. Post-financing scenarios

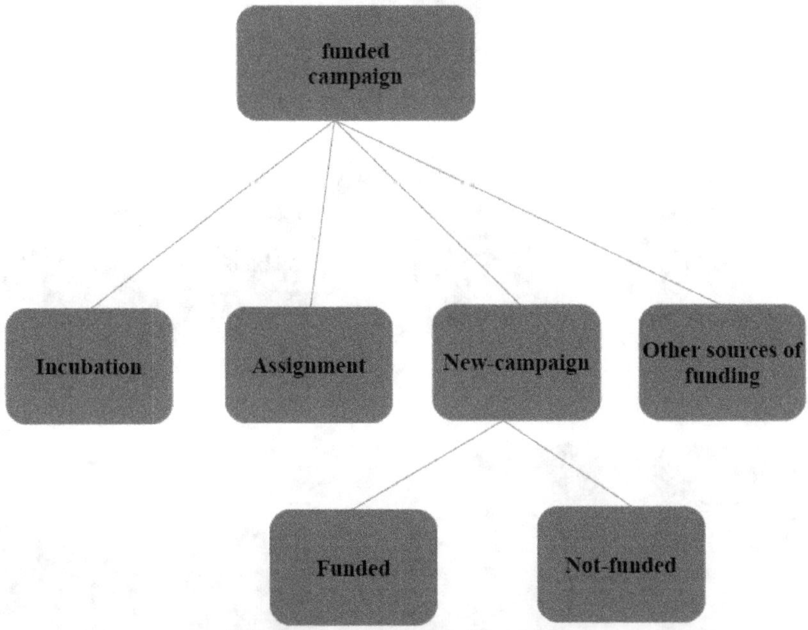

Source: Processing by the author

The successful equity crowdfunding campaign puts the founders in a position to make decisions regarding the development of the company. In fact, the company, and therefore the founder, can propose a crowdfunding campaign again (sometimes even by switching to a different type such as reward crowdfunding in the case of products) to find additional finance necessary for both a consolidation and expansion; sell the company (for example through the acquisition from a big-company or a sale of rights and patents); then be supported by incubators or accelerators that can allow the company to grow and develop; find other sources of financing, for example through venture capitalists and/or business angels, who, as we have seen previously, increasingly come forward to try to grab the most interesting start-ups with high potential and high scalability.

In the case of the reward model, the following two representations are proposed: The first with reference to an initiative with development implications (see Figure: 30), the second a successful pre-ordering initiative in the case of overfunded (see Figure: 31).

Figure 30. Development scenarios

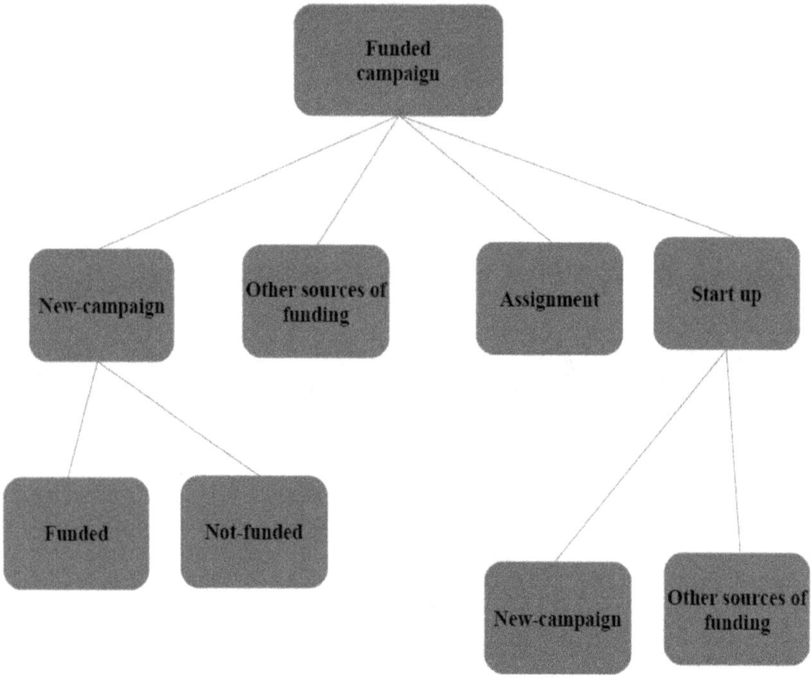

Source: Processing by the author

Figure 31. Overfunded scenarios

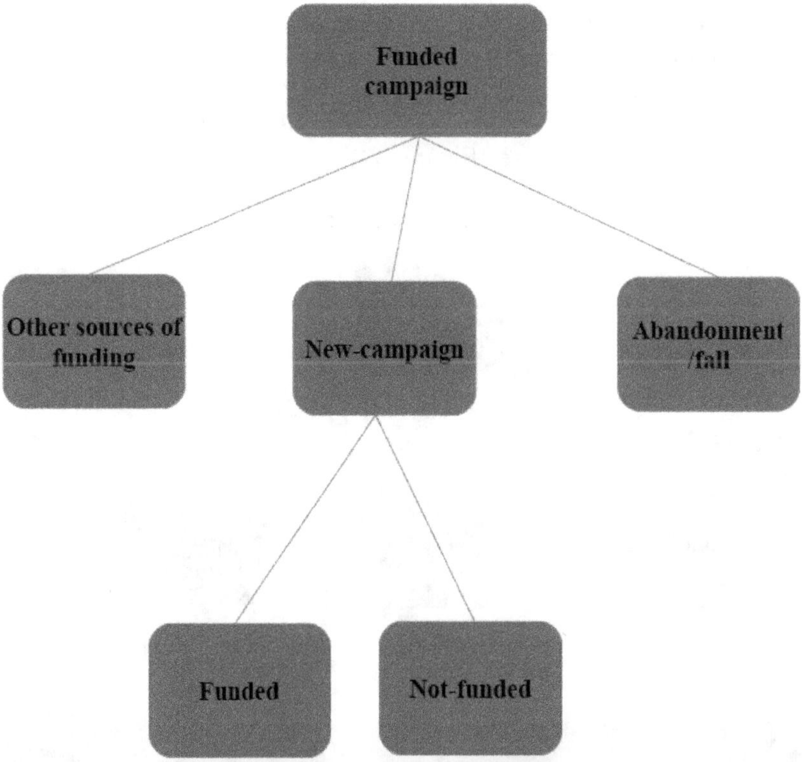

Source: Processing by the author

For the promoters of successful projects, the strategic choice is first of all whether to set up a start-up (if they have not already been founded) or to sell their business or idea. With a view to consolidating and developing the business, the company (or the entrepreneur if not established) may subsequently propose new campaigns using even different models (using for example equity crowdfunding if the company was founded) or find other sources In fact, in this case, success through crowdfunding represents an option for future investments.

Founders who have had success during a campaign must first fulfill the promises made to supporters. In the event that these fail, in particular for campaigns that have foreseen a pre-order, since for example the rewards to be bestowed are more than those that the production system is able to achieve (in case of overfunded), they will they would find themselves in the situation of having to find new finance through other lenders or channels (as in the case of Coolest Cooler with Amazon) in order not to abandon the project and therefore fail.

And what happens after the failures?

In this section some possible post-crowdfunding scenarios in case of campaign failure are proposed.

The following representation is proposed, valid both for rewards and for the equity model (see Figure: 32).

Figure 32. Failure scenarios

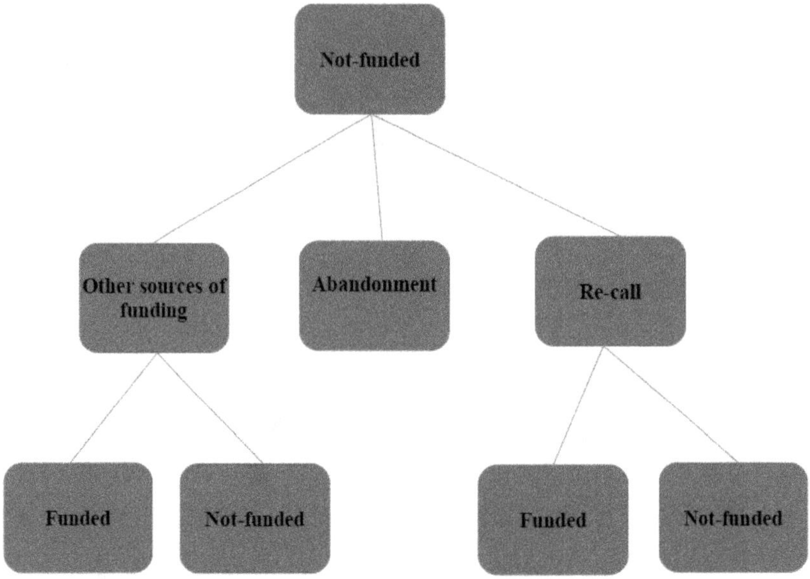

Source: Processing by the author

The failure of a campaign, due to the goal not achieved, implies for the founder the choice, as an alternative to abandoning the business idea, to be able to either search for new sources of funding, or retry with a new crowdfunding campaign, modifying it and working on the critical issues that emerged from the first campaign in order to improve both the initiative and the campaign itself, so that it can be successful.

Entrepreneurs or companies can decide whether or not to propose their project on a platform, according to their needs. Stages of the entrepreneurial path and ambitions. This opportunity is free of costs, if not indirect (in fact there are no plans to take advantage of this type of financing, but only if the goal is reached will a percentage go to the platform) and allows the company and entrepreneurs to gain further options for the future. The focus is on the strategies of the companies, i.e. consolidation or expansion, and the possibility of using the two types of crowdfunding analyzed so far.

The next figure (see Figure: 33) shows the possible strategies (decision-making process) of a company (or entrepreneur) that chooses crowdfunding, in the equity or reward based models depending on the current stage and future prospects.

Figure 33. Corporate strategies

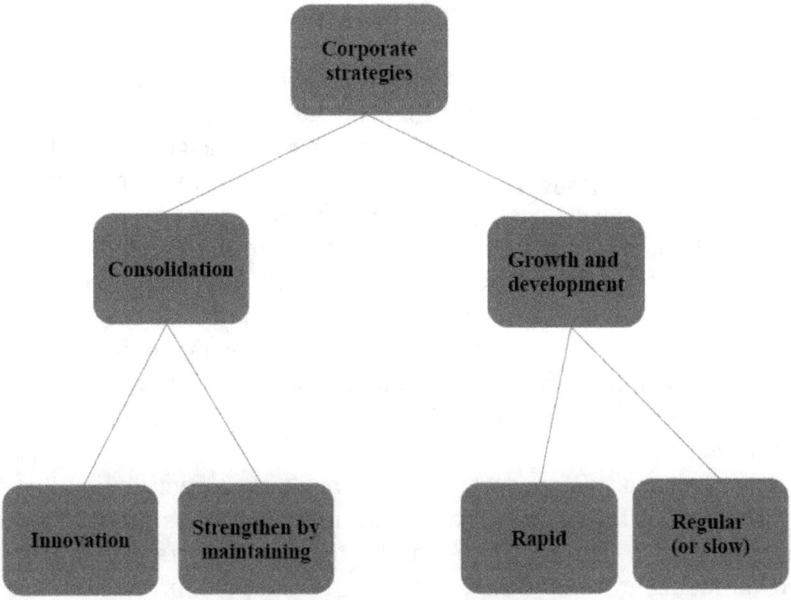

Source: Processing by the author

During the life cycle, companies find themselves having to consider various possible strategies, such as consolidation or expansion. To implement these strategic options, they have the possibility of using crowdfunding both in the equity based and in the reward based typology. From these tools you can find the sources necessary to pursue the set goals. If the company intends to expand, it must consider whether growth can be rapid or slower, and the ways in which to achieve this, while in the case of consolidation it must consider whether to innovate or strengthen by maintaining certain elements, and how to achieve it all. In this regard, crowdfunding can offer a tool capable of supporting the various phases. Elements to be taken into consideration are represented by the nature of the initiatives, the method of requesting and disbursing funding (in the case of equity, for example, there are new entrances to companies), and the duration (both of the campaigns and of the times used subsequently to receive what established, as well as the effects produced). One model can be preferred to the other based on the purposes to be pursued, which make one more suitable than the other.

8. Conclusions and future research

Crowdfunding represents a significant opportunity for many startuppers to embark on their entrepreneurial "path," and for many companies to grow and expand.

This option has considerable implications for a multitude of subjects, primarily founders and funders, but also others such as different types of investors (venture capitalists and business angels), for whom, as we have seen, the projects launched on the market through crowdfunding can be a strong investment opportunity. For entrepreneurs or companies, the crowdfunding campaign can represent a confirmation of the existence of a "market," both in terms of feedback with the audience of "consumers" and as an opportunity to receive support from further forms of funding, and the fact that there are supporters who believe in the initiative.

In this discussion, crowdfunding is interpreted according to the logic of real options, a methodology that until now had not been applied to this theme.

The analysis conducted aims to represent a contribution that can be useful both for policy makers, who make decisions that involve the global economy, and for those who for the first time could approach the crowdfunding system, thus being able to have important information regarding possibilities that derive from it.

It is useful to offer a framework capable of explaining what happens after using the funding mechanism, both in case of success or failure.

This work intends to enter the current debate on crowdfunding and contribute to the knowledge of the phenomenon, which has not yet been fully explored so far, in particular with reference to "post-crowdfunding."

Further developments of the topic include the application of a conditional probability model (bayesian statistic) to a pool of crowdfunding campaigns of different types.

CONCLUSIONS

Crowdfunding as we have seen represents one of the most innovative ways to finance a new activity, allowing the founders of entrepreneurial, non-profit, cultural or artistic activities to finance their project by raising capital through the internet, targeting a large number of individuals requesting relatively small numbers for each of them.

The characteristic of crowdfunding is therefore to range from smaller (such as small campaigns created by artists looking for tens or hundreds of thousands of dollars), to more impressive projects (such as the production of a film or the creation of a video games, activities which can take millions of dollars)

Crowdfunding platforms such as Crowdcube, Ulule and Kickstart have quickly risen to the fore in recent years gaining leadership positions in the US and EU within the means of raising capital.

However, crowdfunding is still a particularly complex and difficult to interpret phenomenon for scholars. In fact, the first studies are empirical and have highlighted what are the factors that determine the success or failure of the initiatives launched through the crowdfunding platforms.

In the first chapter, this work shows the main characteristics of crowdfunding, in particular by describing the models and numbers that underline the incidence of the phenomenon, which has now become internationally relevant, as well as analyzing the reference ecosystem.

Furthermore, in this chapter, the ability of this funding tool to support innovation and be a mechanism of concrete utility also for companies is highlighted, which can use it to support entrepreneurial and innovative processes (corporate crowdfunding).

Successively financed projects were analyzed below, analyzing the determinants that positively affect funding and the investors reached. In fact, the following three chapters highlight the role of the signals, information and qualities of the links of the actors involved to obtain a higher amount of funding. The work developed in the second chapter allows to compare the companies financed through reward and equity model, showing the signals that have determined the success of the initiatives, intended both in terms of investors reached and of funds raised.

In the third chapter the role of internal social capital was taken into consideration, analyzing both the qualities of the founders and the funders.

In the fourth chapter, on the other hand, the networks underlying crowdfunding are analyzed in an innovative way, thus allowing the study of the links between the funders and the founders, as well as between the funders themselves.

These chapters constitute contributions that extend the pre-existing literature, both in terms of signaling theory (second chapter) and on internal social capital (third chapter). Furthermore they show some peculiar aspects that can emerge from the study of crowdfunding through network theory (fourth chapter). These are, by way of example, the role played by the links between the actors of the networks and the possible implications related to entrepreneurship, as in the case of the community's spin offs (fourth chapter) and the transformation of the financiers into founders (third chapter).

The last two chapters analyze what happens after a funding campaign, describing the possible post-crowdunding scenarios, in the event of a positive or unsuccessful outcome of fundraising, and the implications for companies that have used the equity crowdfunding mechanism.

Particularly, we have seen that in order to enhance equity crowdfunding development, it is necessary to balance and to oversee all the different natures. This role, could be assigned only to regulation that should always have as a main purpose the reduction of risks for investors avoiding the imposition of excessive costs on issuers and platforms. This could be done, by inducing issuers in disclosing more financial data, in a way that investors may take more precise and informed decisions. To do so, in order to avoid the introduction of new costs for issuers, a more valid solution could be provide a mechanism of grants or tax relief to compensate the disclosing issuers of the costs of hiring specific consultants.

In this way, not only investors may take more efficient decisions but also the wisdom of the crowd will help in enhancing information quality, notwithstanding the not so deep level of disclosure that could be imposed to the issuer to not increase disclosure costs. In this view, the crowd system, that before could be considered as a source of peril, could function as a catalyst to turn low level financial information in high quality one.

This hypothesis can provide interesting food for thought and be a support both for policy makers who have the task of implementing traditional systems of support for entrepreneurial initiatives, and for users of this financing mechanism, i.e. lenders and promoters. In fact, the latter can draw indications on what are the factors that positively influence the collection of funds and what are the possible options in crowdfunding contexts.

Overall, the crowdfunding phenomenon is constantly evolving and the dynamics of this mechanism can change rapidly. The main platforms are relatively young and consequently the initiatives launched through crowdfunding campaigns have a still short history, therefore it is of considerable interest to consider the future evolution of the companies by referring to a wider time span, an objective that will be sought to achieve in some future works starting from the contributions in this research.

BIBLIOGRAPHY

AGRAWAL A., CATALINI C., GOLDFARB A., *Some Simple Economics of Crowdfunding,* in *Innovation Policy and the Economy,* NBER Books, National Bureau of Economic Research, vol. 14, 2013, pp. 63-97.

AHLERS G.K.C., CUMMING D., GÜNTHER C., SCHWEIZER D., *Signaling in Equity Crowdfunding,* in *Entrepreneurship Theory and Practice,* vol. 39, n. 4, 2015, pp. 955-980.

ALBERT R., BARABASI A.L., *Statistical mechanics of complex networks,* in *Reviews of Modern Physics,* vol. 74, n. 1, 2002, pp. 47-97.

ALLISON T.H., DAVIS B.C., SHORT J.C., WEBB J.W., *Internal Social Capital and the Attraction of Early Contributions in Crowdfunding,* in *Entrepreneurship: Theory & Practice,* vol. 39, 2015, pp. 53-73.

AN J., QUERCIA D., CROWCROFT J. *Recommending investors for crowdfunding projects,* in *WWW' 14: Proceedings of the 23rd international conference on World wide web,* April 2014, pp. 261-270.

BAID C., ALLISON T., *How crowdfunding deals get done: signaling, communication and social capital perspectives,* in *Handbook of Research on Crowdfunding,* LANDSTRÖM H., PARHANKANGAS A., MASON C. (ed. by), Edward Elgar Publishing, Cheltenham, UK Northampton, MA, USA, 2019, pp. 191 ss.

BAUM J.A.C., SILVERMAN B., *Picking winners or building them? Alliance, intellectual, and human capital as selection criteria in venture financing and performance of biotechnology startups,* in *Journal of Business Venturing,* vol. 19, n. 3, 2004, pp. 411-436.

BEAULIEU T.Y., SARKER S., *Discursive Meaning Creation in Crowdfunding: A socio-material Perspective Research-in-Progress,* in *Thirty Fourth International Conference on Information Systems, ICIS,* 2013.

BEBCZUK N.R., *Asymmetric Information in Financial Markets. Introduction and Applications,* Cambridge, Cambridge University Press, 2013.

BECHTER C., JENTZSCH S., FREY M., *From Wisdom of the Crowd to Crowdfunding,* in *Journal of Communication and Computer,* vol. 8, n. 11, 2011, pp. 951-957.

BELLEFLAMME P., LAMBERT T., SCHWIENBACHER A., *Crowdfunding: Tapping the right crowd,* in *Journal of Business Venturing,* vol. 29, n. 5, 2014, p. 585 ss.

BELLEFLAMME P., OMRANI N., PEITZ M., *The economics of crowdfunding platforms,* in *Information Economics and Policy,* vol. 33, 2015, pp. 11-28.

BELLEFLAMME P, OMRANI N., PEITZ M., *Understanding the strategies of crowdfunding platforms,* in CESIfo DICE Report, 2, 2016, pp. 6-10.

BESSIERE V., STEPHANY E., WIRTZ P, *Crowdfunding, business angels, and venture capital: an exploratory study of the concept of the funding trajectory,* in *Venture Capital. An International Journal of Entrepreneurial Finance,* 2019, pp. 1-2.

BORGATTI S.P., EVERETT M.G., FREEMAN L.C., *Ucinet 5.0.*, Natick, MA: Analytic Technologies, 1997.

BORGATTI S.P., JONES C., *A measure of part collaboration,* in *Connections,* vol. 19, n.1, 1996, pp. 58-60.

BORELLO G., DE CRESCENZO V., *The Funding Gap and The Role of Financial Return Crowdfunding: Some Evidence From European Platforms,* in *Journal of Internet Banking and Commerce,* vol. 20, n.1, 2015, pp. 2ss.

BORST I., MOSER C., FERGUSON J., *From friendfunding to crowdfunding: Relevance of relationships, social media, and platform activities to crowdfunding performance,* in *New Media & Society,* vol. 20, n. 4, 2017, pp. 1396-1414.

BOTAZZI L., DA RIN M., *Venture Capital and the Growth of innovative Firms in Europe,* in *Crossroads of Entrepreneurship,* 2004, pp. 83-97.

BOUNCKEN R.B., KOMOREK M., KRAUS S., *Crowdfunding: The Current State of Research,* in *International Business & Economics Research Journal,* vol. 14, n. 3, 2015, pp. 407 ss.

BOWER J.L., CHRISTENSEN C. M., *Disruptive Technologies: Catching the Wave,* in Harvard Business Review, vol. 73, n. 1, 1995, pp. 43–53.

BOWMAN E.H., HURRY D., *Strategy through the Option Lens: An Integrated View of Resource Investments and the Incremental-Choice Process,* in *The Academy of Management Review,* vol. 18, n.4, 1993, pp. 760-782.

BRADFORD C.S., *Crowdfunding and the Federal Securities Laws,* in *Columbia Business Law Review,* n. 1, 2012, pp. 1-150.

BRADLEY D.B., LUONG C., *Crowdfunding: A new opportunity for small business and entrepreneurship,* in *Entrepreneurial Executive,* vol. 19, 2014, pp. 95-104.

BRAET O., SPEK S., PAUWELS C., *Crowdfunding The Movies: A Business Analysis of Crowdfinanced Moviemaking in Small Geographical Markets,* in *Journal of Media Business Studies,* vol. 10, n. 1, 2015, pp. 1-23.

BURKETT E., *A Crowdfunding Exemption? Online Investment Crowdfunding and U.S. Securities Regulation,* in *Transactions: The Tennessee Journal of Business* Law, vol. 13, 2011, pp. 63 – 106.

BURT R.S., *Structural Holes. The Social Structure of Competition,* Harvard University Press, USA, 1995, pp. 324.

BURTCH G., CHOSE A., WATTAL S., *An Empirical Examination of the Antecedents and Consequences of Contribution Patterns in Crowd-Funded Markets,* in *Information Systems Research,* vol. 24, n. 3, 2013, pp. 499-519.

BUSENITZ L.W., FIET J.O., MOESEL D.D., *Signaling in Venture Capitalist-New Venture Team Funding Decisions: Does it Indicate Long-Term Venture*

Outcomes?, in *Entrepreneurship Theory and Practice,* vol. 29, n. 1, 2005, pp. 1-12.

CALDBECK R., *Crowdfunding Won't Solve the Venture Capital Series A Crunch,* available at: http://www.forbes.com/sites/ryancaldbeck/2013/01/23/crown funding-wont-solve-the-venture-capital-series-a-crunch/

CAMBRIDGE CENTRE FOR ALTERNATIVE FINANCE, *Entrenching Innovation-The 4th UK Alternative Finance Industry Report, 2017.*

CARNI U.S., *Protecting the Crowd through Escrow: Three Ways That the Sec Can Protect Crowdfunding Investors,* in *Fordham Journal of Corporate & Financial Law,* vol. 19, n. 3, 2014, pp. 681-706.

CHEMMANUR T.J., CHEN Z., *Venture Capitalists Versus Angels: The Dynamics of Private Frim Financing Contracts,* in *Review of Corporate Finance Studies,* vol. 3, n. 1-2, 2014, pp. 39-86.

CHENG Y.Q., WANG Q., XIE J., *Online social interactions: A natural experiment on word of mouth versus observational learning,* in *Journal of Marketing Research,* vol. 48, n. 2, 2011, pp. 238-254.

CHESBROUG H.W., *Open Innovation: The New Imperative for Creating and Profiting from Technology*. Harvard Business School Press, 2003.

CHISHOLM A., NELSON J., *Platform regulation-Ex-ante versus ex-post intervention: evolving our antitrust tools and practices to meet the challenges,* in *Competition Policy International*, vol. 11, n. 1, 2015.

CHOLAKOVA M., CLARYSSE B., *Does the Possibility to Make Equity Investments in Crowdfunding Projects Crowd Out Reward-Based Investments?,* in *Entrepreneurship Theory and Practice,* vol. 39, n.1, pp. 145-172.

COLLINS L., PIERRAKIS Y., *The Venture Crowd. Crowdfunding equity investment into business,* NESTA, 2012.

COLOMBO M.G., FRANZONI C., LAMASTRA C.R., *Internal Social Capital and the Attraction of Early Contributions in Crowdfunding,* in *Entrepreneurship Theory and Practice*, vol. 39, n. 1, 2015, pp. 75-100.

CORDOVA A., DOLCI J., GIANFRATE, G., *The determinants of crowdfunding success: evidence from technology projects,* in Procedia-Social and Behavioral Sciences, vol. 181, 2015, pp. 115-124.

COSH A., CUMMING D., HUGHES A., *Outside Entrepreneurial Capital,* in *The Economic Journal*, vol. 119, n. 540, 2009, pp. 1494-1533.

CROWDFUNDING CLOUD, *Nuovo regolamento UE sul crowdfunding.* Interview ad D. Valliante. Available at: www.crowdfunding.cloud , 23/04/2018.

CUMMING D. (ed. by), *The Oxford Handbook of Entrepreneurial Finance,* Oxford, UK, Oxford University Press, 2012.

CUMMING D., JOHAN S., *Demand-driven securities regulation: evidence from crowdfunding,* in *Venture Capital. An International Journal of Entrepreneurial Finance,* vol. 15, n. 4, 2013, pp. 361-379.

CUMMING D.J., LEBOEUF G., SCHWIENBACHER A., *Crowdfunding models: Keep-it-All vs. All-Or-Nothing,* in *Financial Management*, 2019.

DE BUYSERE K, GAJDA O, KLEVERLAAN R., MAROM, D., *A Framework for European Crowdfunding.* Resource Document, European Crowdfunding Network, 2012, p. 9.

DEMIRAY M., BURNAZ S., ASLANBAY Y., *The Crowdfunding Market, Models, Platforms, and Projects,* in *Crowdfunding for Sustainable Entrepreneurship and Innovation,* VASSALLO W. (ed. by), IGI Global, 2017, pp. 90-126.

DAVIES W.E., GIOVANNETTI E., *Signaling experience & reciprocity to temper asymmetric information in crowdfunding evidence from 10,000 projects,* in *Technological Forecasting and Social Change,* Elsevier, vol. 133, n. C, 2018, pp. 118-131.

DOMS M., LEWIS E., ROBB A., *Local labor force education, new business characteristics, and firm performance,* in *Journal of Urban Economics,* vol. 67, n.1, 2010, pp. 61-77.

DORFF M.B., *The Siren Call of Equity Crowdfunding,* in *The Journal of Corporation Law,* vol. 39, p. 493.

EISENMANN T., PARKER G.,VAN ALSTYNE M.W., *Strategies for Two-Sided Markets*, in *Harvard Business Review*, vol. 84, n. 10, 2006, pp. 1-11.

ESTELLÉS AROLAS E., GONZÁLEZ-LADRÓN-DE-GUEVARA F., *Towards an integrated crowdsourcing definition,* in *Journal of Information Science,* vol. 38, n. 2, 2012, pp. 1-14.

FIGLIOMENI M., *Grassroots capitalism or: how I learned to stop worrying about financial risk in the exempt market and love equity crowdfunding,* in *Dalhousie Journal of Legal Studies,* vol. 23, 2014, pp. 105-129.

FIROOZI F., JALILVAND A., LIEN D., *Information Asymmetry and Adverse Wealth Effects of Crowdfunding,* in *The Journal of Entrepreneurial Finance,* vol. 18, n. 1, 2016, pp. 1-8.

FREEDMAN D.M., NUTTING M.R., *The growth of equity crowdfunding,* in *Value Examiner,* 2015, pp. 6-10.

GERBER E.M., HUI J.S., HUO P.Y., *Crowdfunding: Why People Are Motivated to Post and Fund Projects on Crowdfunding Platforms,* in *Proceedings of the International Workshop on Design, Influence, and Social Technologies: Techniques, Impacts and Ethics,* Academic Press, 2012.

GIUDICI G., NAVA R., ROSSI-LAMASTRA C., VERECONDO C, *Crowdfunding: the new frontier for financing entrepreneurship?,* in *SSRN Working Paper Series*, 2012.

GOLIC Z., *Advantages of crowdfunding as an alternative source of financing of small and medium-sized enterprises,* in *Proceedings of the Faculty of Economics in East Sarajevo,* vol. 8, 2014, pp. 39-48.

GRELLA S., *Fraudulent Crowdfunding Campaign Sets Precedent,* in *Observer,* September 2015.

GUBLER Z.J., *Inventive Funding Deserves Creative Regulation. The SEC should tread lightly regarding the social-media approach to venture capital,* in *WSJ Opinion,* 31 January 2013.

HAGEDORN A., *The Financing Process of Equity-Based Crowdfunding: An Empirical Analysis,* in *Crowdfunding in Europe. State of the Art in Theory and Practice,* BRÜNTJE D., GAJDA O., (eds), Springer, 2016, pp. 71-85.

HARMS M., *What drives Motivation to Participate Financially in a Crowdfunding Community?,* in *SSRN Electronic Journal*, 2007.

HAZEN T.L., *Crowdfunding or Fraudfunding-Social Networks and the Securities Laws-Why the Specially Tailored Exemption Must Be Conditioned on Meaningful Disclosure,* in *North Carolina Law Review,* vol. 90, n. 5, 2012, p. 1757 ss.

HENDLER J., GOLBECK J., *Metcalfe's Law, Web 2.0, and the Semantic Web*, in *Journal of Web* Semantics, vol. 6, n. 1, 2008, pp. 14 – 20.

HOGAN J., *Like oil and water: equity crowdfunding and securities regulation,* in *Lewis & Clark Law Review,* vol. 18, 2014, pp. 1091-1116.

HOPKINS J., HOPKINS K., *Not all that glitters is gold-Limitations of equity crowdfunding regulations,* in *Business Law Journal*, vol. 16, n. 2, 2014, p. 13 ss.

HORNUF L., SCHWIENBACHER A., *Crowdinvesting-Angel Investing for the Masses?,* in *Handbook of Research on Venture Capital: vol. 3. Business Angels,* 2014.

HORNUF L, SCHWIENBACHER A., *Market Mechanisms and Funding Dynamics in Equity Crowdfunding,* in *Journal of Corporate Finance,* vol. 50, n. C, 2018, pp. 556-574.

HOWE J., *The rise of Crowdfunding,* in *Wired*, 6 January 2006.

HOWE J., *Crowdsourcing: Why the Power of the Crowd Is Driving the Future of Business,* Three Rivers Press, New York, USA, 2008.

HOULIHAN C., CURNEEN D., *The regulation of crowdfunding in Ireland,* Dillon Eustace, 2017.

INGRAM C., TEIGLAND R., *Crowdfunding Among IT Entrepreneurs in Sweden: A qualitative Study of the Funding Ecosystem and ICT Entrepreneurs' Adoption of Crowdfunding,* in *SSRN Electronic Journal,* 2013, pp. 1-49.

INTERREG-CENTRAL EUROPE ARTISTIC, *Strategy Handbook for the Crowdfunding network. Deliverable D.T2.2.5. (WP T2, Activity A, T2.2),* ISN-innovation service network GmbH, PP13, Graz, version 2, 2019.

JENIK I., LYMAN T., NAVA A., *Crowdfunding and Financial Inclusion, Working Paper-CGAP*, 2017, p. 55 ss.

JOHANSON J., MATTSSON L.G., *Interorganizational relations in industrial systems: a network approach compared with the transaction cost approach,* in *International Studies of Management & Organization,* vol. 17, n. 1, 1987, pp. 34-48.

KAHNEMAN D., TVERSKY A., *Prospect Theory: An Analysis of Decision under Risk,* in *Econometrica,* vol. 47, n. 2, 1979, pp. 263-291.

KEUSCHNIGG C., *Venture Capital Backed Growth,* CESifo Working Paper n. 664(5), 2002, pp. 1-27.

KLAPPER L., LUSARDI A.,VAN OUDHEUSDEN P., *Financial Literacy Around the World. Insights from the Standard & Poor's ratings services global financial literacy survey,* Washington DC, 2015, pp. 1-28.

KLEEMANN F., VOß G.G. and RIEDER K., *Un(der)paid innovators: The commercial utilization of consumer work through crowdsourcing,* in *Science, Technology and Innovation Studies,* vol. 4, n. 1, 2008, pp. 5-26.

KOUFARIS M., KAMBIL A., LABARBERA P.A., *Consumer Behavior in Web-Based Commerce: An empirical Study,* in *International Journal of Electronic Commerce,* vol. 6, n. 2, 2001, pp. 115-138.

KOZINETS R., HEMETSBERGER A., SCHAU H.J., *The Wisdom of Consumer Crowds: Collective Innovation in the Age of Networked Marketing,* in *Journal of Macromarketing,* vol. 28, n. 4, 2008, pp. 339-354.

KRAUS S., RICHTER C., BREM A., CHENG C.F., CHANG M.L., *Strategies for reward-based crowdfunding campaigns,* in *Journal of Innovation & Knowledge,* vol. 1, n. 1, 2016, pp. 13-23.

KUPPUSWAMY V., BAYUS B.L., *Crowdfunding creative ideas: The dynamics of project backers in Kickstarter,* UNC Kenan Flager Research Paper, n. 2013-15, SSRN Electronic Journal, 2013, pp. 1-37.

KUTI M., BEDO Z., GEISZL D., *Equity -based Crowdfunding,* in *Financial and Economic Review,* vol. 16, n. 4, 2017, pp. 187-200.

LANDSTRÖM H., PARHANKANGAS A., MASON C. (ed. by), *Handbook of Research on Crowdfunding,* Edward Elgar Publishing, Cheltenham, UK Northampton, MA, USA, 2019.

LAVINSKY D., *Funding Fathers,* available online at: http://www.sbnonline.com/Local/Article/20471/65/0/Funding_fathers.aspx

LEY A., WEAVEN S., *Exploring agency dynamics of crowdfunding in start-up capital financing,* in *Academy of Entrepreneurship Journal*, vol. 17, n. 1, 2011, pp. 85-110.

LI H., LAI V.S., LUO R., *Understanding the Role of Social Situations on Continuance Participation Intention,* in *Journal of Electronic Commerce Research,* vol. 17, n. 4, 2016, pp. 358-380.

LIN N., *Social capital. A theory of social structure and action,* Cambridge, Cambridge University Press, 2001.

LUKKARINEN A., TEICH J.E., WALLENIUS H., WALLENIUS J., *Success drivers of online equity crowdfunding campaigns,* in *Decision Support System,* vol. 87, 2016, pp. 26-38

LYNN D., SABBAGH H., *The JOBS Act opens door for crowdfunding offerings,* in *Morrison & Forrester Social Media Newsletter,* vol. 2, n. 3, pp. 6-8.

MACHT S., *Business angels offer more than money,* 2007.

MACHT S.A., WEATHERSTON J., *The Benefits of Online Crowdfunding for Fund-Seeking Business Ventures,* in *Strategic Change*, vol. 23, n. 1/2, 2014, pp. 1-14.

MACMILLAN I.C., KULOW D.M., KHOYLIAN R., *Venture capitalists' involvement in their investments: Extent and performance,* in *Journal of Business Venturing,* vol. 4, n. 1, 1989, pp. 27-47.

MANCHANDA K., MURALIDHARAN P., *Crowdfunding: a new paradigm in start-up financing,* Global Conference on Business and Finance Proceedings, vol. 9, n. 1, 2014, p. 369.

MASSOLUTION, *2015CF The Crowdfunding Industry Report.* Massolution.com, 2015.

MCGRATH R.G., MACMILLAN I.C., *The Entrepreneurial Mindset: Strategies for Continuously Creating Opportunity in an Age of Uncertainty,* Boston Mass, Harvard Business School Press, 2000.

MEDZIAUSYTE J., NEUGEBAUER P., *Financing success through equity crowdfunding: the case of start-ups and SMEs funded on European crowdfunding platform,* in *International Business School.* Jönköping University, 2017.

METELKA A., *Crowdfunding-Startups' alternative funding source beyond banks, business angels and venture capitalists,* in *School of Management.* Blekinge Institute of Technology, 2014.

METRICK A., YASUDA A., *Venture Capital & the Finance of Innovation,* 2nd edition, Wiley, USA, 2007.

MEYSKENS M., BIRD L., *Crowdfunding and Value Creation,* in *Entrepreneurship Research Journal,* vol. 5, n. 2, 2015, pp. 155-166.

MIGLO A., *Asymmetric Information and Crowdfunding,* 2017, available at SSRN: https://ssrn.com/abstract=3068682

MOLLICK E., *The dynamics of crowdfunding: An exploratory study,* in *Journal of Business Venturing*, vol. 29, n. 1, 2014, pp. 1-16.

MÜLLERLEILE T., JOENSSEN D.W., MÜLLERLEILE A., *Crisis, Co-Financing, and Crowdfunding: Igniting Regional Development,* in *Proceedings of the 7th international conference for entrepreneurship and regional development, ICEIRD 2014,* PAPADOPOULOS G., KETIKIDIS P., KOFTEROS S. (eds.), SEERC, 2014, pp. 277-285.

NASRABADI A.G., *Equity Crowdfunding: Beyond Financial Innovation,* Springer International Publishing, 2016.

NESTA, *The UK Alternative Finance Industry Report*, 2014.

OECD, *OECD Economic Surveys 2002-2003: France, OECD,* vol. 2003/11-July.

OLSON E., *Squalls in the safe harbor: investment advice & regulatory gaps in regulation crowdfunding,* in *Journal of Corporation Law,* vol. 40, 2015, pp. 539-564.

ORDANINI A., MICELI L., PIZZETTI M. and PARASURAMAN A., *Crowd-Funding: Transforming Customers into Investors through Innovative Service Platforms*, in *Journal of Service Management,* vol. 22 , n. 4, 2011, pp. 443 – 470.

OSTERWALDER A., PIGNEUR Y., *Business Model Generation: A Handbook for Visionaries, Game Changers, and Challengers*, Hoboken, Wiley, New Jersey, 2010, pp. 1-288.

PIERRAKIS Y., COLLINS L., *Crowdfunding: A New Innovative Model of Providing Funding to Projects and Business,* SSRN Electronic Journal, 2013.

RALCHEVA A., ROOSENBOOM P., *On the Road to Success in Equity Crowdfunding,* in *SSRN Working Paper,* 2016.

RAMADANI V., *Business Angels-Who They Really Are?,* in *Strategic Change,* vol. 18, n. 7-8, 2009, pp. 249-258.

RAMSEY Y.A., *What the Heck is Crowdfunding?,* in *Business People*, vol. 25, n. 11, 2012, pp. 54-57.

ROBB A.M., ROBINSON D.T., *The Capital Structure Decisions of New Firms,* in *The Review of Financial Studies,* vol. 27, n. 1, 2014, pp. 153-179.

RYU S., KIM K., *Crowdfunding Success as a Quality Signal to Venture Capital,* in *22nd Americas Conference on Information Systems: Surfing the IT Innovation Wave, AMCIS 2016,* Association for Information Systems, United States, 2016.

SAFIRE W., *On Language,* in *New York Times Magazine,* 2009. HOWE J., *Crowdsourcing: Why the Power of the Crowd Is Driving the Future of Business,* Crown Publishing Group New York, NY, USA, 2008.

SALAMPASIS D., MENTION A.L. (Eds.), *Open Innovation. Unveiling the Power of the Human Element,* Open Innovation: Bridging Theory and Practice vol.2, World Scientific Publishing Co., Singapore, 2017.

SAUREMANN H., FRANZONI C., SHAFI K., *Crowdfunding scientific research: Descriptive insights and correlates of funding success,* in *PLOS/ONE*, vol. 14, n. 1., 2019.

SCHENK E., GUITTARD C., *Towards a characterization of crowdsourcing practices,* in *Journal of Innovation Economics & Management,* vol. 1, n. 7, 2011, pp. 93-107.

SCHMID E., COHEN J., *The Digital Disruption. Connectivity and the Diffusion of Power*, in *Foreign Affairs*, Hein Online, 2010.

SCHWIENBACHER A., *Equity crowdfunding: Anything to celebrate?,* in *Venture Capital,* vol. 21, n. 1, 2019, pp. 65-74.

SCHWIENBACHER A., LARRALDE B., *Crowdfunding of Small Entrepreneurial Ventures,* in *Handbook of Entrepreneurial Finance,* CUMMING D., (ed. by), Oxford, Oxford University Press, 2010, pp. 1-23.

SHANE S., CABLE D., *Networks Ties, Reputation, and the Financing of New Ventures,* in *Management Science,* vol. 48, n. 3, 2002, pp. 313-452.

SHNEOR R., MUNIM Z.H., *Reward crowdfunding contribution as planned behavior: An extended framework,* in *Journal of Business Research,* vol. 103, 2019, pp. 56-70.

SOPER T., *Why venture capitalist Marc Andreessen is critical of the "fail fast" startup mentality,* in *GeekWire*, 13 September 2016.

SORRENTINO M., *L'imprenditorialità interna per lo sviluppo*, in LIPPARINI A. and LORENZONI G., (ed. by), *Imprenditori e imprese*, Il Mulino, Bologna, Italy, 2000.

SPENCE M., *Job Market Signaling,* in *The Quarterly Journal of Economics,* vol. 87, n. 3, 1973, pp. 355-374.

STUART T.E., SORENSON O., *Social Networks and Entrepreneurship,* in *Handbook of Entrepreneurship Research. Disciplinary Perspectives,*

ALVAREZ S.A, AGARWAL R., SORENSON O. (ed. by), Springer, Boston, MA, 2005, pp. 233-252.

SUROWIECKI J., *The Wisdom of Crowds: Why the Many are Smarter than the Few and How Collective,* Wisdom Shapes Business, Economies, Societies, and Nations, Doubleday, Anchor, 2005.

TOMCZAK A., BREM A., *A conceptualized investment model of crowdfunding,* in V*enture Capital-An International Journal of Entrepreneurial Finance,* vol. 15, n. 4, 2013, pp. 335-359.

TORABI O., MIRAKHOR A., *Controlling information asymmetry in equity crowdfunding,* in *Journal of Economic and Social Thought,* vol. 5, n. 2018, pp. 32-41.

TRAUTMAN L., AHO W., *Crowdfunding, Entrepreneurship, and Start-Up Finance,* in *Entrepreneur & Innovation Exchange,* published online on 8 August 2019, doi: 10.32617/403-5d4c0e0041267

UNGER J.M., RAUCH A., FRESE M., ROSENBUSCH N., *Human capital and entrepreneurial success: A meta-analytical review,* in *Journal of Business Venturing,* vol. 26, n. 3, 2011, pp. 341-358.

VALANCIENE L., JEGELEVICIUTE S., *Valuation of crowdfunding: Benefits and drawbacks,* in *Economics and Management*, vol. 18, n. 1, 2013, pp. 39-48.

VAN OSNABRUGGE M., *A comparison of business angel and venture capitalist investment procedures: An agency theory-based analysis,* in *Venture Capital. An International Journal of Entrepreneurial Finance,* vol. 2, n.2, 2000, pp. 91-109.

VASSALLO W., *Crowdfunding nell'era della conoscenza. Chiunque può realizzare un progetto. Il futuro è oggi.* Franco Angeli, Milan, 2016, pp. 112.

VOORBRAAK K.J.M., *Crowdfunding for Financing New Ventures: Consequences of the Financial Model on Operational Decisions.* Eindhoven University of Technology, Eindhoven, 2011.

WARDROP R., ROSENBERG R., ZHANG B., ZIEGLER T., SQUIRE R., BURTON J., HERNADEZ E.A., GARVEY K., *Breaking New Ground. The Americas Alternative Finance Benchmarking Report,* Cambridge Centre for Alternative Finance and Polsky Center for Enterpreneurship and Innovation, University of Cambridge-Judge Business School, 2016.

WARDROP R., ZHANG B., RAGHAVENDRA RAU R., GRAY M., *Moving Mainstream. The European Alternative Finance Benchmarking Report,* University of Cambridge, 2015,

WESSEL M., *Crowdfunding: Platform Dynamics under Asymmetric Information,* Darmstadt, Technische Universität Darmstadt, 2016, pp. 1-125.

WORLD BANK, *Global Financial Development Report 2017/2018: Bankers without Borders*, Washington, DC, 2018.

YAMEN S., GOLDFEDER Y., *Equity Crowdfunding. A Wolf in Sheep's Clothing: The implications of crowdfunding legislation under the JOBS Act,* in *Brigham Young University International Law & Management Review*, vol. 11, n. 1, 2015, p. 40 ss.